THE
BLENDER
GAMEKIT
2ND EDITION

Authors:
Carsten Wartmann, Michael Kauppi

Tutorials, game demos, CDROM content:
Campbell Barton, Benoit Bolsee, Jim Coulter, Joeri Kassenaar, Freid Lachnowicz, Reevan McKay, Willem-Paul van Overbruggen, Chris Plush, Randall Rickert, Carsten Wartmann

Editor:
Carsten Wartmann

Design and DTP:
Samo Korošec, froodee design bureau, www.froodee.at

Production:
Ton Roosendaal

Special thanks to:
Benoit Bolsee, Erwin Coumans, Chris Plush, Pablo Vazquez, Campbell Barton, Brecht van Lommel (YoFrankie, Apricot open game)

And very special thanks to the entire blender.org development and documentation crew!

Published by:
Blender Foundation
Entrepotdok 57A
1018 AD Amsterdam
the Netherlands
www.blender.org
foundation@blender.org

Printed and distributed by:
No Starch Press, Inc.
555 De Haro Street, Suite 250
San Francisco, CA 94107 USA
www.nostarch.com

Printed in Canada

13 12 11 10 09   1 2 3 4 5 6 7 8 9

Wartmann, Carsten.
    The Blender gamekit : interactive 3D for artists / Carsten Wartmann, Michael Kauppi. -- 2nd ed.
        p. cm.
    Previous ed.: The official Blender gamekit / edited by Ton Roosendaal and Carsten Wartmann, 2003.
    Includes index.
    ISBN-13: 978-1-59327-205-0
    ISBN-10: 1-59327-205-7
    1. Computer animation. 2. Three-dimensional display systems. 3. Computer graphics. 4. Blender (Computer file) I. Kauppi, Michael. II. Official Blender gamekit. III. Title.
    TR897.7.O38 2009
    794.8'1669--dc22
                        2009010499

Table Of Contents

FOREWORD

Ton Roosendaal & Carsten Wartmann

The first "Blender GameKit" was published end of 2002. It has marked the beginning of a new era for Blender, as an open source project being developed and maintained by the on-line community themselves. It also marked the beginning of the Blender Foundation, as a publisher of Blender books, to enable financing its goals. In just a few months GameKit revenues proved to be sufficient to allow myself to work full-time on Blender projects. So let me begin with thanking everyone who has helped realizing it, and who has supported Blender by purchasing a copy!

The success story of Blender in the six years after are well known now. We've firmly established it in the top ten of 3D creation suites - up-to-par with commercial soft-ware - and we can only be very proud to have helped creating the most popular free and open 3D tool ever!

There was just one aspect of Blender that got stuck behind too much... the logic tools and Game Engine (GE). The complexity of integrating a tool with a GE was just too much of a challenge. Luckily, in a relatively short time, thanks to three remark-able events it came completely back:

- Erwin Coumans, original developer of the GE, helped integrating his new and very advanced collision/physics system in Blender. During 2007 his Bullet library be-came one of the most important reasons of artists to use the GE.
- Early 2008, a new developer Benoit Bolsee fixed like every open bug report in the GE. In just a few months he brought back the open issues from over a 100 to less than 10. Stability and predictability is crucial for game engines!

- The Blender Foundation's "Apricot" Open Game project then decided to start using the GE as well. A lot of work was realized on more advanced logic editing and well integrated usage of materials, shaders and animation features. Apart from Benoit, Brecht van Lommel and Campbell Barton deserve to be credited for this breakthrough. Credits also should go to artist Chris Plush, who proved us the renewed GE's value by creating in a mere four hours work a prototype of the YoFrankie game!

Here's the reason why you're now holding this new and fully revised edition of the Gamekit in your hands. This book always was a great introduction for people into 3D games creation, and with the unleashed power of Blender 2.48, it's more than ever a book that will help you making stunning and advanced interactive 3D environments, multi-level 3D games with menus, or even 3D documentation for industrial products.

I'm also very grateful that we got the interest from the original editor and designer of the GameKit back to update this book. Many thanks go to Carsten Wartmann, renowned author of plenty of Blender books, and to designer Samo Korosec.

I wish you a lot of pleasure reading this book!

Amsterdam, november 2008

Ton Roosendaal

Chairman Blender Foundation

About this book

Blender offers you a new and unique way to explore interactive 3D graphics. This book will guide you through many aspects of making your own games and interactive 3D graphics with Blender.

You can have fun with the ready made games on the DVD instantly, but changing them or creating your own game is also great fun.

Blender is a fully integrated 3D creation suite. It has all the tools for making linear animation and non-linear (interactive) 3D graphics. All of these features are provided in one single application and gives the artist a very smooth workflow from design, to modeling, animating and on-to publishing of 3D content. For example if you needed to make a demo trailer of a game you would need a modeler, a renderer, a video editing application and the game engine itself to produce the video. Blender offers you all these tools combined to produce interactive and linear 3D content.

With Blender, we give you the tools you need to make your creative ideas come true – this book will show you how to achieve this using Blender.

The book contains:

- Example game scenes to play with
- Example games and tutorial scenes to change and personalize
- Blender basics for making interactive 3D graphics
- 3D game technology basics
- Advanced tips and topics from professional Blender artists
- References for the Blender game engine

QUICKSTART

FUN WITH A GAME CHARACTER

Carsten Wartmann

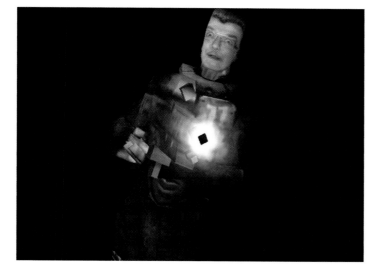

Calli going mad...

Have you ever wanted to personalize a computer game? Well, many game level editors will give you that possibility, but Blender goes a step further, by allowing you to create a completely new game.

In this quickstart chapter, I will show you how to map a face onto a game character.

The game character used here was made by Reevan McKay. You can read more about this in Chapter Game Character Animation, which will show you many other things about character animation.

In Figure "Calli going mad..." you can see an image of an real time 3D animation created using the method which will be briefly described in this chapter. The scene is on the CD and called **Tutorials/Quickstart/CalliGoingMad.blend** .

This quickstart tries to be as self-contained as possible. Although it is good if you already know something about graphics, if you follow the instructions step-by-step all should go well.

If you have not installed Blender yet, please do so.

Simple face mapping

This section will show how to put a new face onto a ready-made character, there are some drawbacks to this method but it will get you started quickly.

Start Blender by double clicking its icon. It will open a screen as shown in the figure.

Blender just after
starting it

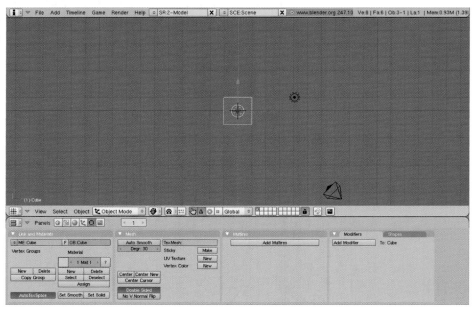

Locate the "File"-menu on the top left of the screen and choose "Open" by clicking it with the left mouse button (**LMB**). A big File Window appears which is used for all Blender loading and saving operations.

The button labeled "P" at the upper left corner of the File Window puts you one directory up in your path. The Menu Button below brings you back to the last directories you have visited, as well as your mapped drives in Windows. Click and hold it with the left mouse button to change to your CDROM drive.

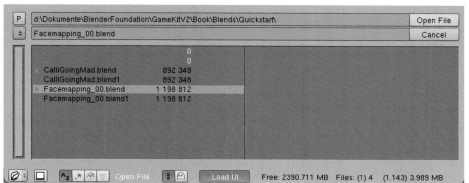

Blender File Window

Now enter the directory **Tutorials/Quickstart/** and click with the left mouse on **Facemapping_00.blend** . Confirm your selection by clicking "Open File" at the top right of the File Window. Blender will load the file needed for the tutorial.

*Please have a look at Section Blender Basics for a explanation on how we will call interface elements and keyboard shortcuts (i.e. **P**) in the tutorials.*

To quickly see what this file is about, press **CTRL - RIGHT**. The window layout changes to a bigger view of the character. Now press **P** and the game engine will start. Using the controls from the table, walk around to have a closer look at the character.

CONTROLS/KEYS	DESCRIPTION
W	Move forward
D	Move left
A	Move right
S	Move backwards
CTRL	Shoot
SPACE	Duck

Stop the game engine by pressing **ESC** when you have seen enough. Press **CTRL - LEFT** to return to the window layout which we will now use to map a different face.

INTRODUCTION

Move your mouse cursor over the left window with the 3D view of the head and press **TAB**. This will start the so-called "Edit Mode", which is used to change the object itself but also manage and change textures on objects.

All polygons which belong to the face are now outlined and you can see them also in the right view showing the 2D texture image of the face. This procedure is called mapping and will make the 2D image appear where we want it on the 3D object.

3D head and
2D facemap

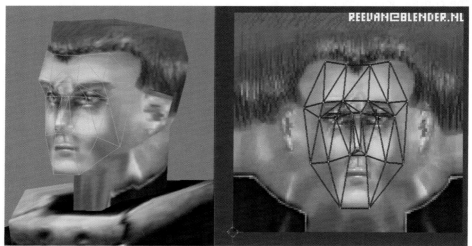

Use the menu "Image → Open..." while holding **CTRL** or press **CTRL**-**ALT**-**O** in the right Image Window. A File Window (in this case an Image File Window) will open and lets you browse through your hard disks and the CDROM again. Go to the directory **Tutorials/Quickstart/textures/** .

If called while holding **CTRL** the Image File Window displays little thumbnail images to ease the choice of images (see Figure "Image File Window").

You can also choose a picture of you or an other person. But if you are a beginner, I would suggest to use the supplied image for your first attempt. Blender can read and write PNG (*.png), Targa (*.tga) and JPEG (*.jpg) and most all other common image formats.

Click on the image **Carsten.jpg** (yes, its me, your tutorial writer making a silly face) and click the "Open Image" Button on the top right of the Image File Window to load it. The image will immediately appear in the 3D view to the left.

Depending on your screen resolution you may need to zoom the right Image Window out a bit. Use the **PAD-** *and* **PAD+** *keys for zooming.*

INTRODUCTION

The dimensions of my silly face don't fit the previous mapping, so it'll look a bit distorted. Also, the color may not match exactly, making it look like a cheap mask.

Now move your mouse over the Image Window on the right and press **A**-**A** (twice **A**), this selects (yellow color) all the control points here, called vertices in Blender. Now press **G** and move your mouse, and all vertices will follow and you can watch the effect on the 3D View. Try to position the vertices in the middle of the face, using the nose as a reference. Confirm the new position with the left mouse button. If you want to cancel the move, press the right mouse button or **ESC**.

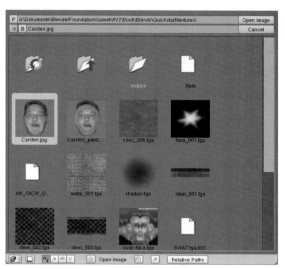

Image File Window

To have a better look at the head in the 3D View, you can rotate the head around using the middle mouse button and moving the mouse (if you are using a 2 button mouse, hold **ALT** *and use the left mouse button).*

To refine the placement of the texture on the head, you may now need to move the vertices more. Move your mouse over to the Image Window on the right and press **A** to de-select all vertices (they will turn purple). Now press **B**. This will start the Border Select, and a crosshair will appear. Press and hold the left mouse button to draw a rectangle around vertices you want to select and release the mouse button. Now you can move these vertices by pressing **G** and using the mouse. Press **LMB** to confirm the move. Control the effect by watching the head on the 3D View. Single vertices can be selected by using the right mouse button, **SHIFT**-**RMB** adds a single vertex or deselects when used on a already selected vertex.

Don't give up too soon! Mapping a face needs practice, so take a break and play with the games on the CDROM, and try again later.

If you want to look at your creation, switch to the full screen scene by pressing **CTRL**-**RIGHT** and start the game engine with **P**.

Using 2D applications to map the face

Maybe you are already an artist for computer graphics who wants to step into the 3D graphics. So it is very possible that you know 2D painting programs well. This part of the tutorial will give you a brief guide on how to use a 2D painting program to montage a face into the facemap. You should know how to work with layers in your application (if not please consult the documentation of your image editing program). I use the free software (GPL) GIMP (**http://www.gimp.org/**) but of course any other image manipulation programs (which support layers) will do.

1. Load the image **swat-face.tga** from the CDROM and the face you want to use in your paint program.
2. Place the new face in a layer below the "swat-face.tga" and make the upper layer slightly transparent so that you can see the new face shining through.
3. Scale and move the layer containing the new face so that it fits to the "swat-face.tga" layer. Use the eyes, mouth and the nose as a guide to match them up. Also try to match the colors of the layers using the color tools of your 2D program.

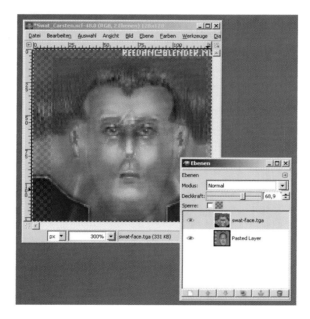

4. Make the upper layer non transparent again
5. Now use the eraser from your 2D paint program to delete parts of the upper layer, the new face will appear at these points. Use a brush with soft edges so that the transition between the two layers is soft.

6. Collapse the layer to one and save the image as a PNG (*.png) or JPEG (*.jpg) image. Maybe do some final touch-ups on the collapsed image, like blurring or smearing areas of transition.

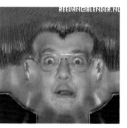

The finished Texture

Now load the scene **Facemapping_00.blend** from the CDROM. Press `TAB` with your mouse over the 3D View on the left to enter Edit Mode.

Move your mouse over to the right Image Window and choose the menu "Image → Replace" this time. This will replace the current texture in the file with your self-made texture. Locate the image with your face on your disks, select it with the left mouse button and press "Open Image" in the Image File Window. The new texture will now appear on the head.

Switch to the full screen again (`CTRL`-`RIGHT`) and test the scene by starting the game engine with `P`.

INTRODUCTION TO 3D

AND GAME ENGINES

Michael Kauppi

Purpose of This Chapter

This chapter will introduce you to the world of three dimensional (3D) computer graphics, first by introducing the general concepts behind 3D and then by showing how those concepts are used in computer graphics. Then, it will introduce you to game engines, especially Blender's game engine, and three aspects that are often found in good games. This chapter is aimed at those who have little or no experience in 3D or with game engines.

General Introduction to 3D

We'll begin our journey into 3D with an overview of 2D because most people reading this should already know the concepts behind 2D or least be able to grasp them fairly quickly.

XY axes

You can think of 2D as being a flat world. Imagine you put a blank piece of paper on a table, and look down at that paper.

If that paper represented the 2D world, how would you describe where things are located? You need some kind of reference point from which to measure distances.

This is generally done by drawing two lines, called axes: one horizontal and the other vertical (see the graph below). The horizontal line is called the X-axis, and the vertical line is called the Y-axis. Where the axes cross is your reference point, usually called the "origin".

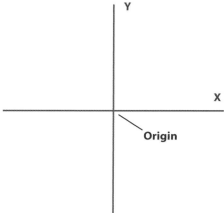

Along these axes, imagine a series of regularly spaced hash marks, like the lines on a ruler. To describe where something is, you count out the distance along the X and Y axes. Distances to the left and below the origin on the X and Y axes respectively are negative, while distances to the right and above the origin on the X and Y axes respectively are positive:

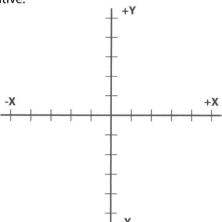

For example, if you wanted to describe where the dot in the graph is located, you would count out 4 units along the X-axis (known as the X coordinate) and 5 units along the Y-axis (known as the Y coordinate).

Now with a default origin and XY coordinates, we can begin to describe 2D geometry.

Points

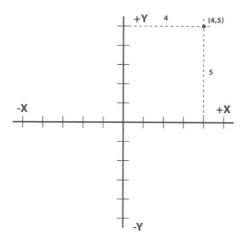

The dot in the graph above is the simplest object that can be described in 2D, and is known as a point. To describe a point you only need an X and a Y coordinate.

Lines

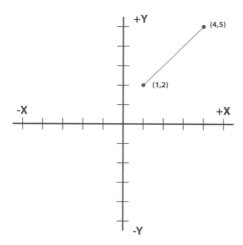

The next simplest object we can describe in 2D is the line. To describe a line, you only need to describe two points (see above).

Polygons

By connecting three or more lines, you can begin to describe shapes, known as polygons. The simplest polygon is the three-sided triangle, next is the four-sided quadrangle, or quadrilateral, (usually shortened to quads), and so on, to infinity. For our purposes, we'll only work with triangles and quads.

With this knowledge, it's now time to expand from 2D to 3D.

3D, the third dimension

As the name implies, 3D has an extra dimension but the concepts we covered in the 2D discussion above still apply.

Z axis

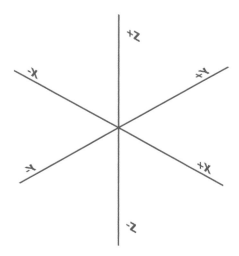

Just like 2D, we need a reference point from which to describe the location of things in 3D. This is done by drawing a third axis that is perpendicular to both the X and Y axes, and passes through the origin. This new axis is usually called the Z-axis, and values above and below the origin are positive and negative respectively (see the graph above). By using this new axis we can describe objects as they exist in the real world.

Points

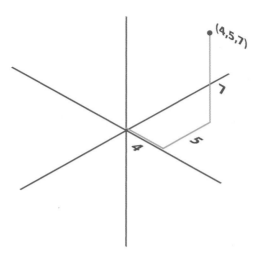

To describe a point in 3D, we now need three coordinates: the X, Y and Z coordinates.

Lines

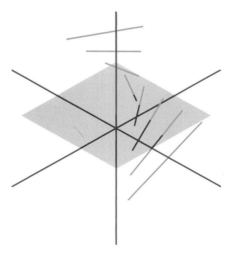

As in 2D, we can describe a line by defining two points, but now our line does not have to lay flat, it can be at any angle imaginable (in the graph above, for example, lines are piercing a plane lying in space).

Polygons

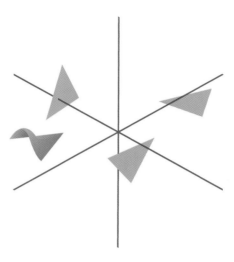

By connecting lines, we can form polygons just like in 2D. Our polygons, just like our lines, are no longer confined to the flat 2D world (see the graph above). Because of this, our flat 2D shapes can now have volume. For example, a square becomes a cube, a circle becomes a sphere and a triangle becomes a cone (as seen below).

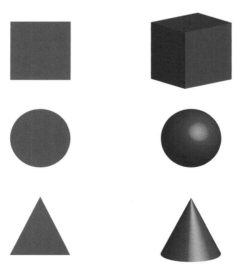

Now with the basics of 3D covered, let's see how they relate to 3D computer graphics.

3D computer graphics

By now, you should have the general concepts of 3D in mind. If not, go back and reread the previous sections. Having these concepts in mind will be very important as you proceed through this guide. Next, we'll show you how the concepts of 3D are used in 3D computer graphics, also known as computer generated imagery (CGI).

Terminology

A slightly different set of terms is used for CGI. The following table shows how those terms relate to what you have learned so far.

3D TERM	RELATED CGI TERM
Point	Vertex
Line	Edge
Polygon	Polygon

Armed with our new terminology, we can now discuss CGI polygons.

Triangles, quads

While theoretically, a polygon can have an infinite number of edges, the more edges there are, the more time it takes a computer to calculate that shape. This is why triangles and quads are the most common polygons found in CGI, they allow the creation of just about any shape and do not put too much stress on the computer to calculate. But how do you form shapes with triangles and quads?

Mesh

As discussed before, our polygons are no longer confined to the flat 2D world. We can arrange our polygons at any angle we choose. By combining a series of polygons together at various angles and sizes, we can create any 3D shape we want.

For example, six squares can combined to make a cube, and four triangles and a square form a pyramid (as seen on the right). By increasing the number of polygons and manipulating their locations, angles and sizes we

can form complex objects (as seen in the arch made out of blocks). As you can see, the more complex an object, the more it takes on a mesh-like appearance. In fact, the object in the following illustration is being viewed in "wire mesh" mode. You'll often hear the term "mesh" used to describe any combination of CGI polygons.

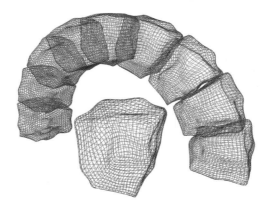

Primitives

As shown above, we can create shapes by combining polygons, but to form basic shapes by hand (such as spheres, cones, and cylinders) would be very tedious. So 3D applications like Blender have preprogrammed shapes called "primitives" that you can quickly add to a 3D scene. Blender's mesh primitives include: planes, cubes, spheres, cones, cylinders and tubes. There are other primitives as well (not all of them mesh based), and you will learn about them as you develop your Blender skills.

Faces

Polygons can be faced or unfaced. You can think of an unfaced polygon as being made of just wire, while a faced polygon has a "skin" stretched over that wire (see above). When you tell Blender to draw your 3D scene, called rendering, the faced polygons will appear solid, while the unfaced polygons will appear as holes (as seen with the orange sphere).

Materials

Look at objects around you, they have many characteristics. Some are shiny, some are matte. Some are opaque, some are transparent. Some appear hard, while others appear soft. To recreate these characteristics in the 3D world, we apply a "material" to an object which tells Blender how to render the object's color, how shiny the object should appear, its perceived "hardness" and other properties.

Textures

Take a look at the things around you again. Besides their material properties, the things around you also have texture. Texture affects not only how something feels (smooth or rough), but also how something looks (colors and patterns). Since we can't touch what we make in the 3D CGI world, we will focus on how things look.

Image maps

A common method for applying textures is through the use of image maps. That is 2D images which we then "wrap" around an object (see right). Image maps allow us to represent minute detail on our models (objects) that would be difficult to model directly and that would greatly increase the number of polygons if we did model them. Using image maps lets us keep the number of polygons low on our models, thus letting Blender render our scenes faster, which is especially important for realtime, quickstart section uses realtime rendering in the game engine.

UV mapping

One common problem with image maps is the accurate wrapping of the maps around an object, especially a complex one. Many times the texture will not be aligned as we wish or it may "stretch" (seen right). A popular method for overcoming this problem is the use of UV mapping.

UV vs. XY coordinates

In order to continue, it is necessary to point out what UV coordinates are. As mentioned in the 3D overview, you can describe a point (vertex) by giving its X, Y and Z coordinates. If you want to ‚map' a 2D image onto a 3D object, the XYZ coordinates have to be transformed into two dimensions. These transformed coordinates are usually called the "UV coordinates". Instead of calculating UV coordinates automatically, you can define them yourself in Blender. This means, that for each vertex, not only a an XYZ coordinate is stored, but also the two values for U and V.

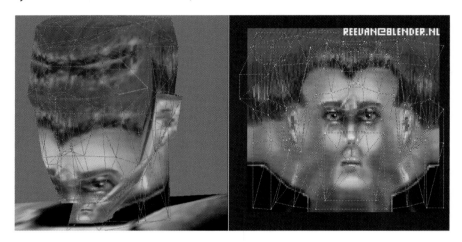

So, how does UV mapping work? Take a look at the head object in the illustration above. Each corner of the faces is a vertex, and each vertex has an XYZ and UV coordinate as explained earlier. Using Blender's UV editor, we unwrap the mesh, much like we do when we take a globe and lay it flat to make a map of the world, and lay that mesh on top of our 2D image texture.

Then, by moving the unwrapped mesh's UV coordinates, we can tell Blender exactly where the texture should go when Blender wraps the texture around our 3D object (left).

The reason it is called a UV editor and not a UVW editor, is that we make our adjustments in 2D (UV) and Blender automatically takes care of the W coordinate when it wraps the texture around our model. Not having to worry about the third dimension makes our job easier in this case.

Viewing 3D space

To do anything in 3D, we need to be able to see what we are doing. This is accomplished using "views". This section will discuss the various views available in Blender ("standard", "interactive" and "camera" views), and the two view modes available. This section will not cover the steps you need to take to use the views. Those will be explained in Chapter 4, " Navigating in 3D". It will also mention the use of lights, which are not actually views but are necessary if you want to see anything when you render your 3D scene and can be used to alter the mood of our scenes.

Standard

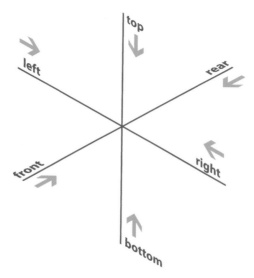

There are six pre-programmed standard views in Blender, each looking along a particular axis as shown above. These views are generally used when modeling objects because they help to provide a sense of orientation. They are also useful if you get disoriented using the interactive view.

Interactive (free)

While the standard views are very useful for modeling, sometimes they don't help us visualize how an object will look in 3D  (left cube). This is when Blender's interactive view becomes useful. Blender's interactive view allows you to rotate your entire 3D scene in any direction interactively (in realtime) to let you view things from any angle (right cube). This helps you visualize how your scenes and models will look.

Cameras

The standard and interactive views are generally not used when it is time to render your scenes (stills, animations or realtime rendering in the game engine). Instead, you use a camera view for rendering. You can think of this like a movie set. You are

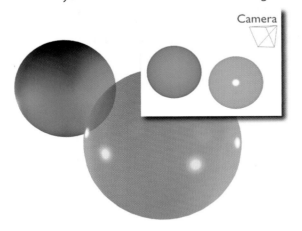

the director and can walk around and look at your set from any direction you want (standard and interactive views) to make sure everything is just as you want it, but when it is time to shoot the scene you need a camera. This is what your audience will see, and the same holds true for camera views.

This is the same image used for explaining Materials — with the additional overlay illustrating the Camera's position used for the rendering.

View modes

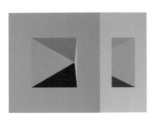 

Here are two viewing modes for all the views in Blender: "orthographic" (left) and "perspective" (right). Orthogonal mode views everything without perspective, whereas the perspective mode, as the name implies, uses perspective. Orthogonal mode is useful when creating your models because there is none of the "distortion" associated with the perspective mode, and this helps your accuracy. The perspective mode, like the interactive view, can help give you a sense of what your model will look like, but without the need to rotate the entire 3D scene. Rotating the entire scene can be slow if it is very complicated.

Lights

Before you can render your scene, or play your game, you will need at least two things: a camera and lights. If you try to render without a camera you will get an error message, but if you try to render without a light all you will get is a black image. This is one of the most common mistakes users new to Blender, so if you try to render something and all you get is a black square be sure to check if you've put in a lamp or not. For the interactive 3D graphics, there can be scenes without light, but they usually look flat.

There is more to lights than just being able to see. Just like in real life, lights can help set the atmosphere or mood of a scene. For example, using a low blue light helps to create a "cool/cold" atmosphere, while a bright orange light might create a "warm" one. Lights can be used to simulate ambient light, muzzle flashes or any other effect where you would expect to see light.

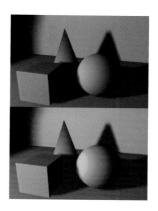

Because you will be creating games with objects that move and change, there is another important concept we must cover.

Transformations

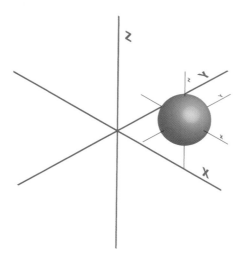

As touched on earlier, we describe the locations of objects in our 3D worlds by using an origin and a XYZ coordinate system to measure with. The coordinates calculated from this default origin are known as global coordinates. In addition, an object's center serves as its own origin, and so the object can have its own XYZ axes (see graph).

This is called a local origin, and a local coordinate system with local coordinates. But why is this important?

A game where nothing moves or changes will not get much of a following. The objects in your games will need to move, and this is one place where the concept of transformations becomes important. The three most common transformations are translation, rotation and scaling:

TRANSFORMATION	DESCRIPTION
Translation	When an object moves from point A to point B.
Rotation	When an object spins around a particular point or axis.
Scaling	When an object increases or decreases in size.

When you make your games, you'll have to keep in mind that transformations are relative and can affect game play. When an object translates from point A to B in the global coordinate system, from that object's point of view, its local coordinate system doesn't necessarily move. For example, a character standing in a moving train seems to be stationary from their point of view. The train's speed may be 100 kph, but the character feels like they are standing still. Their local origin (their center) doesn't move as far as they are concerned.

However, if we look at the same character from the point of view of someone standing still outside the train, the character is moving. From this second character's local point of view, they are standing still and the first character is moving, but neither are rotating. Or are they?

If we look from the point of view of another character, hovering in space, not only are both of the other characters on the Earth, rotating as the Earth rotates on its axis, but also as the Earth rotates around the Sun. So, how does this affect game play? Imagine everyone is trying to hit a stationary target on the train. The first character has the easiest job, a stationary target, the second character has to hit moving target, and the third character has to hit a target that is moving and experiencing two forms of rotation.This shifting of points of view is called "coordinate transformation", and as you can see, it can have an important impact on game play.

In most 3D software packages you can work with these coordinate systems using so-called "hierarchies". You can define one object as being the "parent" of another object; which then becomes a child. Now all transformations of the parent are also applied to its children. That way you only have to define motion for a parent to have all its children moving in the same way. In the solar system example, we humans all are in fact "children" of the Earth, which in turn is a "child" of the Sun.

One last point that needs to mentioned is that transformation is not restricted to just shapes. Materials, textures, and even lights can be moved, rotated and scaled. In fact, anything that exists in your 3D world is actually an object and so is subject to transformations. As your 3D skills develop, you will learn how to use global, local and relative transformations to affect game play and to create interesting effects. Now that you have received a basic introduction to 3D CGI, it's time to talk about game engines and aspects of good games.

Game Engines and Aspects of a Good Game

What is a game engine?

A game engine is software that simulates a part of reality. Through a game engine, you interact with a 3D world in realtime, controlling objects which can interact with other objects in that world. If you have ever played a video game on a computer, a console or in a game arcade, you have used a game engine of some kind. The game engine is the heart of a game and consists of several parts. One part displays the 3D world and its objects on your screen, drawing and redrawing your scenes as things change. Another part deals with decision making (known as game logic), for example, deciding when events like doors opening should occur. Another part simulates physics, such as gravity, inertia, momentum and so on. Yet another part detects when objects collide with each other, while another actually moves objects.

The game engine tries to simulate all these things as quickly as possible to provide a smooth fluid simulation.

For example, in a computer baseball game, the game engine will have the pitcher throw you a pitch (moving an object). As the ball travels the game engine will calculate all the physics that act on the ball, such as gravity, air resistance, etc. Then you swing the bat (or more accurately, you tell the game engine to swing the batter's bat) and hopefully hit the ball (i.e. collision detection between the ball and bat).

This is a very simplified example. The game engines you have used are much more complicated, and can take a team of programmers and a great deal of time to create. Or at least, that was the case until Blender's game engine was released.

Blender's game engine — Click and drag game creation

Blender is the first game engine that can create complete games without the need to program. Through its click-and-drag graphical user interface (GUI), even those with no programming experience can enjoy the challenge of creating fun and exciting games.

After you create your 3D world and 3D objects, you only need to use a series of pull-down menus, simple key strokes and mouse clicks to add behavioral properties to that world and those objects and bring them to life. For professionals, this allows for the rapid prototyping of games, and for non-professionals, it's the first chance to produce their own games without having to spend years learning to program or the need for large programming teams. Of course, for those who can program, Blender uses the Python scripting language to allow programmers to extend Blender's game engine even further.

This relative ease of use, though, hides the Blender game engine's true innovation...

"True" and "fake" 3D game engines

Blender is a "true" 3D game engine. Until recently, game logic (decision making) wasn't done on an object level. This meant that a "higher intelligence" (HI) in the game had to control all the objects, moving them when appropriate or keeping track of their condition (i.e. alive or dead). With the advent of "true" 3D game engines, each object in a game is its own entity and reports such information back to the game engine.

For example, if you are playing a game where you walk through a maze that has hidden doors, in the past the HI would have had to decide when you were close enough to a hidden door and then open it. With Blender's game engine, the door itself can have a sensor function and will determine when another object is close enough, then the door will open itself.

Another example would be a shooting game. The gun has logic attached that detects when you pull the trigger, the gun then creates a new bullet object with a certain starting speed. The bullet, which is now its own entity, shoots out of the gun and flies through the air all the while being affected by air resistance and gravity. The bullet itself has sensors and logic as well, and detects whether it hits a wall or an adversary. On collision, the logic in the bullet and the logic in the collided object define what will happen.

In the past, when you pulled the trigger, the game engine would calculate whether a bullet fired at that time would hit the target or not. There was no actual bullet object. If the game engine determined that a hit would have occurred, it then told the object that had been hit, how to react.

The advantage of Blender's "real" 3D game engine is that it does a better job of simulating reality because it allows for the randomness that occurs in the real world. It also distributes the decision load so that a single HI isn't required to decide everything.

While Blender provides you with the technology to create good games, it doesn't create them automatically. To create good games, you need to understand three important aspects of games.

Good games

If you analyze successful games, you will find that they have three aspects in varying degrees. This is known as the "Toy, immersive, goal" theory of game creation.

Toy • The toy aspect of a game refers to the immediate fun of just playing it. You don't need to think too much, you can just grab the mouse or the game controller and start playing, much like you did with your toys when you were a child. You didn't need to read a manual on how to play with your toy cars, or spend time figuring out complicated strategy. In short, games with a high degree of toy are very intuitive. Think of your favorite arcade game at your local game arcade. Most likely you only needed one joystick and two or three buttons, or a simple gun with a trigger.

> This doesn't mean that such games don't require skill, but that you can gain immediate enjoyment from playing them.

Immersive • The "immersive" aspect of a game is the degree to which a game makes you forget you are playing a game, sometimes called the "suspension of disbelief". Flight simulators or racing simulators are a good example of this. Realism is an important factor in this, and is one of the reasons that simulators have reached such an advanced level in realism. The "Mechwarrior" series and "WarBirds" are two excellent examples of immersive games which have very realistic environments, animations and sounds. They are fairly low on the toy aspect and take some time to learn to play, with almost every key on the keyboard used for some function.

> The old one-button joysticks have been replaced with HOTAS (Hands On Throttle And Stick) systems consisting of a joystick with seven to ten buttons for one hand, a throttle device with an equal number of buttons or dials for the other and even pedals for your feet. These systems combine with the game to create an incredibly immersive environment. These games also often have a high degree of "goal".

Goal • The "goal" aspect of a game is the degree to which a game gives you a goal to achieve. This often involves a lot of strategy and planning. "Age of Empires" and "SimCity" are two games that are very goal oriented. Goal oriented games are often very low on the toy aspect, "SimCity" for example comes with a thick manual explaining all the intricate details of "growing" a successful city. This is not always the case though: "Quake" is a goal oriented game which also has a good deal of toy and immersive aspects to it.

Balance • When you create your games, you will have to strike a balance among the toy, immersive and goal aspects of your games. If you can create a game that has a high degree of each aspect, you'll most likely have a hit on your hands.

Conclusion

In this chapter you have been introduced to the basic concepts of 3D including vertices, polygons, materials, textures, origins, coordinate systems and transformations. You have also been introduced to what makes a game work, both on a technological level with the discussion of game engines, and on a conceptual level with the discussion of what makes good games good.

The rest of this book will show you how to use Blender to put these concepts to work when creating games. Once you have finished this guide, you'll have all the tools you'll need to make games, the rest will fall to your own creativity. Good luck and we look forward to seeing you announce your games on Blender's discussion boards (see Appendix).

BLENDER BASICS

Carsten Wartmann

The Interface

If you are new to Blender, you should get a good grip on how to work with the user interface before you start modelling. The concepts behind Blender's interface are specifically designed for a graphics modelling application and the vast array of features are different and differently grouped from other 3D software packages. In particular, Windows users will need to get used to the different way that Blender handles controls such as button choices and mouse movements. This difference is one of Blender's great strengths. Once you understand how to work the Blender way, you will find that you can work exceedingly quickly and productively. Some features are familiar, like the top menu bar of "File", "Add"..."Help". However, many other features are quite unheard of in most (if not all) other applications. For example: Blender windows cannot overlap and hide each other, one exception being a small number of mini-floating panels which are transparent, fold-able, small, and dock-able. Blender relies heavily on keyboard shortcuts to speed up the work. Blender's interface is entirely drawn in OpenGL and every window can be panned, zoomed in/out, and its content moved around.

Your screen can be organized exactly to your taste for each specialized task and this organization can be named and memorized.

These key differences (and many others) make Blender a unique, powerful, and very nimble application, once you take the time to understand it.

Blender's Interface Concept

The user interface is the vehicle for two-way interaction between the user and the program. The user communicates with the program via the keyboard and the mouse, and the program gives feedback via the windowing system. The interface can be broken down into several key areas: Windows, Contexts, Panels, and Buttons (controls). For example, The Button Window contains Context buttons which show different groups of Panels and the Panels each show groups of Buttons. These principal areas are discussed on the following pages.

Keyboard and mouse

This chapter gives an overview of the general mouse and keyboard usage in Blender and the conventions used in this Manual to describe them, as well as tips on how to use non-standard devices.

Conventions in this Manual

This manual uses the following conventions to describe user input: The mouse buttons are called **LMB** (left mouse button), **MMB** (middle mouse button) and **RMB** (right mouse button). If your mouse has a wheel, **MMB** refers to clicking the wheel as if it were a button, while **MW** means rolling the wheel.

Hotkey letters are shown in this manual like they appear on a keyboard; for example **G** which refers to the lowercase g. When used, the modifier **SHIFT** is specified just as the other modifier keys, **CTRL** and/or **ALT** ; this gives, for example, **CTRL**-**W** or **SHIFT**-**ALT**-**A**. **NUMPAD**-**0** to **NUMPAD**-**9**, **NUMPAD**-**+** and so on refer to the keys on the separate numeric keypad. **NUMLOCK** should generally be switched on.

Other keys are referred to by their names, such as **ESC**, **TAB**, **F1** to **F12** .

Of special note are the arrow keys, **UP**, **DOWN**, **LEFT**, **RIGHT** and so on.

General Usage

Blender's interface is designed to be best used with a three-button mouse. A mouse wheel is quite useful, but not essential. Because Blender makes such extensive use of both mouse and keyboard, a golden rule has evolved among Blender users: **Keep one hand on the mouse and the other on the keyboard**.

If you normally use a keyboard that is significantly different from the English keyboard layout, you may want to think about changing to the English or American layout for your work with Blender. The most frequently used keys are grouped so that they can be reached by the left hand in standard position (index finger on F) on the English keyboard layout. This assumes that you use the mouse with your right hand.

Mouse Button Emulation

It is possible to use Blender with a two-button mouse or an Apple single-button Mouse. The missing buttons can be emulated with key/mouse button combos. Activate this functionality in the User Preferences, View and Controls Context, "Emulate 3 Button Mouse" button.

The following table shows the combos used:

	2 BUTTONS MOUSE	**APPLE MOUSE**
LMB	LMB	LMB
MMB	ALT-LMB	OPTION/ALT-LMB
RMB	RMB	COMMAND/APPLE-LMB

All the Mouse/Keyboard combinations mentioned in this book can be expressed with the combos shown in the table. For Example, SHIFT-ALT-RMB becomes SHIFT-ALT-COMMAND-LMB on a single-button mouse.

NumPad Emulation

The Numpad keys are used quite often in Blender and are not the same keys as the regular number keys. If you have a keyboard without a Numpad (e.g. on a laptop), you can tell Blender to treat the standard number keys as Numpad keys in the User Preferences, System & OpenGL Context, "Emulate Numpad" button.

The Window System

When you start Blender you may see a console (text) window open and, shortly after, the main user interface window will display. You may also see a splash screen announcing the Blender version, but it will disappear as soon as you move your mouse.

The default Blender scene

The default Blender scene shows the screen you should get after starting Blender for the first time. By default it is separated into three windows:

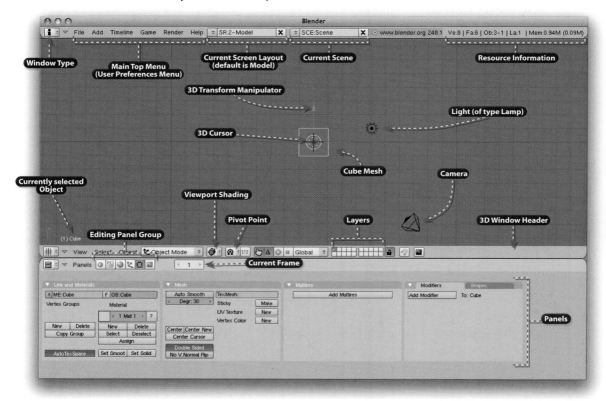

- The main menu at the top is the header part of a User Preferences window
- A large 3D window (3D Viewport window)
- The Buttons Window (at the bottom)
- These windows can be further broken down into separate areas. As an introduction we will cover a few of the basic elements:
    - Window Type: Allows you to change what kind of window it is. For example, if you want to see the Outliner window you would click and select it.
    - Main Top Menu: Is the main menu associated with the "User Preferences" window type. To actually see the information, you need to click and drag the area between the 3D window and menu header; Roll the mouse between them and when it changes to a up/down arrow you can drag and see the "User Preferences" window.
    - Current Screen (default is Model): By default, Blender comes with several

pre-configured Screens for you to choose from. If you need custom ones, you can create and name them.

- Current Scene: Having multiple scenes present allows for you to break up your work into organized patterns.
- Resource Information (found in the User Preferences header): Gives you information about application and system resources. It tells you how much memory is being consumed based on the number of vertices, faces and objects in the selected scene. It is a nice visual check to see if you are pushing the limits of your machine.
- 3D Transform Manipulator: Is a visual aid in transforming objects. Objects can also be transformed (grabbed/moved - rotated - scaled) using the keyboard shortcuts: (**G**/**R**/**S**); **CTRL** **SPACE** will display the manipulator pop-up. The manipulator visibility can also be toggled by clicking the "hand" icon on the toolbar. The translation/rotation/scale manipulators can be displayed by clicking each of the three icons to the right of the hand icon. **SHIFT** **LMB** -clicking an icon will add/remove each manipulator's visibility.
- 3D Cursor: Can have multiple functions. For example, it represents where new objects appear when they are first created; Or it can represent where the base of a rotation will take place.

 The 3D Cursor

- Cube Mesh: By default, a new installation of Blender will always start with a Cube Mesh sitting in the center of Global 3D space. After a while, you will most likely want to change the "Default" settings; This is done by configuring Blender as you would want it on startup and then saving it as the "Default" using **CTRL**-**U** (Save Default Settings).
- Light (of type Lamp): By default, a new installation of Blender will always start with a Light source positioned somewhere close to the center of Global 3D space.
- Camera: By default, a new installation of Blender will always start with a Camera positioned somewhere close to the center of Global 3D space and facing it.
- Currently selected object: This field shows the name of the currently selected object.
- Editing Panel Group: The bottom window displays panels and those panels are grouped. This row of buttons (called Context Buttons) allows you to select which group of panels are shown. Some buttons will display additional buttons (called Sub-Context Buttons) to the right for selection of sub-groups or groups within groups.
- Current frame: Blender is a modelling and animation application; As such, you can animate things based on the concept of frames. This field shows what the current frame is.
- Viewport shading: Blender renders the 3D window using OpenGL. You can select the type of interactive shading (called Draw Type: in the Blender shading list) that takes place by clicking this button and selecting from a variety of shading styles. You can select from boxes all the way to complex Textured shading. It is recommended that you have a powerful graphics card if you are going to use the Textured style.

- Rotation/Scaling Pivot point: Allows you to select where rotation/scaling will occur. For example, rotation could occur about the object's local origin or about the 3D Cursor's position, amongst many others.
- Panels: Help group and organize related buttons and controls. Some panels are visible or invisible depending on what type of object is selected.
- Layers: Make modelling and animating easier. Blender Layers are provided to help distribute your objects into functional regions. For example, one layer many contain a water object and another layer may contain trees, or one layer may contain cameras and lights.
- 3D Window header: All windows in Blender have a header. This is the header for the 3D window.

The Window Header

Most windows have a header (the strip with a lighter grey background containing icon buttons). We will also refer to the header as the window Tool Bar. If present, the header may be at the top (as with the Buttons Window) or the bottom (as with the 3D Window) of a window's area.

Sample Window
Headers using the
Default Theme

Blender is themeable, for this book we use the default theme which is default for a new Blender installation.

When you move the mouse over a window, its header changes to a lighter shade of grey. This means that it is "focused"; All hotkeys you press will now affect (only) the contents of this window.

The icon at the left end of a header, with a click of the **LMB**, allows selection of one of 16 different window types. Most Window Headers, located immediately next to this first "Window Type" Menu button, exhibit a set of menus. Menus allow you to directly access many features and commands. Menus can be hidden and shown via the triangular button next to them.

Changing Window Frames

You can maximize a window to fill the whole screen with the "View → Maximize Window" menu entry. To return to normal size, use the "View → Tile Window". A quicker way to achieve this is to use `SHIFT`-`SPACE`, `CTRL`-`UP` or `CTRL`-`DOWN` to toggle between maximized and framed windows.

You can change the size of a window frame by focusing the window you want to split (moving the mouse to its edge), clicking the vertical or horizontal border with `MMB` or `RMB` , and selecting "Split Area". You can now set the new border's position by moving your mouse to the desired position, and clicking with `LMB`; or you can cancel your action by pressing `ESC`. The new window will start as a clone of the window you split. It can then be set to a different window type, or to display the scene from a different point of view (in the case of the 3D View).

 The Split Menu

You can resize windows by dragging their borders with `LMB`.

You can join two windows into one by clicking a border between two windows with `MMB` or `RMB` and choosing "Join Areas". Then you'll be prompted to click on one of the two windows an arrow will be drawn to visualize which windows will be closed; the one you click will disappear, while the other will be expanded to cover the full area of both windows. If you press `ESC` before clicking on one of the windows, the operation will be aborted.

Console Window & Error Messages

The Console Window is an operating system text window that displays messages about Blender operations, status, and internal errors. If Blender crashes on you, it is a good idea to check the Console Window for clues.

When Blender is started on a Microsoft Windows OS; The Console Window is first created as a separate window on the desktop, then assuming the right conditions are met, the main Blender Application window should also appear.

The Blender Console Window must remain open while Blender is executing; If the Blender Console Window is closed then the Blender Application window will also close, and any unsaved Blender work will be lost!

The Blender Console Window may not be visible, some reasons for this are:

- The Blender Application window may be covering the Console Window. If this is the case just use the Windows task bar to click on the Blender Console Window icon, which should make the Blender Console Window visible.
- The Blender Console Window may be minimized/iconifed when Blender starts. If this is the case again, just use the Windows task bar to click on the Blender Console Window icon, which should make the Blender Console Window visible.

Console Window running Linux

The Blender Console Window in Linux will generally only be visible on the Desktop if Blender is started from a Linux Terminal/Console Window, as Blender uses the Console Window it is started in to display it's Blender Console output.

Most of the different Linux distributions have Blender as one of their applications you can install from their packaging systems. When Blender is installed in this way an icon is usually also installed into their menu systems; Allowing for Blender to be started by clicking an icon rather than having to open a separate Linux Console/Terminal window and start Blender from there; When Blender is started using an icon rather than being started from a Terminal window, the Blender Console Window text will most likely be hidden on the Terminal that the X Window System was started from or in the system console log.

Console Window running Mac OS X

On Mac OS X you also can start Blender from a Terminal to see the output of Blender. However if you start Blender from the finder the console window is hidden. To see the output start the "Console" application, this works for all applications which do outputs to the console.

Window types

The window type selection menu

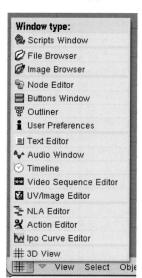

The Blender interface, the rectangular window provided by your operating system, is divided up into many rectangular window frames. Each window frame may contain different types of information, depending upon the Window type.

Each window frame operates independently of the others, and you can have the same type of window in many frames. For example, you may have several 3D windows open but each looking at the scene from a different perspective. You can split and merge and resize window frames to suit whatever you are working on. You can also arrange some window frames to show with or without a header to save screen space.

Window types are broken up by functionality:

- Scripts window - user interface for running Python scripts that extend Blender
- File Browser - for storage and retrieval, especially of .blend files
- Image Browser - search your computer for images, seen as thumbnails
- Node Editor - process/enhance images and materials
- Buttons Window - panels that configure objects and set/select options
- Outliner - Helps you find and organize your objects.
- User Preferences - customize Blender to your work style and computer
- Text Editor - keep notes and documentation about your project, and write Python scripts.
- Audio Window - see sound files and correlate them to frames
- Timeline - jump to different times (frames) in your animation
- Video Sequence Editor - assemble video sequences into a film strip
- UV/Image Editor - edit and paint pictures
- NLA Editor - manage non-linear animation action strips
- Action Editor - combine individual actions into action sequences
- Ipo Curve Editor - make things move or change
- 3D View - graphical view of your scene

You can select the Window type by clicking the window's header leftmost button. A pop-up menu displays showing the available Window types. The tutorials will cover the window types needed for this book.

Button Window Contexts

The Button Window shows six main Contexts, which can be chosen via the first icon row in the header (Contexts and Sub-Contexts Example). Each of these might be subdivided into a variable number of sub-contexts, which can be chosen via the second icon row in the header (Contexts and Sub-Contexts Example), or cycled through by pressing the same Context button again:

Contexts and Sub-Contexts Example

Logic (F4) - Switches to Logic context.
Script - No shortcut. Switches to Script context.
Shading (F5) - Switches to Shading context.
    Lamp - No shortcut.
    Material - No shortcut.
    Texture - Shortcut F6.
    Radiosity - No shortcut.

World - Shortcut **F8**.

Object (**F7**) - Switches to Object context.

Object - No shortcut.

Physics - No shortcut.

Editing (**F9**) - Switches to Editing context.

Scene (**F10**) - Switches to Scene context.

Rendering - No shortcut.

Anim/Playback - No shortcut.

Sound - No shortcut.

Once the Context is selected by the user, the sub-context is usually determined by Blender on the basis of the active Object. For example, with the Shading context, if a Lamp Object is selected then the sub-context shows Lamp Buttons. If a Mesh or other renderable Object is selected, then Material Buttons is the active sub-context, and if a Camera is selected the active sub-context is World.

The Buttons in each context are grouped into Panels.

The menu of available options, shown in a window's header, may change depending on the mode of that window. For example, in the 3D View window, the Object menu in Object mode changes to a Mesh operations menu in Edit mode, and a paint menu in Vertex Paint mode. If you are reading this manual and some menu option is referenced that does not appear on your screen, it may be that you are not in the proper mode, or context, for that option to be valid.

Menus

Blender contains many menus each of which is accessible from either the window headers or directly at the mouse's location using hotkeys.

The Toolbox

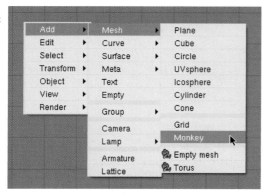

For example, you can access the Toolbox in the 3D window using either the mouse or the keyboard. From the keyboard you would use the **SPACE**. To access it using the mouse just hold down the **LMB** or **RMB** buttons for a few seconds and the Toolbox will pop-up.

Some menus are context sensitive in that they are only available under certain situations. For example, the Booleans menu is only available in Object Mode using **W**. The same hotkey (**W**) in Edit Mode brings up the Specials menu.

While you are using Blender be aware of what mode and types of object are selected. This helps in knowing what hotkeys work at what times.

Panels

Panels generally appear in the Buttons window and by default the Buttons window is at the bottom. The Buttons window includes the Button window header and panels.

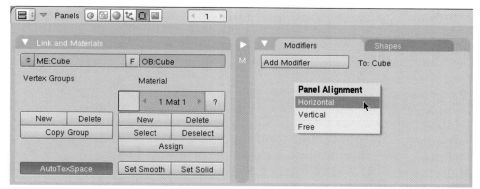

Blender's Panels

Each button on the Buttons header groups panels together into what is called a Context. And those Contexts are grouped further into Sub-Contexts. For example, all Material panels are grouped under the Shading context and Material sub-context.

The panels are not fixed in position relative to the window. They can be moved around the window by **LMB** clicking and dragging on the respective panel header.

Panels can be aligned by **RMB** on the Buttons Window and choosing the desired layout from the Menu which appears. Using MW scrolls the Panels in their aligned direction and **CTRL**-**MW** and **CTRL**-**MMB** zooms the Panels in and out. Single Panels can be collapsed/expanded by **LMB** clicking the triangle on the left side of their header.

Particularly complex Panels are organized in Tabs. Clicking **LMB** on a Tab in the Panel header changes the buttons shown in. Tabs can be "torn out" of a Panel to form independent panels by clicking **LMB** on their header and dragging them out. In a similar way separate Panels can be turned into a single Panel with Tabs by dropping one Panel's header into another.

Buttons and Controls

An operation button   Toggle Buttons   Number Buttons

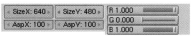

Buttons are mostly grouped in the Button Window. But they can appear in other Windows.These are buttons that perform an operation when they are clicked (with **LMB**, as all buttons). They can be identified by their brownish color in the default Blender scheme (An operation button).

Toggle buttons come in various sizes and colors. The colors green, violet, and grey do not change functionality, they just help the eye to group the buttons and recognize the contents of the interface more quickly. Clicking this type of button does not perform any operation, but only toggles a state.

Some buttons also have a third state that is identified by the text turning yellow (the Emit button in Toggle buttons). Usually the third state means "negative," and the normal "on" state means "positive."

Radio buttons are particular groups of mutually exclusive Toggle buttons. No more than one Radio Button in a given group can be "on" at one time.

Number buttons can be identified by their captions, which contain a colon followed by a number. Number buttons are handled in several ways: To increase the value, click **LMB** on the right of the button, where the small triangle is shown; to decrease it, click on the left of the button, where another triangle is shown.

To change the value in a wider range, hold down **LMB** and drag the mouse to the left or right. If you hold **CTRL** while doing this, the value is changed in discrete steps; if you hold **SHIFT**, you'll have finer control over the values. **ENTER** can be used in place of **LMB** here.

You can enter a value directly by holding **SHIFT** and clicking **LMB**. You can also enter simple equations, like "3*2" instead of 6. Handy geometric constants to remember: pi is "3.14" and the square root of two is "1.414". Press **SHIFT**-**BACKSPACE** to clear the value; **SHIFT**-**LEFT** to move the cursor to the beginning; and **SHIFT**-**RIGHT** to move the cursor to the end. Press **ESC** to restore the original value.

Some number buttons contain a slider rather than just a number with side triangles. The same method of operation applies, except that single **LMB** clicks must be performed on the left or on the right of the slider, while clicking on the label or the number automatically enters keyboard input mode.

Use the Menu buttons to choose from dynamically created lists. Menu buttons are principally used to link Data Blocks to each other. (Data Blocks are structures like Meshes, Objects, Materials, Textures, and so on; by linking a Material to an Object, you assign it.)

Data Block link buttons

1. The first button (with the tiny up and down pointing triangles) opens a menu that lets you select the Data Block to link to by holding down **LMB** and releasing it over the requested item.
2. The second button displays the type and name of the linked Data Block and lets you edit its name after clicking **LMB**.
3. The "X" button clears the link.
4. The "car" button generates an automatic name for the Data Block.
5. And the "F" button specifies whether the Data Block should be saved in the file even if it is unused (unlinked).

Unlinked data is not lost until you quit Blender. This is a powerful Undo feature. if you delete an object the material assigned to it becomes unlinked, but is still there! You just have to re-link it to another object or press the "F" button.

Color Selector

Some controls pop-up a dialog panel. For example, Color controls, when clicked, will pop up a Color Selector dialog.

Color Selector

Screens

Blender's flexibility with windows lets you create customized working environments for different tasks, such as modelling, animating, and scripting. It is often useful to quickly switch between different environments within the same file. For each Scene, you need to set the stage by modelling the props, dressing them and painting them through materials, etc. In the example picture in Window system, we are in the modelling stage.

To do each of these major creative steps, Blender has a set of pre-defined screens, or window layouts, that show you the types of windows you need to get the job done quickly and efficiently:

1. **Animation** • Making actors and other objects move about.
2. **Model** • Creating actors, props, and other objects.
3. **Material** • Painting and texturing surfaces.
4. **Sequence** • Editing scenes into a movie.
5. **Scripting** • Documenting your work, and writing custom animations.

Blender sorts these screen layouts for you automatically in alphabetical order. (A screen name typically starts with a number, which controls the alphabetical order) The list is available via the SCR Menu Buttons in the User Preferences Window header shown in (Screen and Scene selectors). To change to the next screen alphabetically press **CTRL**-**RIGHT**; to change to the previous screen alphabetically, press **CTRL**-**LEFT**.

By default, each screen layout ,remembers' the last scene it was used on. Selecting a different layout will switch to the layout and jump to that scene.

The Screen and Scene selectors

All changes to windows, as described in Window system and Window types, are saved within one screen. If you change your windows in one screen, other screens won't be affected, but the scene you are working on stays the same in all screens.

Adding a new Screen

As you scroll through the Screen list, you will see that one of the options is to Add New - namely, add a new window layout. Click 🖃 and select ADD NEW. When you click this, a new frame layout is created based on your current layout.

Give the new screen a name that starts with a number so that you can predictably scroll to it using the arrow keys. You can rename the layout by **LMB** into the field and typing a new name, or clicking again to position the cursor in the field to edit. For example you could use the name "6-MyScreen".

Deleting a Screen

You can delete a screen by using the Delete Data Block button and confirm by clicking Delete current screen in the pop-up dialog box.

Use the window controls to move frame borders. split and consolidate windows. When you have a layout you like, **CTRL**-**U** to update your User defaults. The buttons window has a special option, if you **RMB** on its background, to arrange its panels horizontally across or vertically up and down.

Scenes

It is possible to have several scenes within the same Blender file. Scenes may use one another's objects or be completely separate from one another. You can select and create scenes with the SCE menu buttons in the User Preferences Window header (usually on top of the screen, also containing the menu bar). For games and other real time content scenes have a important meaning, with scenes you can separate menus, overlays (HUDs, scores etc.), backgrounds from the main scene by layering multiple scenes.

Adding a new Scene

You can add a new scene by clicking the scene menu and selecting ADD NEW. When you create a new scene, you can choose between four options to control its contents (Add Scene menu):

Add scene
Empty
Link Objects
Link ObData
Full Copy

The Add scene menu

- Empty creates an empty scene.
- Link Objects creates the new scene with the same contents as the currently selected scene. Changes in one scene will also modify the other.
- Link ObData creates the new scene based on the currently selected scene, with links to the same meshes, materials, and so on. This means that you can change objects' positions and related properties, but modifications to the meshes, materials, and so on will also affect other scenes unless you manually make single-user copies.
- Full Copy creates a fully independent scene with copies of the currently selected scene's contents.

Deleting a Scene

You can delete a scene by using the Delete Data Block button "X" and confirm by clicking "Delete current scene" in the pop dialog box.

User Preferences

The User Preferences window is where you customize and control Blender. By default this window is located at the top and only the header is visible.

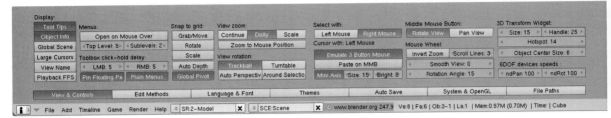

The User Preferences window
To see all of the User Preferences window and its content you need to drag it into view. You can do this by moving the mouse onto the bottom edge of the Info header, or the top of the 3D window, and click the **LMB** and drag downwards.

When viewing all of the Info window you can start to customize Blender to fit your personality or machine capabilities. For example, you may not like the default theme and switch to the Rounded theme. Important is also to configure the paths to enable and save the automatically backup.

Navigating in 3D

Blender is a 3D program, so we need to be able to navigate in 3D space. This is a problem because our screens are only 2D. The 3D Views are in fact "windows" to the 3D world created inside Blender.

Using the keyboard to change your view

Place your mouse pointer over the big window on the standard Blender screen. This is a 3D View used for showing and manipulating your 3D-worlds.

Remember that the window with the mouse pointer located over it (no click needed) is the active window! This means that only this window will respond to your key presses.

Pressing **PAD1** (the number "1" key on the numeric pad) gives you a view from the front of the scene. In the default Blender scene, installed when you first start Blender, you will now be looking at the edge of a plane with the camera positioned in front of it. With holding the **CTRL** key (on some systems also **SHIFT** is possible), you can get the opposite view, which in this case is the view from the back (**CTRL**-**PAD1**).

PAD7 returns you to the view from the top. Now use the **PAD+** and **PAD-** to zoom in and out. **PAD3** gives you a side view of the scene.

PAD0 switches to a camera-view of the scene. In the standard scene you only see the edge of the plane because it is at the same height as the camera.

PAD/ only shows selected objects; all other objects are hidden. **PAD.** (period) zooms to the extent of the selected objects.

Switch with **PAD7** back to a top view, or load the standard scene with **CTRL**-**X**. Now, press **PAD4** four times, and then **PAD2** four times. You are now looking from the left above and down onto the scene. The ‚cross' of keys **PAD8**, **PAD6**, **PAD2** and **PAD4** are used to rotate the actual view. If you use these keys together with **SHIFT**, you can drag the view. Pressing **PAD5** switches between a perspective view and an orthogonal view.

Use **CTRL**-**X** *followed by* **ENTER** *to get a fresh Blender scene. But remember, this action will discard all changes you have made!*

You should now try experimenting a little bit with these keys to get a feel for their operation and function.

Using the mouse to change your view

The main button for navigating with the mouse in the 3D View is the middle mouse button (**MMB**). Press and hold the **MMB** in a 3D View, and then drag the mouse. The view is rotated with the movement of your mouse. Try using a perspective view (**PAD5**) while experimenting -- it gives a very realistic impression of 3D.

With the **SHIFT** key, the above procedure translates the view. With **CTRL**, it zooms the view.

Also explore the View-menu, here you can also change views and control other aspects of the view.

Selecting of Objects

Selecting an object is achieved by **RMB**-*clicking the object.*

This operation also de-selects all other objects. To extend the selection to more than one object, hold down **SHIFT** while clicking. Selected objects will change the color to purple in the wireframe view or an purple outline is drawn around shaded objects. The last selected object is colored a lighter purple and it is the active object. Operations that are only useful for one object, or need one object as reference, always work with the active object.

Objects can also selected with a 'border'. Press **B** to action Border Select, and then draw a rectangle around the objects. Drawing the rectangle with the **LMB** selects objects; drawing with **RMB** deselects them.

Only one Object can be active at any time, e.g. to allow visualization of data in buttons. The active and selected Object is displayed in a lighter color than other selected Objects. The name of the active Object is displayed in the lower left corner of the 3D View. The last Object selected (or deselected) then becomes the active Object.

Copying and linking

Blender uses a object oriented structure to store and manipulate the objects and data. This will affect the work with Blender in many places. For example, the copying of objects or the use of Blender Materials.

In this structure an object can have its own data (in case of the Blender Game Engine Polygon-Meshes) or share this Mesh with more other objects.

So what is the advantage of that system?

1. Reduced size of the scene in memory, on disk or for publishing on the web
2. Changes on the ObData inherits to all Objects on the same time. Imagine you decide to change a house objects you have 100 times in your scene or changing the Material properties of one wall
3. You can design the logic and gameplay with simple place-holder objects and later swap them against the finished objects with a click of the mouse
4. The shape of objects (the Mesh Data) is changeable at runtime of the game without affecting the object or its position itself

Copy

The copy operation you are familiar with from other applications makes a true duplicate of the selected objects. Copying is done fastest with the key command **SHIFT**-**D** or also with the "Duplicate" entry in the Object-menu.

Linked Copy

A linked copy is achieved by using the **ALT**-**D** key command. Unlike copying with **SHIFT**-**D**, the mesh forming the object is not duplicated, but rather linked to the new objects.

Data Browse Button

Another common method to create and change links and Blender
interface element is the User But-
ton . This Menu Button allows to change links by pressing and holding the left mouse
on it and choose a link from the appearing menu. If there are more possibilities than
the Menu can hold, a Data Browse Window is opened instead.

The Data Browse
Button

If an Object has more than one user, the User Button will be blue and a number indicates the number of users (in the above image three). Selecting this number will
make a copy of the Data and makes the object "Single User".

Linking

To link Data from the active to the selected Objects can be done
with the key command **CTRL**-**L**. A "Make Links" menu will ask
what data you want to link. This way you can choose to link the
objects between scenes, or link Ipos (animation curves), MeshData
or Materials.

The Make Links menu

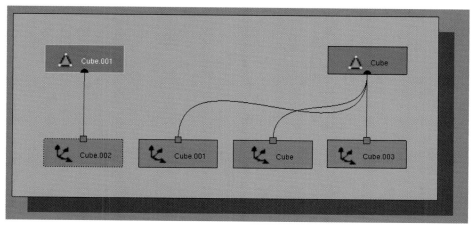

The OOPS window

The object-structure created by copy or linking actions can be visualized in the OOPS
Window. Call the Outliner **SHIFT**-**F9**, then use "View → Show Oops Schematic". Here,
the object "Cube" was copied two times with **ALT**-**D**, you can see that all three objects (Blender automatically generates unique names by appending numbers) are
linked to the same Mesh Data "Cube". The object "Cube.002" was copied with **SHIFT**
-**D** resulting in two objects with their own MeshData.

Manipulating Objects

Most used actions in Blender involve moving, rotating, or changing the size of certain items. Blender offers a wide range of options for doing this. See the 3DWindow section for a fully comprehensive list. The options are summarized here.

Grab

G, Grab mode. Move the mouse to translate the selected items, then press **LMB** or **ENTER** or **SPACE** to assign the new location. Press **ESC** or **RMB** to cancel. Translation is always corrected for the view.

Use the middle mouse button to limit translation to the X, Y or Z axis. Blender determines which axis to use, based on the already initiated movement.

RMB and hold-move. This option allows you to select an Object and immediately start Grab mode.

Rotate

Setting the translation Pivot

R, Rotation mode. Move the mouse around the rotation center, then press **LMB** or **ENTER** or **SPACE** to assign the rotation. Press **ESC** to cancel. Rotation is always perpendicular to the view. Use **X**, **Y** or **Z** to use the global axis for rotation or press the keys two times to rotate around the local object axis.

The center of rotation is determined with the "Pivot"-menu in the 3D View header.

Scaling

S, Scaling mode. Move the mouse from the rotation center outwards, then press **LMB** or **ENTER** or **SPACE** to assign the scaling. Use the **MMB** toggle to limit scaling to the X, Y or Z axis. Blender determines the appropriate axis based on the direction of the movement.

The center of scaling is determined by the Pivot-menu in the 3D View header (see the explanation for the rotation).

Transform Properties

To input exact values, you can call up the Transform Properties with **N**. **SHIFT**-**LMB** to change the buttons to an input field and then enter the number.

Transform Properties

Edit Mode

You can work with Blender Objects in two modes: Object Mode and Edit Mode. Operations in Object Mode affects whole objects, and operations in Edit Mode affect only the geometry of an object, but not its global properties such as location or rotation. You switch between these two modes with the **TAB** key or the Mode-menu in the 3D View header.

Selecting the Edit Mode

Edit Mode only works on one object at a time, the active object. An object outside Edit Mode (i.e. Object Mode) is drawn in purple in the 3D Windows (in wireframe mode) when selected, black otherwise.

In Edit Mode each vertex is drawn in purple, each edge is drawn in black and each face is drawn in translucent dark-blue. Each selected vertex is highlighted in yellow. You can also see a grey shaded face, this is the active face, important for UV texturing.

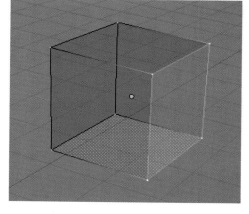

An Object in Edit Mode

If multiple objects are selected and Edit Mode is entered then the last Object selected (the Active Object) enters Edit Mode. The other Objects remain purple and in Object Mode.

If enough vertices are selected to form a face then that face is highlighted in translucent purple while the remaining faces are highlighted in translucent dark-blue. This helps give you a frame of reference when selecting vertices, edges or faces. The translucent effect indicates that you have selected enough vertices to imply one or more faces. See Edge and Face Tools for further details on implicit selections.

If the Buttons Window is visible and Editing (**F9**) is activated then two panels appear while in Edit Mode (Mesh Tools and Mesh Tools More):

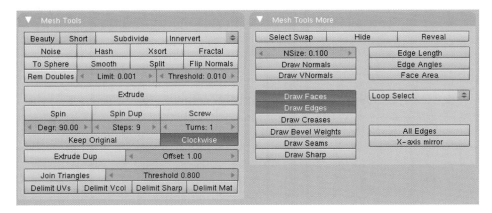

By default the buttons (Draw Faces and Draw Edges) are pre-selected and any selected edges and faces are highlighted.

Vertices, Edges and Faces

In basic meshes, everything is built from three basic structures: Vertices, Edges and Faces. We are not talking about Curves, NURBS, and so forth here as they are currently not supported in the game engine. But there is no need to be disappointed: This simplicity still provides us with a wealth of possibilities that will be the foundation for all our models.

You can convert all Blender Object types down to a Mesh using **ALT**-**C**

Vertices

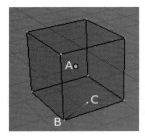

A Vertices is primarily a single point or position in 3D space. It is usually invisible in rendering and in Object Mode. Don't mistake the center point of an object for a vertex. It looks similar, but it's bigger and you can't select it. The image shows the center point labeled as "A". "B" and "C" are vertices.

To create a new vertex, change to Edit mode, hold down **CTRL**, and click with the **LMB**. Of course, as a computer screen is two-dimensional, Blender can't determine all three vertex coordinates from one mouse click, so the new vertex is placed at the depth of the 3D cursor ‚into' the screen. Any vertices selected previously are automatically connected to the new one with an edge. Vertex labeled "C" is a new vertex added to the cube with a new edge (B to C)

Edges

An edge always connects two vertices with a straight line. The edges are the ‚wires' you see when you look at a mesh in wireframe view. They are usually invisible on the rendered image. They are used to construct faces. Create an edge by selecting two vertices and pressing **F**.

Faces

A Face is the highest level structure in a mesh. Faces are used to build the actual surface of the object. They are what you see when you render the mesh. A Face is defined as the area between either three (triangle) or four vertices (quad), with an Edge on every side. Triangles always work well, because they are always flat and easy to calculate.

Take care when using four-sided faces (quads), because internally they are simply divided into two triangles each. Four-sided faces only work well if the Face is pretty much flat (all points lie within one imaginary plane) and convex (the angle at no corner is greater than or equal to 180 degrees). This is the case with the faces of a cube, for example. That's why you can't see any diagonals in its wireframe model, because they would divide each square face into two triangles.

While you could build a cube with triangular faces, it would just look more confusing in Edit mode. An area between three or four vertices, outlined by Edges, doesn't have to be a face. If this area does not contain a face, it will simply be transparent or non-existent in the rendered image. To create a face, select three or four suitable vertices and press **F**.

Vertex Modes, Edge Modes and Face Modes

In Edit Mode there are three different selection modes, Vertices, Edges or Faces. The mode can be chosen with **CTRL**-**TAB** and using the "Select-Mode"-menu or with the icons in the 3D View header.

The Select Mode menu and icons

Vertices • The selected vertices are drawn in yellow and unselected vertices are drawn in a pink color.

Edges • In this mode the vertices are not drawn. Instead the selected edges are drawn in yellow and unselected edges are drawn in a black color.

Faces • In this mode the faces are drawn with a selection handle in the middle which is used for selecting a face. Selected faces are drawn in yellow with the selection point in orange, unselected faces are drawn in black.

Almost all modification tools are available in all three modes. So you can Rotate, Scale and Extrude etc. in all modes. Of course rotating and scaling a single vertex will not do anything useful, so some tools are more or less applicable in some modes.

Basic Editing

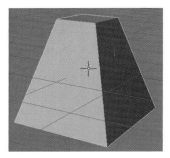

Most simple operations from Object mode (like selecting, moving, rotating, and scaling) work the same way on vertices as they do on objects. Thus, you can learn how to handle basic Edit mode operations very quickly. The only notable difference is a new scaling option, **ALT**-**S** which scales the selected vertices along the direction of the normals (shrinks-fattens). The truncated pyramid shown here, for example, was created with the following steps:

- Add a cube to an empty scene. If not in Edit mode then use **TAB** to enter Edit Mode.
- Make sure all vertices are deselected (purple). Use border select (**B**) to select the upper four vertices.
- Check that the scaling center is set to anything but the 3D cursor, then switch to scale mode (**S**), reduce the size, and confirm with **LMB**.
- Exit Edit Mode by pressing **TAB**.

All operations in Edit Mode are ultimately performed on the vertices; the connected edges and faces automatically adapt, as they depend on the vertices' positions. To select an edge, you must select the two endpoints or place the mouse on the edge and press **ALT**-**RMB**. To select a face, each corner must be selected.

Edit Mode operations are many, and most are summarized in the Editing Context Buttons window, accessed via the header button or via **F9** (Edit Context).

Specials

With **W** you can call up the Specials menu in Edit Mode. With this menu you can quickly access functions which are frequently required for polygon-modelling.

Subdivide • Each selected edge is split in two, new vertices are created at middle points, and faces are split too, if necessary.

Subdivide Multi • This is identical to Subdivide except a dialog pops up asking for the number of cuts or repeated subdivisioning. The default is "2".

Subdivide Multi Fractal • As above, but new vertices are randomly displaced within a user-defined range.

Subdivide Smooth • Same as Subdivide, but new vertices are displaced towards the barycenter (center of mass) of the connected vertices.

Specials
Subdivide
Subdivide Multi
Subdivide Multi Fractal
Subdivide Smooth
Merge
Remove Doubles
Hide
Reveal
Select Swap
Flip Normals
Smooth
Bevel
Set Smooth
Set Solid
Blend From Shape
Propagate To All Shapes
Select Vertex Path

The Specials menu

Merge • Merges selected vertices into a single one, at the barycenter position or at the 3D cursor position.

Remove Doubles • Merges all of the selected vertices whose relative distance is below a given threshold (0.001 by default).

Hide • Hides selected vertices.

Reveal • Shows hidden vertices.

Select Swap • All selected vertices become unselected and vice-versa.

Flip Normals • Change the Normal directions of the selected faces.

Smooth • Smooths out a mesh by moving each vertex towards the barycenter of the linked vertices.

Bevel • Bevels the entire object regardless of the selected vertices, edges or faces.

Set Smooth • Changes the selected faces to smoothing shading.

Set Solid • Changes the selected faces to faceted or flat shading.

Blend From Shape • Mixes between two shape keys

Propagate To All Shapes • Copies the changes to all shape keys

Select Vertex Path • Select a path of vertices between two selected vertices

You can access the entries in a Popup-menu by using the corresponding numberkey. For example, pressing **W** *and then* **1** *will subdivide the selected edges without you having to touch the mouse at all.*

PUMPKIN RUN

PLAYING WITH 3D GAME TECHNOLOGY

Carsten Wartmann

Using the "Pumpkin-Run" example file, most of the core techniques for making a 3D game will be explained and illustrated. However, we can't make you a professional game designer in a few pages, or even with a complete book. But you can learn the basics here and have fun at the same time! You are also encouraged to experiment and play with Blender.

Things you will learn here:

- Loading and saving Blender scenes
- Manipulating objects and navigating in the scene
- Basic Texture mapping
- Playing interactive 3D in Blenders integrated 3D engine
- Adding interactivity to control game elements
- Camera control and lights
- Object animation
- Adding and using sound

And there is more! Many things will be covered in later chapters. But don't despair the most important thing is the gameplay. Even technically simple games can be entertaining for long times ("Tetris" for example). So concentrate on making the game fun for others or just enjoy creating stuff yourself!

Modeling an environment

Start Blender by clicking its Icon. Blender will start with its default scene as shown in the following image. Depending on your installation, screen display ratio and how you installed Blender there may be some slightly differences or a splash-screen will appear.

Blender just after starting it

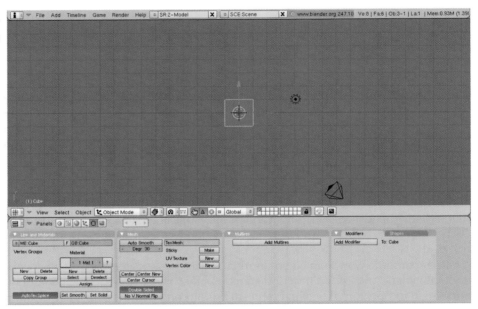

The big window is the 3D View, our window to the world of 3D inside Blender scenes. The pink square is a cube, we are currently looking onto the scene from above, a

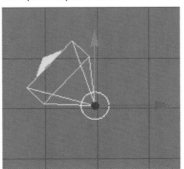

so called "Top View". The line drawn object to the lower right of the cube is the representation of a Blender Camera. The object right of the cube is a light source.

Now move your mouse cursor over the Camera and press your right mouse button, this selects the Camera which is now drawn pink. The colored arrows are so called 3D-handles, by dragging them with the left mouse button you can move the selected object along one axis.

*Blender uses the right mouse button (**RMB**) for selecting objects!*

Now we will change the view of the scene. Move the mouse cursor into the big 3D View and press and hold the middle mouse button (**MMB**) and move the mouse to rotate the view.

*Blender is designed to work best with a three buttons mouse. However, if you have only a two buttons mouse you can substitute the middle mouse button by holding **ALT** and the left mouse button (**ALT**-**LMB**).*

Now return to the top view of the scene by pressing **PAD**-**7**. These actions should give you a basic idea of how navigating in the 3D space through a 2D window works. More on this topic is covered in the Blender Basics Chapter.

In the next steps we will create a ground for our game. Select the cube again by pressing **RMB** with your mouse over it. The cube will be drawn in pink when your selection has been successful. Now press **X** or **DEL** to delete the cube. Blender will ask you for confirmation, if you move the mouse out of the pop-up, the deletion will be canceled, if you agree with **LMB** or **ENTER** the cube will be deleted.

 Newly added objects will always appear at the 3D-Cursor. The 3D-Cursor is placed by a click with the left mouse button, **LMB**. Now place the 3D-Cursor in the middle of the 3D-view by clicking **LMB**.

Now press **SPACE** to call the Toolbox, this is something like the main menu of Blender. Choose Add → Mesh → Plane and confirm the selection with **LMB**. A plane appears, you can check that it is really a plane by rotating the view using the **MMB** and mouse movements. After that switch back to a top view using **PAD**-**7**.

Move the mouse over the selected plane, press **S**, and move the mouse. You can see that the plane changes its size according to your mouse

Scaling info in the 3D View Header

moves. Now hold **CTRL** while moving the mouse. The scale will only change in steps of 0.1. Scale the plane until the size is 10.0 for all axes. To do so look at the scaling information in the bar below the 3D View then press the left mouse button to finish the scaling operation.

*If you can't reach a scale of 10.0 or want to stop the scaling action, press **RMB** or **ESC**. Furthermore, **ESC** will abort every Blender procedure without making any changes to your object.*

In case you can't reach a scale of 10.0, you can try to zoom out using the mouse-wheel. Furthermore it is important where you locate the mouse cursor when calling scale with **S**. If your mouse cursor is close to the center of the object, you will be able to scale in big steps, if your mouse cursor is located away from your object you scale in small amounts, but with a higher accuracy.

I will now show you how to customize the Blender screen, and especially, the window layout.

 Move your mouse slowly over the lower edge of the 3D View until it changes to a double arrow.

Now press the **MMB** or **RMB**, a menu will appear:

Click on "Split Area". Move the appearing line to the middle of the 3D View and press **LMB**, Blender splits the 3D View into two identical views of the 3D scene.

Move your mouse over the right window and press **SHIFT**-**F10**. The window will change to an UV/Image Editor this is the place in Blender to work with images and textures, which will color our real-time models.

All key presses in Blender will be executed by the active window (that is the window with the mouse over it). There is no need to click a window to activate it.

Move your mouse back to the plane in the left 3D View and select it again in case it is not selected anymore (i.e. not pink). Now press **ALT**-**Z**, the plane is now drawn shaded according to the light in the scene. Press **TAB** and the plane will be drawn with a overlay pattern, the edges yellow and the vertices (the points that span the face) as yellow dots. This indicates that the face is selected.

Now with your mouse over the plane, press **U** and choose "Reset" from the "UV Calculation"-menu. A representation of the 3D coordinates of the plane will appear in the UV/Image Editor on the right, this step is needed for mapping a 2D image (texture) onto a 3D object (in our case only a plane). This so called UV mapping is covered in depth in further tutorials and the reference part.

Move your mouse to the right window and select Open from the Image-menu or use **ALT**-**O**.

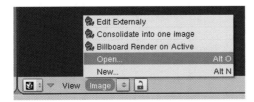

A File Window opens where we can navigate on our disks and select and load images. Pressing and holding the Menu Button on the top left with the left mouse button will give you a choice of recently-browsed paths and on Windows operating systems, a list of your drives.

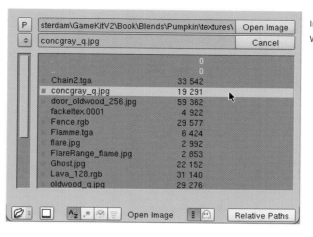

Image File Window

The directory you are currently in, is shown in the top text-field. The "P" button allows you to go up one directory (parent directory).

Using these methods, go to your CDROM drive and browse for the folder **Tutorials/Pumpkin/textures/** and locate the **concgray_q.jpg** image. Click on it with the left mouse button and then choose "Open Image", alternatively you could also click on the filename with the **MMB**.

The texture now shows up in the 3D View to the left. Now leave Edit Mode by pressing **TAB**.

We have just created a very simple environment, but we used many of the steps

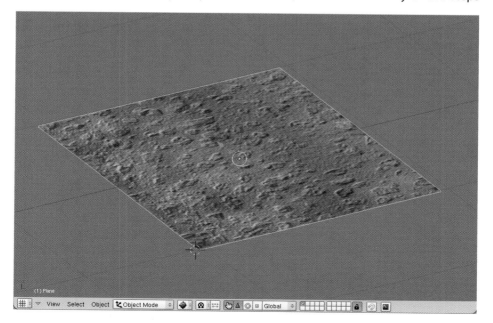

needed to create more complex game levels, which is in fact only a good combination of the simple things we just practised!

It is now time to save your scene. To ease the process we will include the texture in the saved scene. To do so, choose the menu "File → External Data → Pack into .blend file". A little parcel-icon will appear in the menu bar to indicate that this scene is packed. Now use the "File → Save As" or **F2** to open a file window, browse to your hard disk (as described above), enter a name in the filename field (currently "untitled.blend") and click the "Save File" Button in the File window.

Appending an object from an other scene

Because we can't cover modeling and the general use of Blender as a tool to create whole worlds, we load ready-made objects. In fact, there is no special file-format in Blender to store objects, so all scenes can be used as archives to get objects from.

Move your mouse over the UV/ Image Editor window (the right one from the last step) and press **SHIFT** - **F5** to change it to a 3D View.

Press **SHIFT** - **F1** with your mouse over one of the 3D Views, a File Window will appear in "Append" mode (see Figure "File window in append mode"), which allows us to load any Blender object from a scene into the current scene.

You can also use the File menu to access the Append function, but mostly a shortcut is faster.

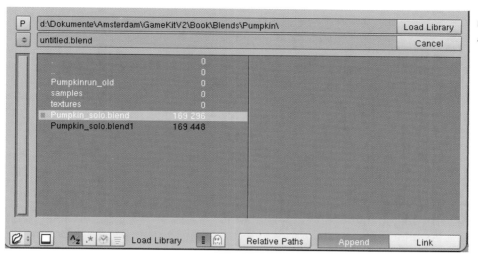

File window in append mode

Pressing and holding the Menu Button on the top left with **LMB** will give you a choice of recently browsed paths and, on Windows operating systems, a list of your drives.

The directory you are currently in is shown in the top text-field. The parent directory "P" button allows you to go up one directory.

Using these methods, go to your CDROM drive and browse for the folder **Tutorials/Pumpkin/** . Now click with the left mouse button on the filename " **Pumpkin_Solo.blend** ". The file will be opened immediately an its contents shown in the file window.

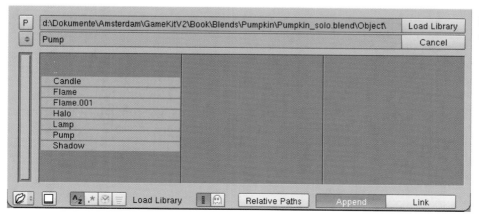

Browsing in a *.blend file

When you have entered the file, the File Window will show you all the parts of the scene like in a file-browser. Now click on "Objects" with **LMB**. You will see the objects contained in that scene (see Figure "Browsing in a *.blend file"). Select all objects by pressing **A**. Confirm by pressing **ENTER** or clicking with **LMB** on the "Load Library" button.

You can now see the pumpkin as an orange spot, sitting in the middle of the plane in the left 3D View.

Switch the right window to a second 3D view by pressing **SHIFT**-**F5** with the mouse over the window. You will get the same top view as in the left 3D view but drawn only shaded. Now select the camera with **RMB**. Move your mouse back to the left (textured) 3D view and press **CTRL**-**PAD 0**. This switches the view to a camera view.

Start your (Game) Engines!

We can now start the Blender game engine already! While pointing with the mouse over the camera view, press **P** and you can see the pumpkin on our textured ground. The pumpkin character has an animated candle inside and you will see it flicker. To stop the game engine and return to Blender press **ESC**.

The Logic Buttons

I hear you saying "That's nice, but where is the animation?" Well, give me a minute.

Move your mouse over the right 3D view and press **PAD**-**3** to get a view from the side. Zoom into the view by pressing **PAD +** a few times or hold **CTRL**-**MMB** and move the mouse up, which will give you a smooth zoom. You also can move the view with the **MMB** and mouse movements while holding **SHIFT**. This way we prepare the view to move the pumpkin up.

Select the character with the **RMB** (click somewhere on the pumpkin), and it will outlined pink to indicate that it is selected.

We will now enter the main command center for interactive 3D in Blender. To do so press **F4** or click the Logic Buttons icon in the icon bar.

Use the menu on the left labeled "Static" to change the pumpkin to "Dynamic". This setting will enable the character to follow the laws of physics, like falling, bouncing and reaction to collisions.

If you now start the game engine you will not see much difference, but we will change that in a minute.

Zoom the right 3D View out a bit (do you remember? Use **CTRL** - **MMB** or **PAD+** / **PAD-** to zoom). Make sure that the pumpkin is still selected (pink, if not then click it with **RMB**), press **G** over the right 3D View and move the mouse. The character will follow your mouse movements in the 3D View. The **G** starts the so called "grab-mode" which allows you to move objects within the 3D space.

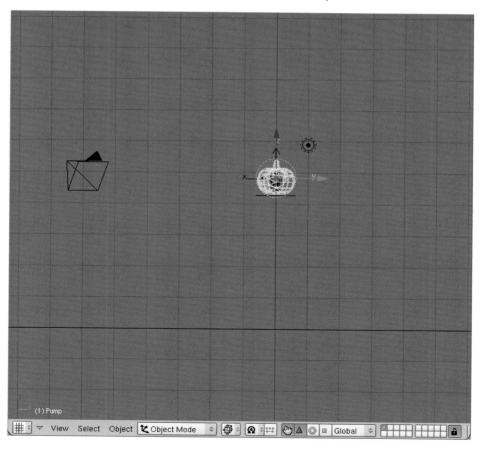

Move the object straight up until it disappears on the top of the camera view (left 3D Window) and confirm the new position with **LMB** . If you are unsure you can always cancel the operation with **ESC** or **RMB** and try again.

Now move the mouse to the left 3D View (the camera view) and press **P** to start the game engine. The Pumpkin falls and rests on the ground. Press **ESC** to exit the game engine.

Realtime Materials

To refine the movement we need some restitute so that the pumpkin would bounce. These settings can be found in the Materials Buttons **F5** . Select the ground plane and press **F5** to access the Material Buttons. Currently there is no material, so click "Add New" to add a new one. If you now start the game you will notice that the texture is gone while the game runs. This is because by default Blender uses a bit more advanced material system by default, the "Blender Multitexture Materials" (see in the Game-menu and in the reference chapter). To solve this we could use the old "Texture Face Materials" or we can just add a texture channel to the material. This can be done by locating the "Texture"-panel on the right of the Material Buttons and click "Add New" there.

If the "Texture"-panel is out of reach you can pan the contents of a button window by holding **MMB** *and moving the mouse or using the mouse wheel. Button windows can also be zoomed with* **PAD -** *and* **PAD +** *!*

Next we will now define the restiute of the ground plane. Locate the "DYN" Button in the "Material"-panel of the Material Buttons and activate it. The buttons in the panel are changing and we can now crank up the "Restitut" slider up to 0.8. This is a factor on how much energy the material will give back on a collision. Two objects with both a restitute of 1.0, will bounce forever, 0.0 means no bounce back.

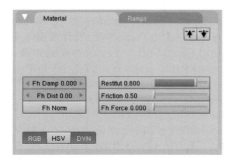

The pumpkin already has a material with a restitute set to 0.8, so if you now start the game engine, it will fall and bounce like a rubber ball, just right for our fun game.

Interactivity

The Logic Buttons (**F4**) are logically divided into four columns. We have already used the leftmost column to set up the object parameters to make the pumpkin fall. The three right columns are used for building the interactivity into our game.

So lets move the pumpkin at our request.

The columns are labeled as "Sensors", "Controllers" and "Actuators". You can think of Sensors as the senses of a life form, the Controllers are the brain and the Actuators are the muscles.

Press the "Add" button once for each row with the left mouse button to make one Logic Brick for the Sensors, Controllers and Actuators (see below).

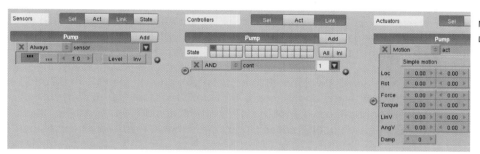

Newly-created Logic Bricks

The types of the added Logic Bricks are nearly correct, for our first task, only small changes are needed. Press and hold the Menu Button now labeled with "Always Sensor" and choose "Keyboard Sensor" from the pop up menu.

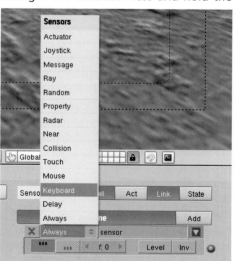

Now **LMB** click into the "Key" field of the Keyboard Sensor. The text "Press any key" appears. Press the key you want to use to move the player forward (I suggest **UP**).

Now have a closer look at the Motion Actuator. We will now define how the player should move. The third line of numbers labeled "Force" defines how much force will be applied when the Motion Actuator is active. The three numbers stand for the forces in X, Y, and Z-Axis direction.

If you look closely at the wire frame view of the player you can see that the Y-axis is pointing forward on the player. So to move forward we need to apply a positive force along the Y-axis. To do so, click and hold on the second number in the "Force" row with the left mouse. Drag the mouse to the right to increment the value to about 10. You can hold the **CTRL** key to snap the values to decadic values. Another way to enter an exact value is to hold **SHIFT** while clicking the field with the left mouse. This allows you to enter a value using the keyboard.

Having created the configuration shown in Figure "Newly-created Logic Bricks", we now need to "wire" or connect the Logic Bricks. The wires will pass the information from Logic Brick to Logic Brick, i.e. from a Sensor to a Controller.

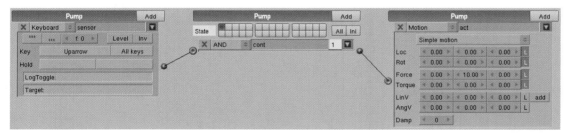

Logic Bricks to move
the player forward

Click and hold the left mouse button on the yellow ball attached on the Keyboard Sensor and drag the appearing line to the yellow ring on the AND Controller. Release the mouse and the Logic Bricks are connected. Now connect the yellow ball on the right side of the AND Controller with the ring on the Motion Controller.

To delete a connection, move the mouse over the connection. The line is now drawn highlighted and can be deleted with an **X** or **DEL** key-press.

Always name your Objects and Logic Bricks, this will help you to find your way through your scenes and refer to specific Logic Bricks later. To name a Logic Brick click into the name field with **LMB** *(see figure above) and enter the name with the keyboard. However, Blender will name objects and Logic Bricks automatically with generated unique names like "sensor1", "sensor2" or "act", "act1" etc., so you don't have to fear about name-collisions.*

Now press **P** to start the game engine and when you press the **UP** key briefly, the player moves passing the camera.

To make the movement more interesting, we can now add a jump. To do so en-ter a 20.0 in the third (z-Axis, up) field of the Motion Controller. If you try it again in the game engine, you can see that there is a problem: If you hold the key pressed, the pumpkin will take off into space. This is because you also apply forces when in the air.

To solve this we have to ensure that the forces only get applied when the pumpkin touches the ground. That's where the Touch Sensor kicks in. Add a new Sensor by clicking on "Add" in the Sensors row. Change the type to "Touch" like you did for the Keyboard Sensor (see Figure "Logic Bricks for adding a constant jump").

Wire the Touch Sensor to the AND Controller. Now the Keyboard and the Touch Sensor are connected to that controller. The type "AND" of the controller will only trigger the Motion Actuator when the key is pressed AND the player touches the ground. This is an easy way to add logic to your interactive scenes. As well as the AND Controller there are also OR, Expression and Python (Blender's scripting language) Controllers which all offer more flexibility to make your game-logic. Because the forces are now applied only a fraction of a second we might adjust them to higher values, 50.0 for force Y and 100.0 for force along the Z-axis should get you started, feel free to experiment here to get a idea how the forces work.

At this moment, space in the Logic Buttons can get sparse. But besides changing the window layout we also can collapse the Logic Bricks. To do so press the little orange arrow right beneath the brick's name (so that you are still able to see the connections, though the content is hidden).

To make the movement more dynamic, we will now add Logic Bricks to make the pumpkin jump constantly. Add a new Controller and a new Actuator by clicking "Add" in the appropriate row. Name the new Actuator "AlwaysJump". Wire the Touch Sensor with the new AND Controller input and the output of the Controller to the new Motion Actuator "Always Jump".

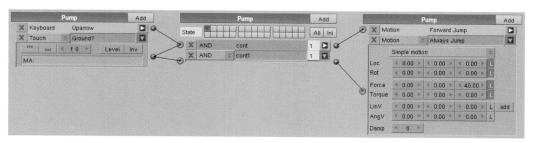

Logic Bricks for adding a constant jump

Yes, not only one Controller can be connected to two Sensors, a sensor can also "feed" two or more controllers. Start the game again with **P**, the pumpkin jumps, **UP** moves it forward

More control

Now we add more Logic Bricks to steer the player with the cursor keys.

Add a new Sensor, Controller and an Actuator by clicking on the "Add" Buttons. Change the Sensor type to "Keyboard" with the Menu Button and assign the left cursor key to the Sensor. Don't forget to name the Logic Bricks by clicking on the name field in the bricks. Wire the Sensor ("LeftArrow") with the Controller ("pass2") and the Controller output with the Actuator ("Left")

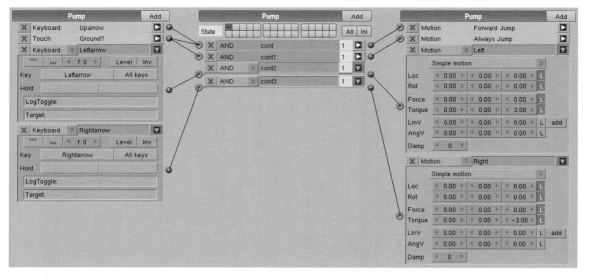

Logic Bricks to steer the player

Enter "3.0" in the third field (Z-axis) in the "Torque" row. Torque is the force that turns the object. In this case it will turn the actor around its longitudinal axis. Try it in the game engine, the pumpkin will turn left when you press **LEFT**. Repeat the steps but change it to turn right. To do so use **RIGHT** and enter a torque of "-3.0". See Figure above.

It is most likely that we need to adjust or fine tune the controls later in the game, this is a iterative process which need some experience.

Camera control

In this section, I will show you how to set up a camera which follows the actor, trying to mimic a real cameraman.

Move your mouse over the right 3D view (the wire frame or shaded view) and zoom out with **PAD-** or **CTRL**-**MMB** movements. Locate the camera and select it with **RMB**.

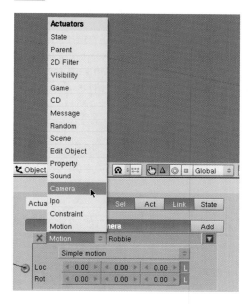

Ensure that the Logic Buttons (**F4**) are still open. Now add a Sensor, Controller and an Actuator as you learned above. Wire the Logic Bricks and Change the Actuator into a Camera Actuator. The Camera Actuator will follow the Object in a flexible way which gives smooth motions.

Click the "OB:" field in the Camera Actuator and enter the name of the pumpkin object, here "Pump". The camera will follow this object. Click and hold the "Height:" field with the **LMB** and move the mouse to the right to increase the value to about 2.0. This is the height the camera will stay at.

Holding **CTRL** *while adjusting a Number Button will change the value in stages making it easier to adjust the value.* **SHIFT**-**LMB** *on a Number Button lets you use the keyboard to enter values.*

Logic Brics for the camera

The Min: and Max: fields determine the minimal and maximum distance the camera will get to the object. I chose "Min: 4.0" and "Max: 7.0". Start the game engine to test the Camera Actuator. Experiment a bit with the values.

Real-time Light

Real-time lighting in Blenders game engine is performed by the OpenGL subsystem and takes advantage of hardware accelerated transform and lighting if your graphics card provides it.

Locate the lamp in a 3D View and select it with **RMB**. Use **G** to move it and watch the effect on the textured view on the pumpkin. For reference, the left pumpkin in Figure "Logic Brics for the camera" is lit, the right one is not. Try to move the light around in the 3D Views so you can see that the textured view gets updated in real-time. Moving the light under the pumpkin gives a scary look, for example.

Difference between a lit and unlit pumpkin

In this example, the real-time lighting doesn't cast shadows. The shadow of the pumpkin is created differently. Also, bear in mind, that real-time lights cause a slowdown in your games. So try to keep the number of objects with real-time light as low as possible.

More options for lamps and real-time lighting are covered in the Reference section.

Object Animation

Here I will cover the basics of combining Blenders animation system with the game engine. The animation curves (Ipos) in Blender are fully integrated and give you full control of animations both in conventional (linear) animation and in the interactive 3D graphics covered by this book.

Use **SHIFT**-**F1** or use the File-menu "Append or Link". Browse to the book's disk, choose **Tutorials/Pumpkin/Door.blend**, click on Object, select all objects with **A**, confirm with **ENTER**. This will append a wall with a wooden door to the scene. The pumpkin will bump against the walls and the door. The collision detection is handled by the Blender game engine automatically.

Switch the right 3D View to a Top View (**PAD7**) and zoom (**PAD+** or **PAD-**) as needed to see the appended door completely. The door has the name and the axis enabled, so it should be easily visible, for easier access switch the view to a wire frame view (**Z**). Select the door with **RMB** (it will turn pink).

We will now make a simple key frame animation:

The Frame Slider

1. Ensure that the Frame Slider (the current animation frame) is at frame 1 by pressing **SHIFT**-**LEFT**
2. **I**, select "Rot" from the menu
3. Now advance the animation time by pressing **UP** five times to frame 61. With the game engine playing 60 frames per second our animation will now play 2 seconds.

The Insert Key Menu

4. Press **R** (be sure to have your mouse over the top view) and rotate the door 150° clockwise. You can see the degree of rotation in the Header of the 3D View. To make it easier to rotate exactly, hold **CTRL** while rotating.
5. Now insert a second key by pressing **I** and again choosing "Rot"
6. Move to frame 1 by pressing **SHIFT**-**LEFT** and press **SHIFT**-**ALT**-**A**, you will see the animation of the door being played back. After 51 frames the animation will continue to frame 250 and then repeat.
7. Press **ESC** to stop the playing animation.

With the door still selected switch the Buttons Window to the Logic Buttons, by pressing **F4**. Add a Sensor, Controller and Actuator, wire them, name them, change the Sensor to a Keyboard Sensor and change the Actuator to "Ipo" type.

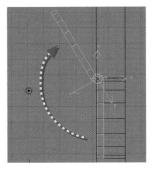

Rotating the door

Change the type of the Ipo Actuator to "Ping Pong" mode using the Menu Button. **SHIFT**-**LMB** "End" and change the value into "61". This way the Ipo Actuator plays the door animation from frame 1 to 61 which opens the door. A new invocation of the Ipo Actuator will then close the door (because of playing it "Ping Pong").

Logic Bricks for playing an Ipo in "Ping Pong" mode

Play the scene **P** in the textured view, and the door will now open and close when you press **SPACE** and can push the actor around if he gets hit by the door. To visualize the animation curves (Ipos) switch one window to an Ipo Window by pressing **SHIFT**-**F6**.

Refining the scene

You may have noticed there is currently a problem in the file: The actor can "climb" (nearly takes off like a rocket) the wall because we can jump on every touch of any object even on a wall.

Select the pumpkin and look at the Touch Sensor, the "MA:" field is empty. "MA:" stands for a material name. If you fill in a material name here, the Touch Sensor will only react to objects with this material. In our scene this would be the ground we created at the beginning.

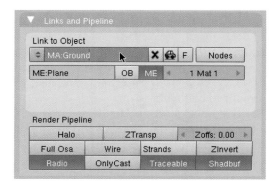

So now select the ground plane and change to the Material Buttons **F5**. Locate the "Links and Pipeline"-panel and change the name of the material by clicking it with the left mouse button and entering "Ground".

Now, select the pumpkin again, switch back to the Logic Buttons **F4** and enter "Ground" into the "MA:" field of the Touch Sensor.

Whether a name is capitalized or not makes a difference in Blender. So a Material called "ground" is not the same as "Ground". Blender will blank a button when you enter an object name which does not exist. This may sound frustrating but it really helps while debugging, because it prevents you from overlooking a simple typo.

Try again to hop around, now you now cannot climb the wall anymore.

At this point you may want to place the camera more behind the pumpkin, so that the view during the game is better, and also move the light in a way that the pumpkin gets lit better. It is best to do such things in the top view, using **G** to move and **R** to rotate and controlling the effect in the camera view.

One last thing: it would be nice if the door would only open when the actor is close to it. The Near Sensor will help us here.

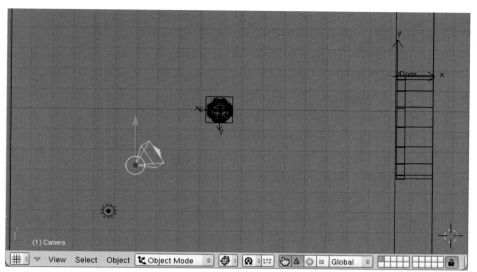

Moving the Camera in the Top View

Add a new Sensor to the door and change the Sensor type to "Near". Wire it to the existing AND Controller (see Figure "Near Sensor"). The "Dist:" field gives the distance at which the Near Sensor starts to react to the actor. By the way, it will react to every actor if we leave the "Property:" field empty. The "Reset: 12.0" field is the distance be-

tween the Near Sensor and the object where the Near Sensor "forgets" the actor. Try to set the "Dist:" setting to 4.0, now you need to come close to the door first but then you can back up before you press **SPACE** to open the door without the danger of getting hit. Now the door only opens when you press **SPACE** and the pumpkin is near the door, good for levels with more than one door.

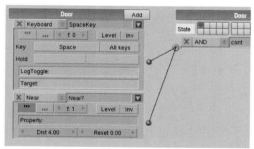

Near Sensor

Adding Sound to our scene

There is no game without sound, so I will show here how to add a sound to an event in Blender.

Locate the Sound Buttons icon in the icons of the Display Buttons **F10**. Click the icon with the left mouse button to switch to the Sound Buttons. Because there is no sound in the scene the "Sound"-panel will be near empty. Use the Menu Button under "Blender Sound block" (click and hold) to

The Display Buttons

choose "OPEN NEW". A file window opens, browse to get to the CDROM and load **DoorOpen.wav** from the directory **Tutorials/Pumpkin/samples/** .

The Sound Buttons with a sound loaded

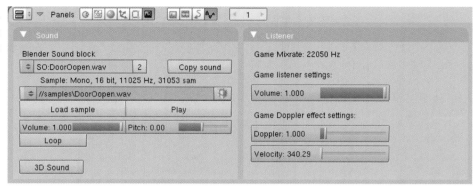

Blender is capable of creating 3D sound (Sound located spatial in the scene) and provides many ways to influence the sound. But for the moment we can go with the defaults and don't need to touch any of these buttons. Of course you can play the sound by clicking on the big "Play" button.

Select the door object (**RMB**) and switch to the Logic Buttons with **F4**. Add a new Actuator and change the type to "Sound". Wire it to the Controller (see Figure "Door Sound"). Click and hold the solitary Menu Button in the Sound Actuator and choose the sound file "DoorOpen.wav" from the pop-up menu. As a last step before you can try it, change the mode "Play Stop" to "Play End" this means the whole sound is played without stopping too early.

Door Sound

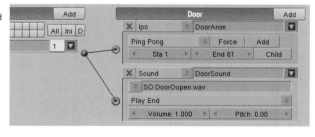

In the same manner you can load the sound "bounce.wav" and add this sound to the pumpkin. Just make sure that you connect the Sound Actuator with the right Controller, the one which is also connected to the "Always Jump" Actuator. This way every time the pumpkin touches the ground, a bumpy sound will be played.

Last words

After this chapter you should have an idea what it is about to make a game with Blender. We did some of the basic steps and you are now prepared to do other tutorials or start playing with ready made scenes or your own ideas. I would encourage you to experiment a bit more with the pumpkin scene, also check out the additional scenes in the pumpkin folder on the disk.

I suggest that you continue with the chapter "The Blender Basics", and read it at least one time so that you know where to look when you face problems. Also don't hesitate to use our support, see the Appendix for links to the forums and online resources.

TUBE CLEANER

A SIMPLE SHOOTING GAME

Carsten Wartmann

Tube Cleaner was designed by Freid Lachnowicz. The game is a simple shooter game that takes place in a tube. Three kinds of enemies are present. Try to collect as many points and bullets as you can on your way up the tube!

To play the game in its final stage load the scene **Games/TubeCleaner.blend** from the CDROM. It includes instructions.

This Tutorial is not supposed to explain how to make the full game. But you should be able to understand the extensions in the final result (you can also look for cheat codes in the game...) with the help of this book and this tutorial. And of course you are encouraged to change and extend the game to your liking!

Tube Cleaner game controls

CONTROLS	DESCRIPTION
CURSOR KEYS	rotate the cannon left, right, up and down
SPACE	Shoot

Loading the models

Tube Cleaner game

Start Blender and load **Tutorials/TubeCleaner/TubeCleaner_00.blend** from the disk. This scene contains all models to start. To make the scene interactive, this tutorial will lead you through the following tasks:

1. Adding game logic to the gun, allowing it to move up, turn and shoot
2. Adding game logic to the enemies
3. Creating the score system including display

The scene contains a camera view on the left, a wireframe view (view from top) on the right and a the Logic Buttons on the bottom. In the top view (Figure " Wireframe top view in the Tube Cleaner scene") you can see the "Base" object is already se-lected and active (purple color in wireframe). The "Base"-object will carry the cannon

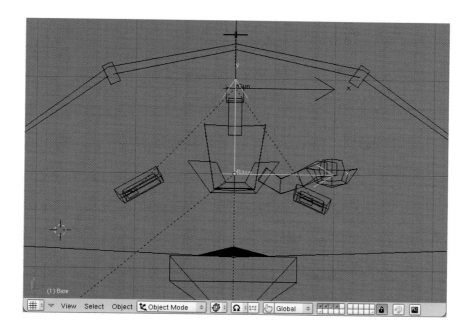

Wireframe top view
in the Tube Cleaner
scene

and will contain some of the global logic of the game. The cannon itself is parented
to this "Base". This hierarchy will make our job later easier because we won't have to
worry about composite movements.

Controls for the base and cannon

We start with the rotation around the vertical axis of the base. This will also rotate the
cannon and the camera because they are parented to the base.

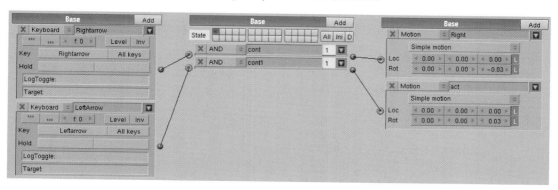

Logic Bricks to
Make sure that the "Base" object is selected (pink, **RMB** to select if not) and click on   rotate the gun
the "Add" Buttons in the Logic Buttons **F4** for each row of Sensors, Controllers and

Actuators. In every row a new Logic Brick will appear.

Now link (wire) the Logic Bricks by clicking and drawing a line from the little yellow balls (outputs) to the yellow donuts (input) of the Logic Bricks. These connections will pass the information between the Logic Bricks. Change the first Logic Brick to a Keyboard Sensor by click and hold its Menu Button with the left mouse button and select "Keyboard" from the pop up menu.

Please (re)do the tutorial in the "Pumpkin Run" chapter if you have problems with the creating, changing and linking of Logic Bricks.

Now, click the "Key" field with the **LMB** and press the **RIGHT** key when prompted by "Press any key" in the Keyboard Sensor. The "Key" field now displays "Rightarrow" and the Keyboard Sensor now reacts to this key only.

Now change the third number (Z-Axis) in the "dRot" row of the Motion Actuator to -0.03. Do this by using **SHIFT**-**LMB** on the number and entering the value with the keyboard. The three fields always denote the three axis (X,Y,Z) of an object. So we will rotate around the Z-axis.

Now move your mouse cursor over the camera view and press **P** to start the game. You should now be able to rotate the gun with the right cursor key.

You should always name your Logic Bricks and other newly created elements in your scenes (click on the default name and edit with your keyboard). This will help you to find and understand the logic later. Take Figure "Logic Bricks to rotate the gun" as a reference.

Use the same procedure as above to add Logic Bricks to rotate the gun to the left. Use **LEFT** as key in the Keyboard Sensor and enter "0.03" in the third "dLoc" field of the Motion Actuator.

As you can see the space in the Logic Buttons is getting sparse with only six Logic Bricks. Use the little orange arrow icon in the Logic Bricks to collapse the Logic Bricks to just showing a title. Now you also see another good reason for properly naming Logic Bricks.

Upwards Movement

In "Tube Cleaner" we want to have a continuous upwards movement within the tube. We could achieve this similarly to the rotation of the gun, but there is another way which will give us much more control over the movement and also allows you to move down to a specific level of the tube.

The method used here is to combine the possibilities of Blender's game engine and its powerful animation system. Move your mouse cursor over the camera view and press **ALT**-**A**, Blender will play back the animations already defined in the scene. Press **ESC** to stop the playback. But so far none of these animations is played back by the game engine. We have to tell the objects to play the animation. This way we can interactively control animations, for example play, stop or suspend.

Move your mouse cursor over the wireframe view and press **SHIFT**-**F6**. The window will change to an Ipo Window (see the Ipo Figure below), meant for displaying and editing Blender's animation curves. The Ipo Window is organized into axes, here the axes are the horizontal axis, showing the time in Blender's animation frames and the vertical axis showing Blender units. The yellow vertical line is the animation curve for the movement along the Z-Axis of the "Base" object, meaning upward move-ment for our object. So to move the object 10 units up you can move the Ipo cursor (green line) with a left mouse click to frame 10. The camera view will reflect this im-mediately.

To play this animation in the game engine, we use a special Logic Brick the "Ipo Actuator", set to "Property play" type. A Property is a variable owned by a game object, which can store values or strings. We will now create a new property which will hold the height (zLoc(ation)) of the "Base" object. To do so click on "ADD property" in the Logic Buttons for the "Base" object.

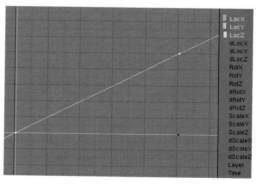

Ipo Window with the animation curve for upward movement

Click on "Name:" and change the default name "prop" to "zLoc", this Property will hold the height of the gun in the tube.

Blender uses capitalization to distinguish between names of Objects and Properties. So "zloc" is not the same as "zLoc".

Continue creating the Logic Bricks from Figure "Logic Bricks for the upward move-ment". The Always Sensor triggers the logic for every frame of the game engine ani-mation, ensuring constant movement. The AND Controller just passes the pulses to two Actuators, both are connected to the Controller and will be activated at the same frame.

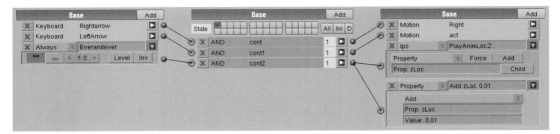

Logic Bricks for the
upward movement

The Ipo Actuator will play the Ipo animation according to the value in the Property "zLoc". To get a constant motion we increase the "zLoc" Property every frame with the Property Actuator . In this case it is of the type "Add" which adds "Value:" (here 0.01) to the "zLoc" Property every frame. Try to change the "Value:" to get a feeling for the speed of the animation. If you'd like to move the cannon downwards try entering -0.01 into the "Value:" field. After experimenting a bit please use 0.01 for the value field as shown in the Figure. To play the game at this stage move your mouse to the camera view and press **P**.

Blender can show you the used Properties and their values while the game runs. To do so, choose "Show debug properties" from the "Game" menu and activate the "D" Buttons (Debug) for every Property you'd like to have printed on screen

Shooting

Switch the Ipo Window back to a 3D View by pressing **SHIFT**-**F5** over the Ipo Window. Now select the "Gun" object with the right mouse. You can click on every wire from the "Gun" object, a proper selection will be reflected in the lower left corner of the 3D View and in the Logic Buttons where "Gun" will appear in the columns for the Logic Bricks.

Now add a Sensor, Controller and Actuator to the "Gun" object and wire them as you learned earlier in the tutorials. Change the Sensor to a Keyboard Sensor (please name the Sensor "Space") and choose (click in the "Key" field) Space as trigger for the gun. Change the Actuator to an "Edit Object" Actuator. The default type is "Add Object" which adds an object dynamically when the Actuator is triggered.

Logic Bricks to fire
the gun

Enter "bullet" into the "OB:" field by clicking it with **LMB** and using the keyboard to enter the name. This will add the object "bullet", a pre-made object, which is on a hidden layer in the scene. Enter 18.00 as the second number in the "linV" fields. This will give the bullet an initial speed. Also activate (press) the little "L" button behind the "linV" row. This way the bullets will always leave the gun in the direction aimed. Enter 50 in the "Time:" field. This will limit the life time of the bullets to 50 frames, avoiding ricochets to bounce forever. As usual, try to run the game now and shoot a bit.

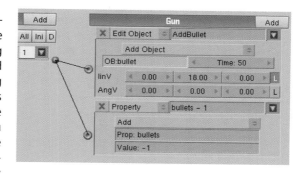

So far we have unlimited ammunition. To change this we again use a Property storing the number of bullets left. Add a new Property by clicking on "ADD property". Name this Property "bullets" and change its type to "Int" with the Menu Button now labeled "Float" (the standard type for new Properties). An "Int(eger)" Property only holds whole numbers, this is ideal for our bullets as we don't want half bullets. **SHIFT-LMB** on the field to the right of the "Name:" field to enter 10 here. This is the initial number of bullets available at the start of the game.

To actually decrease the number of bullets on every shot we use the "Property Add" Actuator that we also used to make the base of the cannon move up. So add another Actuator by clicking on "Add" in the Actuator's column of the gun. Wire it to the AND Controller we created in the last step. Change the Actuator type to "Property" choose "Add" as the action. Enter "bullets" in the "Prop:" field and -1 in the "Value:" field. This will subtract 1 (or add -1) from the Property "bullets" on every shot triggered by Space.

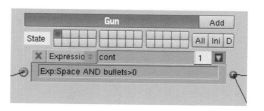

So far the gun doesn't take any notice of the number of bullets. To change this we will use an Expression Controller which allows to add single line expressions to process game logic. Change the AND Controller with the Menu Button to an Expression Controller. Then click on the "Exp:" field and enter "Space AND bullets>0" (without the quotation marks) and press **ENTER**. Here "Space" is the name (exactly as you typed it in the Logic Brick) of the Keyboard Sensor and "bullets" is the bullets Property. The Controller now only activates the following Actuators if the Sensor "Space" is active (meaning that Space is pressed) AND bullets is bigger than zero. Try again to run the game, you now can only shoot 10 times. Read more about Expressions in Section [Expressions].

The last step to make the gun work is to make the bullets display functional. Select the display (the right one with the flash on it) with the right mouse button. It is best to hit the little dot on the "@" sign (which is a visual hint for placing the object). The name "BulletsDisplay" should appear in the Logic Buttons and in the 3D View. Alternatively you can zoom into the wireframe view to make the selection easier.

You can see in the Logic Buttons that there is already a Property called "Text" for the display object. The object has a special text-texture assigned which will display any information in the Property called "Text" that is on it. You can test this by changing the value "10" in the Property, the change will be displayed immediately (a bit covered by the "@" sign) in the camera view and also during runtime of the game.

Because Properties are local to the object they are owned by, we have to find a way to pass the values of Properties between objects. Inside a single scene this can be done with the Property Copy Actuator. Another way would be to use messages, in this case you can also pass information between multiple scenes.

Add a line of Logic Bricks to the "BulletsDisplay" like you did before and wire them. Change the Actuator to a Property Actuator, type "Copy".

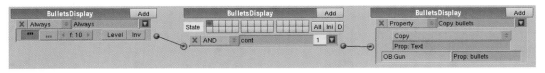

Logic Bricks to display the amount of bullets

Enter "Text" into the first "Prop:" field, this is the name of the Property we copy into. Enter "Gun" into the "OB:" field, again watch for correct capitalization, Blender will blank the input field if you enter a non-existing object. From this object we will get the value. Enter "bullets" into the field "Prop:" beneath "OB:" this is the Property name from which we get the value. It is not needed to actually copy the information in every frame, so enter a 10 in the "f:" field of the Always Sensor, this will copy the Property every 10th frame (about 1/6 of a second) and will so preserve performance.

Start the game and shoot until you have no more bullets.

More control for the gun

Tilting the gun will add more freedom in movement and dynamic to the game. We will use a similar technique as for the movement up, by combining animation curves and Logic Bricks.

Select the gun and collapse the Logic Bricks by clicking their arrow icons 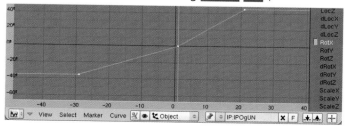, this will give us more space for the coming logic.

As for the upward movement of the gun, it already contains a motion curve that we can use. We also need a Property which contains the actual rotation (tilt, rotation around x-axis). So add a new Property by clicking on "ADD property" and name it "rotgun".

Again use the "Add" Buttons to add a Sensor, Controller and one... nope, you are right this time two Actuators. You already know this from the upward movement. We need one Actuator to change the Property and one to play the Ipo. Wire the new Logic Bricks, as shown in Figure "Logic Bricks to rotate the gun upwards". The collapsed Logic Bricks are the ones you made for shooting.

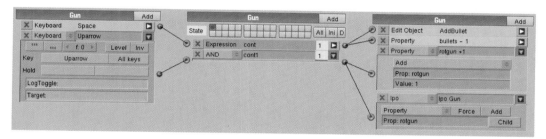

Logic Bricks to rotate the gun upwards

Change the Bricks according to the Figure above and enter all the necessary information. Using the Property Add Actuator we increase "rotgun" by one every time **UP** is pressed and then play the Ipo according to the "rotgun" Property, this will rotate the gun up.

Now test the game. Every time you press **UP** the gun will rotate a bit up. Stop the game with **ESC**. To get a continuous motion we have to activate the pulse mode icon for the Keyboard Sensor, this will give a keyboard repeat here, so the gun will rotate as long as you press the key without the need to release it.

Now test the rotation again, and you will see that the gun only rotates a specific amount and then stops. This is because of the animation curve (Ipo), you can visualize the curve when you switch a window to an Ipo Window using **SHIFT**-**F6** (use **SHIFT**-**F5** to return to the 3D View). You can see that the curves are horizontally from frame 21 (horizontal axis), meaning no further rotation is possible. You also see that we need to make the "rotgun" negative to rotate down.

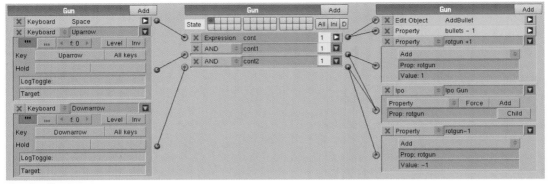

Again add a Sensor, Controller and one (yes, this time, it's really only one) Actuator. Wire and name them as shown in Figure "Completed Logic Bricks to tilt the gun". Note that we use the Ipo Actuator for the tilting down also. This is perfectly ok, this way we can save a Logic Brick. It would have also been working ok to use a second Ipo Actuator here.

If you prefer "pilot-controls" just swap the UpArrow and DownArrow in the Keyboard Sensors.

Expressions to
correctly stop the
rotation

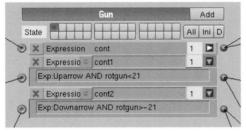

There is one drawback: if you press **UP** for too long the gun will stop rotating but "rotgun" is still incremented. This will cause that the cannon is not rotating back immediately when you press **DOWN** again. To prevent this we can use an Expression Controller again, see the Figure to the left for the correct Expressions.

These Expressions will prevent "rotgun" from counting when "rotgun" is already greater than 21 or less than -21.

It is time to save your project now! Blender scenes are usually very compact so saving only takes seconds. First you need to pack (include in the Blenderfile) the textures, use the "File-menu → External Data → Pack into .blend file" to do so. Then save the file to your hard disk. This makes sure that all textures (and in case also sounds and fonts) will be on your harddisk, so that opening the file again will not need the books disk inserted.

This way you can also send the file to a friend by e-mail and he will get all textures with the game.

For further working on the scene it is recommended to unpack the data again with "File-menu → Data → Unpack into Files...", then choosing "Use files in current directory (create when necessary)".

An enemy to shoot at

It is now time to add something to shoot at. Select the "Target" object with the right mouse, it may be needed to rotate the view a bit using **MMB** and mouse movements to get a good view.

The tasks a game logic on the enemy has to do are:

1. React on hits (collisions) with the bullets
2. Make a silly face when hit, and die
3. Add some points to the players score

You can see that I try to keep the game logic on the target itself. Although it is possible to put all that to the player or any other central element, it would make a very complex and difficult to maintain logic for this object. Another advantage of using local game logic is that it makes it much easier to re-use the objects and the logic, even in other scenes.

We start again by adding a Sensor, Controller and an Actuator and wiring them. You should be familiar with that procedure by now. To react to a collision, change the Sensor to a Collision Sensor. Enter "bullet" into the "Property:" field, this is the name of a Property carried by the bullet, this way the Collision Sensor will only react to collisions with bullets.

Logic Bricks to make the target look silly

Change the Actuator to an Edit Object Actuator and choose "Replace Mesh" as the type. Enter "TargetDead" into the "ME:" field. This mesh show the dead target and will be shown from now on when you hit the target with a bullet. The dead target is on a hidden Layer, you can look at it when you switch Layer 11 on by pressing **SHIFT** -**ALT**-**1**.

*Don't forget to switch of Layer 11 again with **SHIFT**-**ALT**-**1**, or shooting will not function properly. This is because all added objects need to be in a hidden layer to make the Add Object Actuator work.*

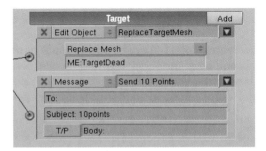

To actually score a hit we will use Blender's messaging system. This allows us to send messages from objects to objects. In this case we will signal the score-display to add some points to our score. So add a second Actuator to the target, wire it with the existing Controller and change it to a Message Actuator.

We can leave the "To:" and "Body:" fields blank, just fill in the "Subject:" field with "10points". This is equal to shouting into the room and the score-keeper will note the score.

We now need to set up the score display to react to the score messages. Select the "Score-display" object and add Logic Bricks as shown in the following Figure:

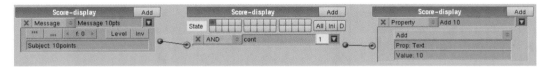

The "Score-display" is again an object with a special texture on it showing the content of the "Text" property as explained for the bullets display. Be sure to change the 999 to zero or the score will start with 999 points. The Message Sensor will only hear messages with the "10points" subject and then trigger the Property Actuator to add 10 to the "Text" Property which is then displayed. This way it is also very easy to add different scores to different actions, just add a new line of Logic Bricks listening for different subjects and then add the appropriate amount of points.

You should now try out the game so far and shoot at the enemy. This should add 10 points to your score. If anything fails to work, check especially the correct wiring, and that the names and capitalization of Properties and message subjects are as they should be.

In the final game the targets start to slide down the tube, look at Figure "Advanced animation for dead targets" for a possible solution for that. The simple target also has the drawback that it will still add a score when you hit a dead target.

We have already used most of these Logic Bricks. Basically it just uses an Expression Controller to avoid counting scores by shooting on dead targets. This is done by checking the frame Property for being zero which gets increased by one when a hit occurs. As soon as frame is one a Property Sensor type "Interval" fires as long as

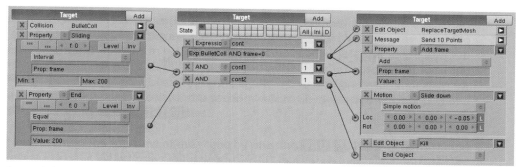

frame is between 1 and 200, this triggers adding frame by one and sliding the target a bit down in every frame. When frame reaches 200 the object gets killed by the Edit Object Actuator.

Advanced animation for dead targets

Now you can place more targets in the tube. For that select the target, then use **ALT**-**D** to copy it. Now use grabbing (**G**) and rotating (**R**), use **CTRL** for a snap) to place the new enemy.

Together with the reference part of this book and the final game on the disk you can now try to extend the file or just enjoy playing the game. Don't desperate and keep on experimenting. By breaking the task into small steps, even complex logic is possible without getting lost.

PINBALL

Carsten Wartmann

Pinball

A pinball game is a nice thing to test a physics engine. The fast motions will stress the collision system to the max.

As the theme I chose a construction site, I did not try to mimic a real pinball that much but looked for some special effects like the accident mode in the tunnels, the sewer mode or the brickmode which would be not possible in a real arcade flipper. Load the file **Games/Pinball.blend** and press **P** to play.

FUNCTION	KEY
Add Ball	**B**
Flipper left	**C**
Flipper right	**M**
Shoot Ball	**RETURN**

Use of the elements

All elements like the bumpers, flippers etc. in the game are groups in hidden layers (see layers 11-20) for easy re-use. This also allows to quickly change already placed elements without a hassle.

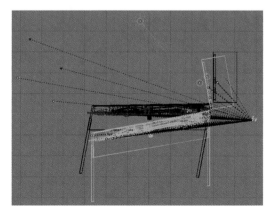

For easily constructing the game and placing the elements, I parented all elements to a master empty, then before playing I rotate the master empty so that the desired slant is achieved. So the usual way to edit look like this:

1. switch to frame 2, the pinball table is now leveled
2. add element or group
3. parent the element or group (**CTRL**-**P**) to the master empty

4. if wanted, now copy the element or group with **ALT**-**D**, all copies are automatically parented also to the master empty
5. switch to frame 1
6. play the game

Other ideas for elements could be:

- construction site sounds
- pipes (working as ball ramps)
- sand „hills" or sand ground (slows the ball)
- caterpillar (moving, can manipulate the ball or „protect" an extra)
- scaffolds
- ramps made of shelves
- containers

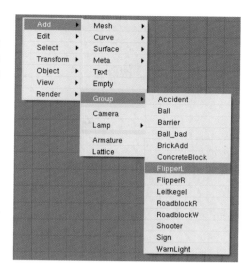

Bumpers

All bumpers follow the same principle, the objects itself has no collision set, instead an invisible simple object surrounds them. This surrounding object plays an Ipo upon contact to give the ball an extra hit.

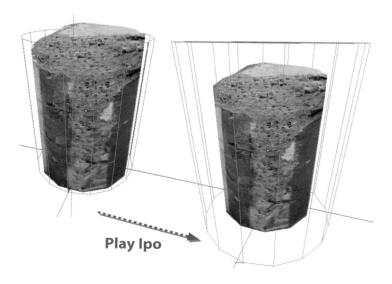

Play Ipo

The Logic Bricks are only a Collision Sensor which triggers the Ipo, plays a sound and sends a score message.

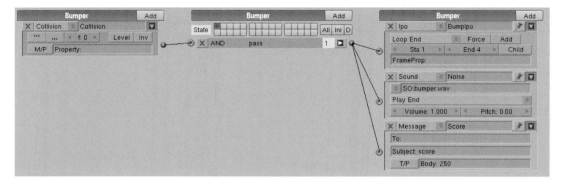

The Sewer

The sewer effect is played when the ball falls into the hole on the street. Here we just have an object which kills the ball (all objects having a Property „kill" will kill the ball, the logic is on the ball itself) and sends a message to the sewer.

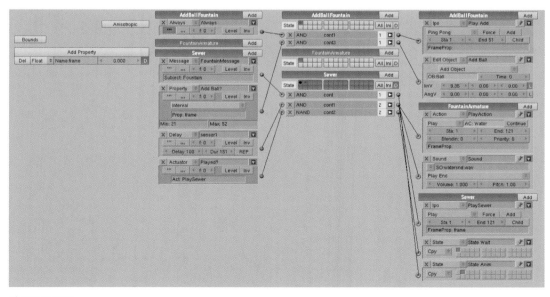

The Sewer Logic

The sewer is assembled out of four parts, the manhole cover, an Empty which will add a new ball with the Add Object Actuator and a water fountain which is deformed by an Armature.

The Sewer Objects

The logic of the sewer contains four new logic elements which were developed by Benoit Bolsee for the Apricot Project and are now part of Blender 2.48: The NAND Controller, the Delay Sensor, the State system and the Actuator Sensor.

Let's start with the easy part, how the ball is added:

AddBallFountain • This is just an Empty, it has an Ipo which is always played in Ping Pong mode so that the new added ball will start with a new direction (pseudo randomly) every time. At a specific time (depending on the whole animation) the ball is added by triggering a Add Object Actuator.

Now the complicated part, syncing the Actions and Ipos of the fountain:

Sewer • This object is the manhole cover and contains the most complicated logic. It has two states, the initial one which just sits there and waits for a message with the subject „Fountain" and triggers the second state when it arrives. The second state plays an Ipo animation of the manhole cover and an action on an Armature which deforms the water fountain.

   The Delay Sensor • waits some seconds then it triggers the water sound, the Ipo animation of the manhole cover and the Action for the Armature

   The Actuator Sensor • is triggered as long as the sewer Ipo Actuator is played. When the Ipo is over, it will trigger the State Actuator to go to state 1 again. This is achieved with the use of a NAND Controller.

SUBRACER

AN UNDERWATER RACING GAME

Carsten Wartmann

The "Subracer" game features some recent developments which were made for the Apricot Project. This includes GLSL Materials (normal maps, caustic maps, reflection maps), GLSL mist (nicer and more flexible than the normal BGE mist) and GLSL Shadows.

Concept art

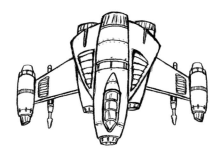

The game idea, concept, game logic, physics, scripts, the ship, the HUD and the cockpit, the gates, mines and special effects were made by me, Carsten Wartmann.

The level (the rocks, sandy ground, plants, ancient columns) and the ship design was made by Chris Plush (blengine), thank you Chris!

Originally it was planned as a (contemporary) submarine game, where you are supposed to perform missions under water, however, it turned more and more into a SF-racing-arcade game and as the ship design was looking more like an aircraft I switched the idea to the current one. For the short amount of time I am pleased whith the game play, at least there is a goal in having a good round time. Beside of that the game demonstrates many things common for games, like the working HUD (Head Up Display), multiple camera perspectives, scripts for timing and organizing.

So now load the game from the books disk (**Games/Subracer.blend**) and drive around a bit. You need to go through the gates in the specified sequence to complete a round. The indicator in the middle of the HUD will tell you which gate is next, the rough direction of the next gate and if you are on a course towards the gate (green gate indicator) or away from the gate (red indicator). Collect the crates, they will give you 100 units turbo fuel. After completing a round your time will be displayed in the "R-TIME" field. Note that with no thrust the ship is hard to control, so use small thrust strokes to keep your ship on course in slow passages.

Subracer game controls:

CONTROLS	DESCRIPTION
CURSOR KEYS	Turning left/right and pitch up/down (pilot controls)
W	Forward thrust
Q	Turbo speedup (as long there is enough turbo fuel, see HUD)
A/D	Roll the ship, this is not needed always but can save you in some situations
SPACE	Fire the sonic gun to blast mines
R	Restart the game
F1	First person perspective
F2	Third person perspective

This game is based on advanced GLSL materials and lights. So if your graphic card does not support this you can switch of GLSL (Texture Face Materials) or parts of (GLSL Material Settings) it in the "Game"-menu. However, the game will then not look very good anymore.

Ship setup

The ship consists of several objects, have a look at the Figure "Ship setup" for an overview.

The main ship object is only a invisible cage surrounding roughly the ship mesh you will see in the game. This is to lower amount of collision detection for the physics engine, we use a "Triangle Mesh" bounds type (see Ship physics and Properties), so we don't get stuck with the tanks on the wings for example at other objects. The ship you see in the game has a much higher resolution but all faces are set to "no collision".

You can also see the two cameras and two spotlights, one from above for generating the shadow of the ship on the ground and one which is the search headlight. The shadow from the ship is important to give the eye a hint how near the ground is, of course it does not look too realistic but a global light

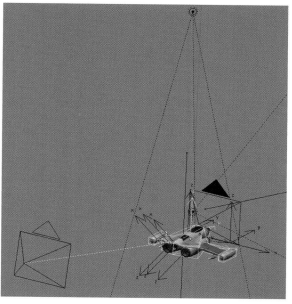

Ship setup

for the whole scene would be too expensive. At the back of the thrusters you can see three Empties which generate the exhaust of the engines using an AddObject Actuator. Similar in front of the ship are two Empties attached which will act as guns.

The physics properties are set to "Rigid Body", so we can have our ship behave correct at collisions and on gravity. The "Mass:"-field is set to 5 which does give it a higher inertia compared to other objects. You see it is not always needed to use "real" weights, we rather want to make it good looking and playable than being a precise physical simulation. I am using relatively high values for Damp and RotDamp to simulate the water friction. The ship is set to "Actor", so that Near sensors can see it, this is used for the mines. I also activated "No sleeping" we don't want to see the ship lazy sleeping on the ground.

Ship physics and Properties

Rigid body	⬍	Actor	Ghost	Advanced Settings
◀ Mass: 5.00 ▶	◀	Radius: 0.04 ▶	No sleeping	
Damp 0.300 ▬		RotDamp 0.600 ▬		
Do Fh	Rot Fh ◀	Form: 0.40 ▶	Anisotropic	

Bounds	Triangle Mesh	⬍	Compound

		Add Property			
Del	Float ⬍	Name:uboot	◀	0.000 ▶	D
Del	Int ⬍	Name:turbo	◀	300 ▶	D
Del	Int ⬍	Name:damage	◀	0 ▶	D
Del	Int ⬍	Name:next	◀	0 ▶	D
Del	Float ⬍	Name:head	◀	0.000 ▶	D
Del	Float ⬍	Name:incl	◀	0.000 ▶	D
Del	Timer ⬍	Name:time	◀	0.000 ▶	D
Del	Float ⬍	Name:roundtime	◀	-1.000 ▶	D
Del	Int ⬍	Name:round	◀	0 ▶	D

We have a bunch of Properties for the ship. The Property "uboot" is just a marker for other objects to filter out collisions of the ship so that they can react on the collision properly. The other Properties are really containing values. "turbo", "damage", "head"

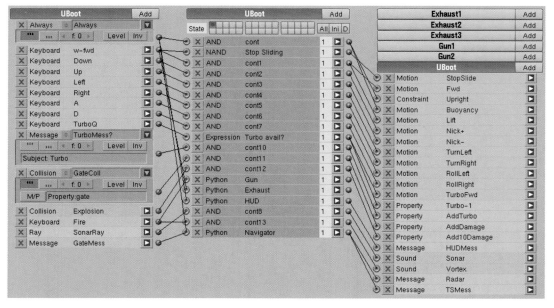

The ship's
Logic Bricks and "incl" are used to store the values for the functions, for example the turbo value is used to decide if you still have enough turbo-fuel left to use the turbo. The value is also passed to the HUD to be displayed. "next" contains the number of the next gate you need to pass. "time" is a timer and the value is stored into "roundtime" every time you complete a race round correctly. The number of rounds are counted in the Property "round".

As you can see in the Logic Bricks figure there are quite a bunch of Logic Bricks involved. However not quite as many as in a more complete character setup, like the one in the "Yo Frankie!" game.

Sensors

Most of the Sensors are Keyboard Sensors to control the ship. Then there are two Collision Sensors to detect collisions with other objects and a Ray Sensor which detects other objects in range and is used to play a sonar sound. The two Message Sensors are reacting on messages if new turbo-fuel is found and when the ship passed a gate. You can see at "GateMess" that I decided not to let the ship detect a pass through a gate but let the gate detect it and then notify the ship. This is just a matter of taste but will certainly reduce the complexity of the ship logic. In a multi player game this would also open the way to use the messages to compare the players ships and to stat the success.

Controllers

Most of the Controllers are simple AND Controllers and they just pass the pulses to the Actuators because they only have one input connected. At second position there is a NAND Controller, used to fire a Motion Actuator when the Forward Key **W** is **not** pressed, I will come back to this topic later. There is one simple Expression Controller "TurboQ and turbo>0.0" which will only allow to use turbo-boost if there is enough turbo fuel left.

Last but not least we have four Python Controllers. Some of the functionality in these scripts could have been done with just Logic Bricks, but this would have resulted into a quite complex and hard to maintain logic. But some of the functions in the scripts are just impossible to do with Logic Bricks, like the calculation of the angle to the next gate. The scripts "Gun" and "Exhaust" are just simple scripts to add bullets and exhaust "particles" but overcome a limitation of the Add Object Actuator. The other scripts are a bit more complicated, it would have been possible to combine them into one script but this also results into a hard to maintain big script.

Actuators

Most of the Actuators are just Motion Actuators directly connected to the Keyboard Sensors to move and rotate the ship. There is also an Actuator called "Buoyancy" which is used to add some uplift to the ship so that it will not follow the gravity too fast.

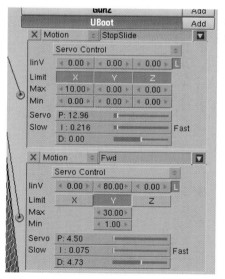

Logic Bricks to drive the ship

The Actuators to get the ship going are using the new "Servo Control" Actuators. These will bring the ship to the wanted speed using forces, this will lead to a maximum top speed without caring for problems with collisions or damping. Using the "Limit Y" in the "Fwd" Actuator we can also control how fast the ship can accelerate. The "StopSlide" Actuator will prevent the ship sliding sideways (along the ships X-axis) to much, which would make the control of the ship almost impossible. This simulates (roughly) the water dynamics (as in aerodynamics) in reality where a ship has less drag along the center line and much drag caused by fins etc. at the cross axis.

The Property Actuators are adding to the turbo and damage Properties. The Message Actuators are passing information to the Cockpit and HUD overlay scenes.

Guns

As I told you above we have two Empties parented to the ship which form the guns of the ship. The exhaust of the turbines is done in a similiar way.

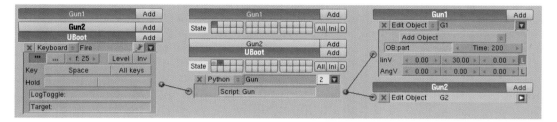

As you can see a Keyboard Sensor on the ship (object "UBoot") is connected to a Python Controller (see the Python Code Listing) and the Controller connects with one Edit Object "Add Object" Actuator on every gun Empty.

Script driving the guns:

```
1.   # Gun script
2.   # This script takes the velocity of the ship into account for fir-
        ing the cannons
3.   # also uses instantAddObject to prevent 1 frame lag of the Add Ob-
        ject Actuator
4.
5.   import GameLogic
6.
7.   cont = GameLogic.getCurrentController()
8.   me   = cont.getOwner()
9.
10.  fire = cont.getSensor("Fire")
11.  g1 = cont.getActuator("G1")
12.  g2 = cont.getActuator("G2")
13.
14.  if fire.isPositive():
15.      ys = me.getLinearVelocity(1)[1]
16.      g1.setLinearVelocity(0,30+ys,0)
17.      g2.setLinearVelocity(0,30+ys,0)
18.      g1.instantAddObject()
19.      g2.instantAddObject()
```

So why do we use a Python script here? There are two reasons:

1. The Add Object mechanism leads to at least one frame lag or delay, that is not visible (the lag is visible for the exhaust) but can lead to the situation that the ship, especially when moving quite fast, runs into it's own bullets.
2. We can give the bullets a initial speed which is the same as the ship has and adds to the bullet speed.

We use the function `instantAddObj()` (lines 18-19) to avoid the lag of the Actuator. This function calls the Actuator immediately and adds the object given in the Actuator (here the object "part" which needs to be in a hidden layer). The object will have a life-time of 200 frames as entered in the "Time:" field.

In line 15 we get the actual ship speed in forward direction and add that speed in lines 16-17 to the desired bullet speed of 30. The function `setLinearVelocity()` set the speed like the input fields "linV" in the Actuator.

Game Objects

Turbo crate

The logic for the turbo fuel crates is quite simple. The upper row of logic bricks is just for rotating the box. When an object with the Property "uboot" collides with the box (which has the "Ghost" physical property to avoid any restitute) a message is sent which tells the ship that it got 100 "liter" turbo fuel, and then the crate object is deleted from the scene (End Object).

So why is the crate also deleted when a message with the subject "Init" is received? We need to make sure that in every race round new crates are there, so on a init or game start we delete all left over crates and add new ones, which leads us to the logic on how we add these crates.

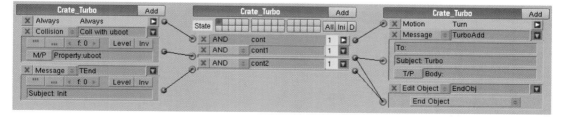

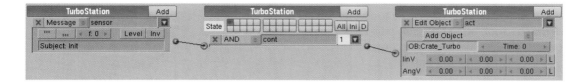

You can see, it is just an Empty placed everywhere in the level where a turbo-crate should be. At game start and when a round is completed an "Init" message is sent, which causes all existing crates to vanish and new ones to be created at the Empties. This can work because there is a lag or delay of one frame in between receiving the message and creating new objects, that way the init message can't destroy the new created objects.

Mine

The mine is made up from a few objects, the mine itself, two pieces of chains (so they can be animated moving in the waves) and the anchor block. The logic for the mines is basically just a Near Sensor which works as a proximity fuse, it only reacts to objects with the "uboot" Property. So what happens then?

First of all an explosion sound is played, then we remove the mine and the chain objects, the lower chain is replaced (using an Edit Object Actuator type "Replace Mesh") by a mesh of a chain laying on the ground. Then an object with the fireball is added and an object which builds the shockwave.

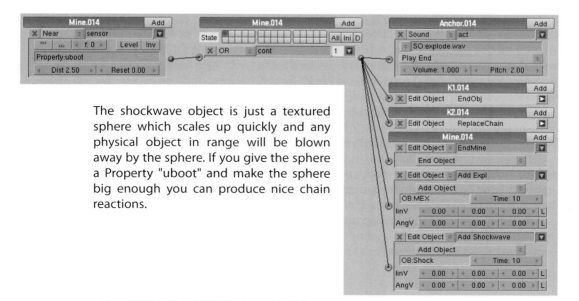

The shockwave object is just a textured sphere which scales up quickly and any physical object in range will be blown away by the sphere. If you give the sphere a Property "uboot" and make the sphere big enough you can produce nice chain reactions.

Gate

The gates in the game have a quite simple logic. If you look at the Logic Bricks (I removed the LBs to rotate them here) you can see that the logic again is spread over different parts of the gate. The gate itself has an Always Sensor, a Python Controller and a Message Sensor. Interconnected are an Always Sensor from the gate number display and a Collision Sensor from the green "energy" surface.

The "Init" Sensor fires one time at game start and then the script is used to register the gate to a global variable (lines 15-23). After game start, all gate-objects are then stored into a Python Dictionary where they can be accessed by their names. Beside that, the gate number display is filled with the current gate name.

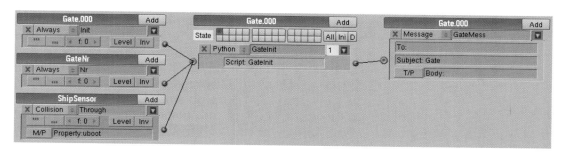

Gate's init script

```
3.    # This handles the gates
4.
5.    import GameLogic
6.
1.    me = GameLogic.getCurrentController().getOwner()
2.    cont = GameLogic.getCurrentController()
3.
4.    init      = cont.getSensor("Init")
5.    nr        = cont.getSensor("Nr")
6.    through   = cont.getSensor("Through")
7.    gate      = cont.getActuator("GateMess")
8.
```

```
9.      # the (random number) of gates are registering themselves
10.     # be sure to name the gates Gate.000...Gate.XXX
11.     if init.isPositive():
12.       # set the visible gate name
13.       nr.getOwner().Text = me.name[2:]
14.       try:
15.         GameLogic.gates[me.name]=me
16.       except:
17.         # first gate?
18.         GameLogic.gates={}
19.         GameLogic.gates[me.name]=me
20.
21.
22.     # ship has passed the gate, send message to the ship
23.     if through.isPositive():
24.       gate.setBody(me.name)
25.       GameLogic.addActiveActuator(gate,1)
```

GLSL Mist

To achieve a nice underwater looks with dimminishing blue colors for objects further away it is possible to use the standard mist in the World Buttons. With some tweaking this really looks nice. However, the standard mist has the disadvantage that it works not well together with faces set to "Add" and also shows some problems with alpha-faces. This is the reason I decided to use GLSL-mist, which is in fact just a Node-material. Further to the compatibility with "Add"-faces, it is also possible to make multi-color mist and other advanced stuff, on the "Yo Frankie!" DVD Pablo explains in a tutorial how to do this. Another advantage is that you can exclude objects from the mist.

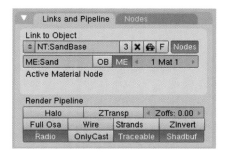

The mist is a Node group named "Mist" which you can append to your own scenes.

To use Node materials you can first set up all your materials as you are used to do. Then activate the "Nodes" Button in the Material Buttons **F5**, "Links and Pipeline"-panel.

Next change one window to a Node Editor and chose your base material in the Input

Node. When you now render with **F12** or start the game with **P** nothing has changed, but in fact we are now using the Node material system. Now back in the Node Editor cut the wire between Input and Output Node and add the Mist group which you appended from the scene on the books disk.

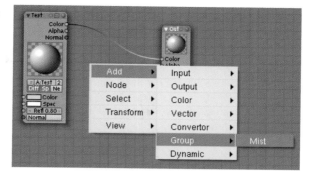

Connect the yellow Color connections from Input to the "Mist"-Group and then to the Output Node. The effect should be visible immediately in the 3D View when you have activated "GLSL Materials" in the Game-menu.

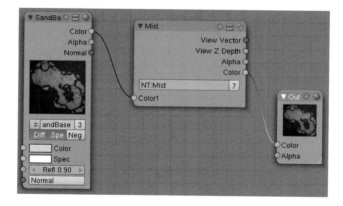

This procedure you have to repeat for all materials which should be affected by the mist.

When you open the "Mist"-Group you can see how this effect is achieved. The strength of the mist should be dependent on the distance camera to object, a farther away object will become more blue (or other colors for other types of mist). This distance we get from the "Camera Data" Node, "View Distance". Of course this distance can be quite big and depends on the overall scene scale, so we most probably need to scale it to our needs, which is done by the "Mapping"-Node. Notice the ``0.01´´ at the third place (Z coordinate) in the "Size" row, this means that the view distance value is divided by 100. So why "Z"? This is because the cameras in Blender always look along their Z-Axis.

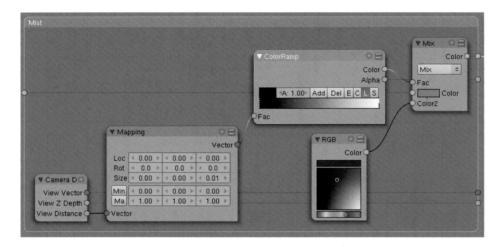

Next we pass the value through a "Color Ramp"-Node which will clip the value to a range between 0 and 1.0 and can also be used to fine tune the mist appearance. Next we mix the original color of the material (Color1) with a blueish color (Color2) coming from a "RGB"-Node with the "Mix"-Node. The amount of mixing is controled (Fac) by the value derived from the view distance. And thats it!

For the best effect you should set the color of the world to exactly the same color as in the RGB Node. To achive this just pick the color from the RGB Node with the "Sample"-tool of the color-picker in the World Buttons.

BOIL IT DOWN TO THE BASICS

BLENDER BASIC NETWORK SETUP

"Old Jim" Coulter

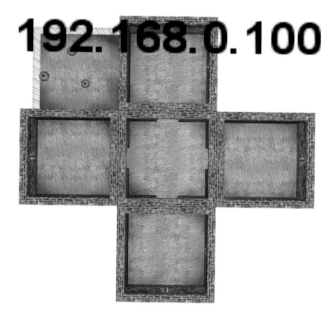

192.168.0.100

Making games and playing them is a lot of fun, but it is even more fun if you can make games to play together with your friends. I will show you how to "cook" a basic network setup in blender. Since Blenders game engine has no build in network support we have to do it in Python, for this you need a matching Python installation for Blender. Take a close look at the terminal or dos-box output when Blender starts, it will tell you which version it needs and if the import worked.

Ingredients:

IP • Unique Computer name

> **LAN IP** • Only accessible inside the local network
> **Internet IP** • Accessible form all over the world (when routers and firewalls allows it)

Port • Access line to a specific communication

Socket • Transmitting and receiving station.

Libraries • Importing cookbooks (modules) from the Python Library gives blender info on how to prepare a special meal

Logic Bricks • central switching station of the Blender game engine.

Objects • We will use 2 cubes which we can move around and these movements we will send over the Network.

If you load the file **Tutorials//WSAGNetwork/BasicNetwork.blend** you can find 2 scripts in there which are relevant to our network setup. (Server.py and Client.py). These scripts show what you get if you boil a network down to its basics. So what do they do?

Server.py

```
#------------SETUP-------------#
1.    from GameLogic import *
2.    from socket import *
3.    from cPickle import *
4.    cont = GameLogic.getCurrentController()
5.    obj = cont.getOwner()
6.    if obj.OneTime == 0:
7.        Host = ''
8.        ServerPort = 10000
9.        GameLogic.sServer = socket(AF_INET,SOCK_DGRAM)
10.       GameLogic.sServer.bind((Host,ServerPort))
11.       GameLogic.sServer.setblocking(0)
12.       obj.OneTime = 1
13.   PosYou = obj.getPosition()
14.   scene = getCurrentScene()
15.   Client = scene.getObjectList()["OBClient"]
16.   PosClient = [0,0,0]
```

```
       #------------RECEIVE/SEND-------------#
17.    try:
18.        Data, CLIP = GameLogic.sServer.recvfrom(1024)
19.        UPData = loads(Data)
20.        PosClient = [UPData[0],UPData[1],UPData[2]]
21.        Client.setPosition(PosClient)
22.        Data = dumps((PosYou))
23.        GameLogic.sServer.sendto(Data,CLIP)
24.    except:
25.        pass
```

```
1.      from GameLogic import *
```

From the library we import the book (module) called GameLogic. By importing this book we have access to all the information about the blender game engine.

```
2.      from socket import *
```

Gives us all the information about network socket setups

```
3.      from cPickle import *
```

Gives us information on how to pack data in to a container (similar to a zip program)

```
4.      cont = getCurrentController()
```

This command gets the Controller for the script and saves it to the variable cont. The logic brick we just made accessible, is the Controller that gave the order to execute the python script.

```
5.      Obj = Cont.getOwner()
```

Gets us the owner of this script. That would be the object that owns the logic brick.

```
6.      if Obj.OneTime == 0:
12.         Obj.OneTime = 1
```

Line 6 calls up the property OneTime and if its value is equal to 0 it will execute the lines below that are indented. Line 12 will change the value of the property OneTime to 1. By changing the property we make sure that the indented lines below line 6 only run one time.

```
7.          host = ''
```

Saves a empty text holder in to the variable host. The purpose of this empty text holder is to make a place where later the computer name can be written in to. So you may ask; why not write the computer name in to it right away? Well you could do that but then this script would only run on your own computer. So that's why we leave it empty and let the socket fill it out later all by it self. You also would have the option to write localhost between the ", that would say the script right a way to enter the name of the local computer in there… But why write more then necessary?

```
8.          ServerPort = 10000
```

Saves the value 10000 in to the variable ServerPort. This value will be the port number over witch the socket will communicate. That's why you will have to make sure that your firewall and your router won't block this and the other ports that will be added later. Information on how you can setup your firewall and router to forward information over this port, can be found in the manuals of your firewall and router. If any questions or problems come up then you can ask them in the gameblender.org forum.

```
9.          GameLogic.sServer = socket(AF_INET,SOCK_DGRAM)
```

This code will create a socket that uses the protocol that is defined inside of the brackets and saves it to the global variable GameLogic.sServer.

`AF_INET,SOCK_DGRAM` is the definition for the UPD protocol. We will use this protocol because it is very fast and will keep on working even if it once can't send or receive a packet.

```
10.         GameLogic.sServer.bind((Host,ServerPort))
```

The code `.bind((host,Serverport))` is used to bind the information that we have saved in to variable host and Serverport to the socket. Now the socket knows on what computer and over witch port he should communicate.

```
11.         GameLogic.sServer.setblocking(0)
```

The socket will already work with the lines above. But as I already mentioned by line 8 we would like to make sure that the script will keep on running even if the socket did not send or receive a packet. This can happen very easy, if the connection has a problem, the client and server have different streaming rates, the connection is temporary used by a different program… That's why we will use the code .setblocking(0). The 0 in the brackets will tell the script that it should not block even if it did not send or receive anything. If you would put a 1 there, the script would try to receives/send a packet until it has had success. If you would do this everything would be as slow as the slowest client that is connected with the server.

```
13.      PosYou = obj.getPosition()
```

Gets the position of servers cube (the server controls the blue cube)

```
14.      scene = getCurrentScene()
15.      Client = scene.getObjectList()["OBClient"]
```

The command getCurrentScene() will get all the elements of the current scene in to the script. These elements will be saved in the variable scene. The variable scene contains all the elements of the current scene, now we would like to have access to all the Objects in the scene, this will happen by using the command getObjectList(). In the square brackets we write the name of the object that we would like to save to the variable objPump1. Its important that you put the letters "OB" in front of the objects name.

```
16.      PosClient = [0,0,0]
```

In the variable PosClient we provide a list with 3 elements. This list will be later filed with the coordinates of the player. The 3 elements [0,0,0] stand for the X, Y and Z coordinates.

```
17.      try:
```

Line 17 starts to try to execute the indented lines below. If one of the lines fail lines 24 and 25 come in to action telling the script to just pass on. The only line below that actually can fail is the Line 18. It will fail when it tries to receive and there is no data there to receive. This can for example happen if no Client is sending any data.

```
18.          Data, CLIP = GameLogic.sServer.recvfrom(1024)
```

The variable GameLogic.sServer contains the information about the socket. The code .recvfrom commands the socket to receive data. (1024) defines the maximal size, that the buffer can receive at once.

Every time we receive data we get 2 blocks. The first block contains the data and is saved in the variable Data. The second block contains the sender address and is saved in the variable CLIP (= Client IP)

```
19.          UPData = loads(Data)
```

Now we will use the methods from the cPickle module for the first time. The received data will be unpacked and saved to the variable UPData, As you will see in line 22, data that is send over the network is first packed in to a container.

```
20.          PosClient = [UPData[0],UPData[1],UPData[2]]
```

The received and now unpacked data is saved in to the list we made in line 16.
UPData[0] = Position on the world axis X
UPData[1] = Position on the world axis Y
UPData[2] = Position on the world axis Z

```
21.          Client.setPosition(PosClient)
```

The list we just filled out is now used to set the position of the clients player.

```
22.          Data = dumps((PosYou))
```

The command dumps will pack any data inside the double brackets in to a container and save it to the variable Data. Important: You have to use double brackets here "((PosYou))" and not single brackets "(PosYou)". The Variable PosYou that we are packing here contains the information of the coordinates of the Server cube (blue) see line 13.

```
23.          GameLogic.sServer.sendto(Data,CLIP)
```

To send Data we use GameLogic.sServer to call up the socket and give it the command .sendto. To send data do it just as in line 18, you need 2 things: The data and the address that this packed should be send to. This information you put inside the brackets.

```
24.      except:
25.          pass
```

These lines work together with line 17 and were already explained.

The client script.py is very similar to the server.py script, the only real difference is that it sends data to the server first, so it does not have an already received package that contains the servers address; so this will have to be entered manually. We do this in the script setup.py line 10. By entering the servers IP address there behind the global variable GameLogic.IP. If you now study the script below you may say he way not just write it in to line 7 instead of putting the global variable GameLogic. IP there. You are right, you can do so but by having the IP entering in the setup.py script it makes it easier to find it. Also the setup.py script contains other informationsthat help a user to start this program in any network. See lines that are behind a comment mark "#". They are not part of the script, but give you information on how to use this script. So that's why we will have the 3D window on the left side and the setup.py script on the right side when we open the **Tutorials//WSAGNetwork/ BasicNetwork.blend** file.

Client.py

```
          #------------SETUP-------------#
1.        from GameLogic import *
2.        from socket import *
3.        from cPickle import *
4.        cont = GameLogic.getCurrentController()
5.        obj = cont.getOwner()
6.        if obj.OneTime == 0:
7.            ServerIP = GameLogic.IP
8.            Serverport = 10000
9.            Clientname = ''
10.           ClientPort = 10001
11.           GameLogic.sClient = socket(AF_INET,SOCK_DGRAM)
12.           GameLogic.sClient.bind((Clientname,ClientPort))
13.           GameLogic.host = (ServerIP,Serverport)
14.           GameLogic.sClient.setblocking(0)
15.           obj.OneTime = 1
16.       PosYou = obj.getPosition()
17.       scene = getCurrentScene()
18.       Server = scene.getObjectList()["OBServer"]
19.       PosServer = [0,0,0]
          #------------RECEIVE/SEND-------------#
20.       Data = dumps((PosYou))
21.       GameLogic.sClient.sendto(Data,GameLogic.host)
22.       try:
23.           Data, SRIP = GameLogic.sClient.recvfrom(1024)
24.           UPData = loads(Data)
25.           PosServer = [UPData[0],UPData[1],UPData[2]]
26.           Server.setPosition(PosServer)
27.       except:
28.           pass
```

Since all the commands in this script where explained in the server.py script I will only give a short summary on these lines of code:

Lines 1 – 5: Basic setup to access the Object, its properties and logic bricks

Lines 6 + 15: Make sure that the intended lines below Line 6 only run once.

Line 7: Saves the global Variable that contains the IP to a local Variable.

Lines 8 – 12: Setup the Socket

Line 13: Saves the complete Server address to a variable.

Line 14: Tells the script to just keep running even if no data was sent/received.

Line 16: Gets the position of the red cube.

Line 17 + 18: Make the blue cube accessible by this script.

Line 19: Makes a empty list, that will be used to set the servers cube (blue cube)

Line 20 + 21: Packs your position in a container and sends it to the server.

Line 22, 27, 28: Will try to run the intended lines below line 22, if they fail the script will just pass on.

Appetite for more

I hope this little starter whetted your appetite for more. There is a more complete tutorial on the CDROM (**Tutorials//WSAGNetwork/PumpkinRun_MP.blend**) and a lot of information about more complex network "meals" can be found at **http://www.wsag.ch.vu** If any questions come up you can ask them at the **http://gameblender.org** forum.

GAME CHARACTER ANIMATION

USING ARMATURES

Reevan McKay

The armature system opens up many possibilities for character animation in the Blender game engine, but can be somewhat intimidating for new users. This tutorial guides you through the steps involved in building an armature and creating actions that can be used for smooth character animation in the game engine.

Preparing the Mesh

This tutorial assumes you have already modeled a character that you want to use in an animation. Due to the high cost of calculating skeletal deformation, you will get better performance by using fewer vertices in your meshes. It pays to spend some time to optimize your models before continuing. You can use the file **Tutorials/ CharacterAnimation/Characteranim00.blend** as base for this tutorial.

Many aspects of Blender's game and animation engines depend on the fact that you have modeled your character and armature using the correct coordinate system. The front view (**PAD1**) should show the front of your character and armature. If this is not the case, you should rotate your mesh so that the front of the character is displayed in the front view, and apply the rotations as described in the next step.

Before adding bones and animating a mesh, it is a good idea to make sure that the base mesh object does not have any rotation or scaling on it. The easiest way to do this is to select the mesh and apply any existing transformations with **CTRL**-**A** → "Scale and Rotation to ObData".

Working with Bones

The next step is to build the skeleton or "armature" that will be used to deform the character. A single armature object can contain an entire hierarchy of bones, which makes editing animations easier. Select your character, then position the 3D-Cursor on it using **SHIFT**-**S** → "Cursor to Selection". Add an armature object from the tool-box by pressing **SHIFT**-**A** → "Armature".

You will see an Armature with one bone appear. Armatures have an Edit Mode similar to meshes. As with meshes, you can toggle in and out of Edit Mode using **TAB**. While you are in Edit Mode, you can add and remove bones, or adjust the rest position of existing bones. The rest position of your armature should correspond to the untransformed position of the mesh you want to deform, and you should build the armature inside the mesh, like a skeleton inside a human body.

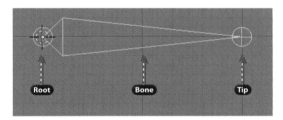

While you are in Edit Mode, you can reposition a bone by selecting one or more of its endpoints and using the standard transformation tools such as scaling (**S**), rotation (**R**) and translation (**G**).

You can also extrude selected points to form new bones with **E**.

Now enter Edit Mode and select the tip of the bone. Move the tip to the position shown in figure "Adding bones". Now click with **CTRL**+**LMB** to the place where the tip of the new bone should be. At this point a new yellow bone will appear, attached to the end of the first bone. You can continue to add connected bones in this fashion.

One or more bones can be selected by selecting their start and end points. Like meshes, you can select all of the bone points within a region by using **B** or you can select or deselect all bones in an armature with **A**. You can also select an entire bone chain at once by moving the mouse over any one of the chain's points and pressing **L**. Selected bones can be deleted with **X** or duplicated with **SHIFT**-**D**.

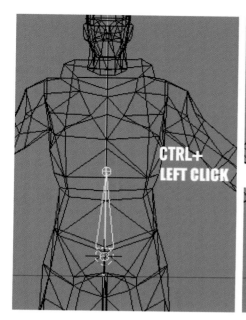
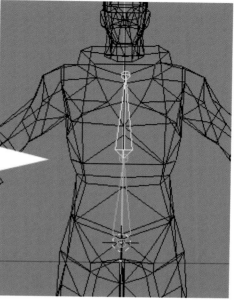

Adding bones

Bone Hierarchy and Rest Positions

Naming Bones

It is a good idea to give meaningful names to the bones in your armature. This not only makes it easier to navigate the hierarchy, but if you follow a few simple naming rules, you can take advantage of the pose-flipping features. You can have the bone names displayed on the model by selecting the armature, switching to the Edit Buttons **F9** and clicking the green "Names" button in the "Armature"-panel.

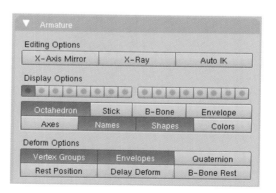

For symmetrical body elements such as arms or legs, it is a good idea to append ".left" or ".right" (or simply ".l" and ".r") suffixes to each part. This information is used when flipping poses. An example of this would be to name the right arm "Arm.Right" and the left one "Arm.Left". Non-paired limbs such as the head or chest do not need any special naming.

When re-using the same action on different armatures, the engine looks at the names of the bones in the armature, and the names of the animation channels in the action. When there is a perfect match (capitalization matters), the animation data in the action will be applied to the appropriate bone. If you want to take advantage of action re-use, make sure that all your skeletons use the same naming convention.

Parenting Bones

Parenting bones
in the Edit Buttons

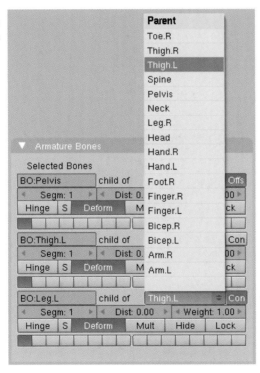

To establish parenting relationships within an armature, you must first make sure the armature is in Edit Mode. Select from the bones you wish to modify (or if you prefer, select all bones with **A**) and switch to the Edit Buttons with **F9**. You will see a list (Figure "Parenting bones in the Edit Buttons") of the selected bones in the "Armature Bones"-panel and next to each bone in the list you will see a "child of" label and a pull-down menu. To make a bone the child of another bone, simply select the appropriate parent from the pull-down menu. Note that the menu only contains the names of bones that could be valid parents. This prevents you from accidentally making a loop in parents (such as making an arm the parent of the chest, which should be parent of the arm).

To clear a parenting relationship, set the "child of" menu to the first (empty) choice in the menu.

Parenting is much quicker with the shortcut **CTRL**+**P**, where the last selected bone becomes parent.

Basic Layout

For a typical humanoid character, the following hierarchy is recommended. Some characters may benefit from additional bones for elements such as flowing skirts or hair.

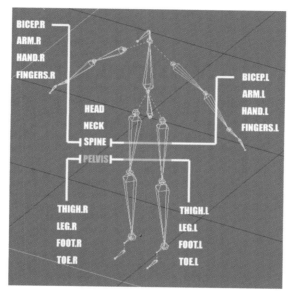

Typical bone layout for a humanoid character

Coordinate System Conventions

Before going on, it is a good idea to clear any rotation or scaling that may have been assigned to the armature. Leave Edit Mode and with the armature object selected, apply the transformations with **CTRL**-**A** → "Scale and Rotation to ObData".

The center point of the armature (represented by a purple dot) should be located on the ground, between the character's feet. If this is not the case, enter Edit Mode for the armature, select all bones with **A** and move the bones so that the center point is at the correct location.

The final step before preparing the mesh for deformation is to ensure that the bones in the armature have consistent orientations. Each bone is like an individual object with its own coordinate system. You can see these coordinate systems (in Edit Mode) by selecting the armature object, switching to the Edit Buttons with **F9** and clicking on the green "Draw Axes" button in the "Armature"-panel.

Generally you want to make sure that the Z-axis for each bone points in a consistent direction. In most cases this means having the Z-axis point upwards. You can adjust the roll angle of a bone by selecting it in Edit Mode, pressing **N** and adjusting the "roll" field.

If you are going to be re-using actions on different armatures, it is very important that both armatures have their bones oriented in the same way. If this is not the case, you will notice a lot of strange flipping happening when you assign the action.

Mesh Deformation Vertex Groups

Creating Groups

Once your armature is established, it is time to specify which bones will affect which vertices of the mesh. This is done using vertex groups.

Attaching the Mesh to the Armature

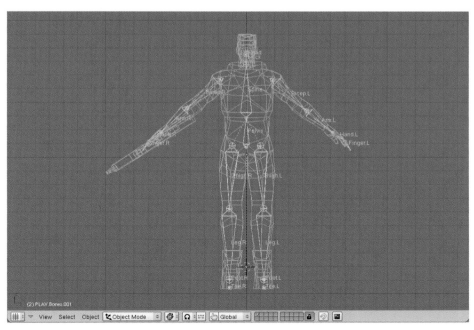

At this point, we should attach the mesh to the armature. Make sure that the mesh and the armature are correctly lined up and that you are not in Edit Mode.

Select the mesh first and while holding **SHIFT**, select the armature and press **CTRL**-**P** → "Use Armature". Blender now asks if he should create vertex groups automatically for you.

There are different options:

Don't Create Groups • no groups are created, use this if your character already has groups or you like to keep total control on the whole process.

Name Groups • create groups with the names of the bones, there are no vertices in the groups!

Create From Envelopes • create groups and assign all vertices to them lying in the range of the bones envelope

Create From Bone Heat • an attempt to assign vertices automatically to bones. This will often lead to a nice starting point for further work

For editing and refining the groups you can assign vertices to the currently active deformation group by selecting vertices and clicking the "Assign" button. The selected vertices will be assigned to the active group with the weight specified in the "Weight" slider. You can remove vertices from the current deformation group by selecting them and clicking the "Remove" button.

If you prefer the total control of the process, create vertex groups for all of the bones in your armature (making sure the names of the groups and bones match) and assign vertices to the appropriate groups. Make sure that every vertex is affected by at least one bone. For this "first pass" of the deformation process, try to keep things simple by leaving the weight set to "1.000" and avoid having vertices being assigned to more than one group.

To access the vertex grouping features, select the mesh you will be deforming and enter Edit Mode. Switch to the Edit Buttons and find the "Group" column. Normally you will have one vertex group for each bone in the armature. A vertex can belong to more than one group, which is how smooth deformation is achieved. In order to be recognized

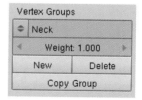

by the armature, the vertex groups must have exactly the same names as the bones they are associated with (capitalization matters). To create a new vertex group, click on the "NEW" button and edit the name in the text button that will appear.

You can see a list of all of the current deformation groups by clicking on the menu next to the group name button. Selecting an item from this menu changes the active deformation group.

Testing the Skinning

Once you have attached the mesh to the armature, you are ready to start testing the deformation. It often takes a fair amount of tweaking to get satisfying results. You want to avoid the excessive pinching or stretching that can occur when vertices are not assigned to the right bones. We'll spend more time on that later. For now, we'll take a look at how to pose the armature, which is a skill needed for testing the deformation.

Pose Mode

In addition to Edit Mode, armatures have a Pose Mode. This is used to position bones within the armature. Setting key frames in Pose Mode defines an "action" for the armature, and the game engine will use these actions to animate the character.

Note that only transformations performed in Pose Mode will be incorporated into the action (and therefore the game engine). Rotations, scalings and translations performed in Object Mode cannot be recorded in actions.

Armature in Pose Mode

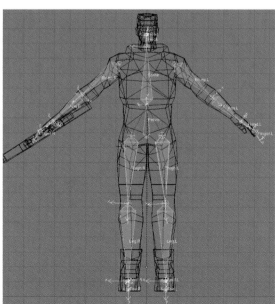

You can toggle in and out of Pose Mode by selecting an armature and pressing **CTRL**-**TAB** or by selecting Pose Mode with the mode-menu in the 3D View header. When in Pose Mode, the armature will be drawn in blue, with selected bones drawn in a lighter shade.

To manipulate bones in Pose Mode, select bones by using **RMB** on them and use the standard transformation keys for scaling, rotation and translation. Note that you cannot add or remove bones in Pose Mode, and you cannot edit the armature's hierarchy. At any time,

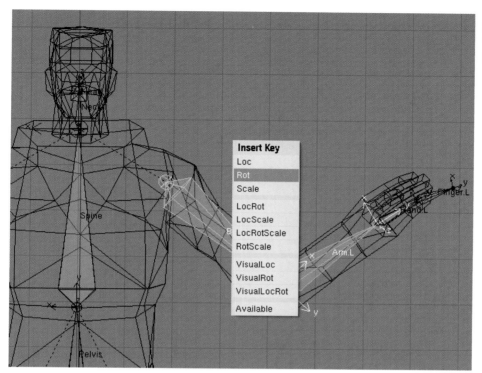

Insert a key for "Arm.L" and "Bicep.L" bone

you can clear the pose you have made and return to the armature's rest position by clearing the rotation, scaling and translation components using **ALT**-**R**, **ALT**-**S** and **ALT**-**G** respectively.

You can set key frames for a pose by selecting one or more bones and pressing **I** and choosing one of the transformation channels to key from the pop up menu.

Weight Editing

In Pose Mode, manipulate the limbs of the armature through their typical range of motion and watch carefully how the mesh deforms. You should watch out for deformation artifacts caused by any of the following:

- Vertices that are not assigned to any bones can be easily detected by moving the root of the character's hierarchy (usually the hips or pelvis) and seeing if any vertices are left behind.

• Vertices that are not connected to the correct bones. If you move a limb (such as the arm) and notice vertex "spikes" protruding from other parts on the body, you will have to enter Edit Mode for the mesh and remove the offending vertices from the vertex group.

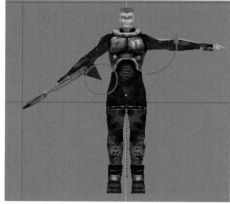

• Pinching or creasing caused by inappropriate vertex weighting. This effect is most visible in the joints of limbs such as arms and legs. Often it is a symptom of vertices that are members of too many groups. The easiest way to fix this is to use the weight painting tool.

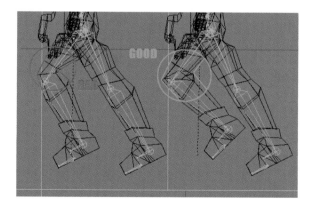

To adjust vertex weights, you have the choice of manually assigning weights using the method outlined above, or you can use the weight painting tool.

This feature lets you "paint" bone influence onto the mesh and see the resulting deformation in real-time. Make sure you are in wireframe or untextured mode with **Z** or **SHIFT**-**Z**. Access weight painting mode by selecting the mesh and clicking on the weight-paint icon in the 3D View header.

In Weight Paint Mode the mesh is displayed with a "false color" intensity spectrum similar to the view from an infrared camera (see figure). Blue areas have little or no influence from the current deformation group while red areas have full influence. As you change the active deformation group in the Edit Buttons **F9**, you will see the coloring on the model change.

Painting weights onto the model works somewhat similarly to vertex painting. **LMB** paints onto the area beneath the cursor. Pressing **U** or **CTRL**+**Z** works to undo painting operation. The cursor size and opacity settings in the Vertex Paint Buttons are used to determine your brush settings and the "Weight" field in the Edit Buttons is used to determine the "color" you are using (0.000 is the blue end of the spectrum and 1.000 is red).

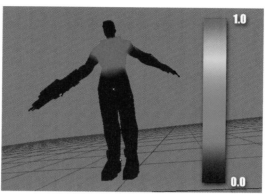

Weight painted character

To remove weight from a group of vertices, set the vertex weight to 0.000 and paint over the area. Note that you do not need to have the mesh in Edit Mode to change the active deformation group, or to change the weight.

There are two ways to quickly select vertex groups.

- Using **SHIFT**+**LMB** will give a menu showing all vertex groups under the mouse cursor.
- If the armature is in PoseMode, **RMB** select on a bone will activate the associated vertex group.

Animation

Animation is very important for conveying the impression of life in a game world, and for giving the player an immediate reward for his or her decisions. Game characters typically have a set of animated actions they can perform, such as walking, running, crawling, attacking or suffering damage. With the armature system, you can design each animation in a separate action and define which actions play at which times using Logic Bricks.

At the time of writing, animation constraints (including teh IK Solver) only work in the game engine as long as you use loose bones in the Armature as targets for the constraints. Enter the armature name into the OB: field, of the constraint, then a BO: field appears, where you can enter a bone name of the current armature.

Multiple Actions and Fake Users

Structure of the file in the Data Select Window

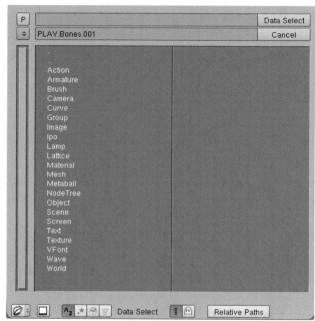

If you want to create multiple actions in a blender file, remember that only one action can be assigned to an armature at a time. If the other actions do not have any users, they will not be saved when the file is saved. To prevent additional actions from disappearing a fake user is automatically added to Actions.

To create or remove a fake user for an action, press **SHIFT**-**F4**. This lets you browse the various objects and data blocks in the blender file. You may need to click on the "P" button once or twice to find the root of the file's structure, which should look like the Figure to the left. From there, descend into the Action directory, and select the actions you want to protect or unprotect with **RMB**. Pressing **F** will add or remove a fake user to the selected items (indicated by the capital "F" that appears next to the action name), preventing them from being accidentally removed from the file.

Creating an Idle Cycle

The simplest action to create for a character is the "idle" or "rest" position. This action can be played when the character is not doing any other action. A good idle animation gives the game character the illusion of life by keeping it moving even when the player is not actively issuing any control commands.

Since the character is not moving through the level while playing the idle animation, we don't have to worry about syncing the animation with the physics system.

To create a new action, split the view by clicking with **MMB** on one of the window borders, selecting "Split Area", and **LMB** to set where the split will appear. Change the type of the newly created window to Action Window by **LMB** on the window-type icon in the Header and choosing the Action icon.

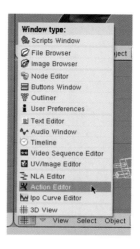

Go to a 3D View and select the armature you wish to animate. Enter Pose Mode and make sure that Blender is on frame 1 by changing the number in the frame counter button in the header of the Buttons Window, or by using **SHIFT**-**LEFT**.

You are now ready to make the first frame of the idle animation, using the Pose Mode techniques described earlier. What this pose looks like will depend largely on the personality of your character and the type of game you are making. Consider which actions might immediately follow the rest position. If the character is supposed to be able to fire a weapon quickly, the rest position might involve holding the weapon in a ready-to-fire stance. A less fast-paced game might have the character adopt a more relaxed "at-ease" pose.

When you are satisfied with the first frame, select all of the bones in Pose Mode and insert a rotation key by pressing **I** → "Rot". Next, deselect all bones and select only the character's root bone (usually the pelvis or hips) and insert a "Loc" key. Normally only the root bone gets location keys, while all bones get rotation keys.

When you insert keys, you should notice that new channels appear in the action window (right Figure). The yellow rectangles represent selected key frames and gray rectangles represent unselected key frames. You can move key frames in the action window by selecting them and grabbing them with **G**.

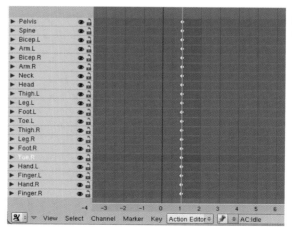

Keys in the Action Window

Key frames can be deleted by selecting them and pressing **X** → "Erase selected".

You can erase an entire action channel (all key frames for a particular bone), by selecting one or more action channels by **SHIFT**-**RMB** on the channel names in the column at the left. Selected channels are displayed in blue, while unselected channels are displayed in red. Pressing **X** → "Erase selected channels" with the mouse over the channel list deletes the selected channels.

In order to create an action that loops smoothly, you will need to copy the first frame and duplicate it as the last frame of the animation. There are two main ways of doing this.

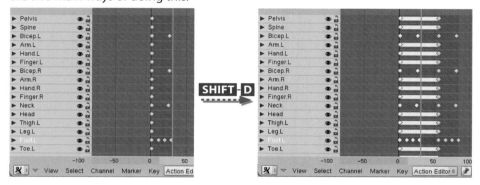

- The first way is to select all of the bones in Pose Mode and click on the "Copy Pose" button. This will copy the transformations from the selected bones into a temporary buffer. You can paste the pose at another keyframe by changing the frame and clicking the "Paste Pose" button. Note that this doesn't necessarily set key frames at the new point in time, unless you have activated the "Auto Keying" option in the preference window. If you have not activated "Auto Keying" and you want to make key frames after pasting the pose, you can press **I**-"Avail".
- The second way to copy a block of key frames is even easier. In the Action Window, select the vertical column of key frames for all channels (hint: use **B** to select with a bounding rectangle). Pressing **SHIFT**-**D** will duplicate the key frames. You can move the block to a new point in the timeline and drop them by **LMB**. To ensure that the key frames stay on whole frame increments, hold down **CTRL** while dragging.

Idle animations tend to be fairly long, since the motion involved is typically subtle and shouldn't be seen to loop too often. The last frame should be at least 100 or higher.

While animating, you can "scrub" through the animation by holding the left mouse button and dragging the mouse in the action window. This will move the position of the green "current frame" indicator. In this way you can test parts of the animation to make sure they play smoothly. You can also play the whole animation by moving to the first frame and pressing **ALT**-**A** with the mouse over a 3D View. To see the animation in a loop, set the "Sta" and "End" values in the Display Buttons (**F10**) window to match the start and end frames of your loop.

At this point you can go back in and add additional key frames between the start and end. Remember to keep the motion reasonably subtle so that the player doesn't notice the repetitive nature of the action. Good elements to add are breathing effects, having the character adjust its grip on any weapons or equipment, and slight head turns.

When you are satisfied with the action, give it a name by editing the name field in the Action Window Header:

Action Editor | AC:Idle | 2 | X | F

Creating a Walk Cycle

Another very important action is the character's walk cycle. This animation will be used when the character is moving through the level. This animation is somewhat more complicated, since we have to consider how the animation will interact with the physics system.

When creating the walk cycle, it is generally best to animate it in such a way that the character seems to be walking on a treadmill. The forward motion will be provided by the game's physics system at run time.

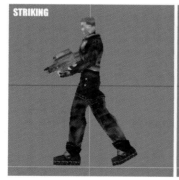

Striking and crossing

A walk-cycle actually consists of two steps. One for the left foot and one for the right foot. For each step there are two main key frames: the striking pose and the crossing pose (Figure " Striking and crossing"). The striking pose represents the moment when one foot has just been planted on the ground and the other is about to be lifted. The crossing pose represents the moment when the two legs cross each other under the character's center of gravity: one foot is on the ground and moving backwards, while the other is lifted and is moving forwards.

To start creating this animation, switch to the action window and create a new blank action by clicking on the Action menu and choosing "Add New". This will create a copy of any action that may have already been on the character. Name the action and make sure the animation is blank, by moving the mouse over the channel list, selecting all channels with **A** and deleting them with **X** → "Erase selected channels".

Key frames for the walk cycle

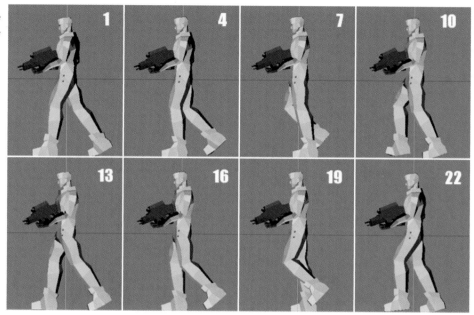

For this animation, we'll make a 24 frame walk cycle. We'll set five key frames to get a basic walking motion established. Once that's done you can go back and add additional key frames to smooth out the motion and improve the animation.

The first thing to do is to set the striking pose for the left foot. This pose will be copied and pasted as the last frame of the action to ensure the animation loops smoothly. Note that if you later make changes to this first frame, you should copy those changes to the last frame again.

The striking pose has the following characteristics:

- The leading leg is extended and the foot is firmly on the floor.
- The trailing foot has the toes on the floor and the heel has just left the ground.
- The pelvis is lowered, to bring the feet down to the level of the floor.
- If the walk cycle incorporates arm swinging, the arms oppose the legs. If the left leg is advanced, the left arm will be swung back, and vice versa.

When you are satisfied with the pose, insert rotation key frames for all bones, and insert an additional location keyframe for the pelvis bone. Copy this pose to the end of the animation loop, which will be frame 25. Frame 25 will not actually be played however; we will end the loop at frame 24 when playing. Since frame 25 is a duplicate of frame 1, the animation should play back seamlessly.

If you built the character's armature using the naming conventions and coordinate systems recommended earlier in the tutorial, you can take advantage of the character's axial symmetry by copying the striking pose and pasting it flipped. To do this, go to the first frame, and select all bones in Pose Mode. Click the "Copy Pose" button and set the active frame to the middle of the animation (in this case, frame 13). To paste the pose, click the "Paste Flipped" button.

Set "Avail" key frames for the appropriate bones. Note that if your animation does not incorporate arm swinging (for example if the character is carrying a weapon), you might choose to only select the pelvis and legs when copying and pasting the pose. Otherwise, the character will seem to switch the weapon from one hand to the other.

The next task is to create the crossing pose. The first one will occur halfway between the first frame of the animation and the flipped pose you just created (i.e. frame 7). The crossing pose has the following characteristics:

- The planted foot is underneath the character's center of gravity.
- The lifted foot is crossing past the planted leg.
- The pelvis is raised to bring the feet up to the level of the floor.
- If the arms are swinging, the elbows will be crossing each other at this point.

Set "Avail" key frames for all bones on this frame and copy the pose. Advance the active frame to halfway between the end of the animation and the second striking pose (frame 19) and paste the pose flipped.

At this point test your animation loop. It is a good idea to go in and look at it frame by frame with **LEFT** and **RIGHT**. If you see frames where the feet seem to push through the floor, adjust the height of the pelvis accordingly and set "Loc" key frames, or adjust the rotation of the bones in the offending leg and set "Rot" key frames for them (See Figure "Bad positions of the character's legs" on the next page).

Bad positions of
the character's
legs

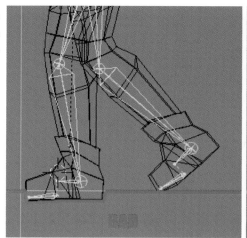

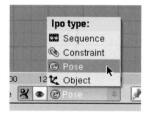

If you prefer working with Ipo Windows, you can edit action channel Ipos directly, though this is not always required. To do this, select an action channel in the Action Window, switch one window into an Ipo Window with **SHIFT**-**F6** and choose "Pose" from the Ipo-type menu.

- Note that Action Ipos display rotations in quaternions instead of Euler angles. This gives nice predictable results when working with complex combinations of rotations, but can be a bit unusual to work with. The best tactic is to set the action value of the quaternions by inserting "Rot" key frames in pose mode, and only using the Ipo Window to adjust the way the curves are interpolated.
- To view several different Ipos in different windows, you can use the "pin" icon in the Ipo Window Header buttons to prevent the displayed Ipo from changing when you change object selection.

Game Logic

When adding game logic to your character, make sure to put the game logic on the armature object itself, rather than on the mesh.

If you are making your character a dynamic physics object, you may need to adjust the center point of the armature based on the size of the dynamic object to make sure that the character's feet touch the floor. The character's feet should touch the bottom of the dotted dynamic object bounds.

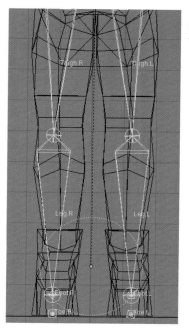

Dynamic object for the character

Generally speaking, you will need to add an Action Actuator for each different action that your character can perform. For each actuator, you will need to set the start and end frames of the animation, as well as the name of the action.

Blender has the ability to create smooth transitions or to blend between different game actions. This makes the motion of game characters appear much more natural and avoids motion "popping". To access this functionality, all you have to do is adjust the "Blending" parameter in the Action actuator. This field specifies how long it will take to blend from the previous action to the current one and is measured in animation frames. A value of "0" indicates that no blending should occur. Note that this blending effect is only visible in the game engine when the game is run.

Action actuators have many of the same playback modes as Ipo actuators, including looping, playing, flippers and property- driven playback.

You should try and design your game logic so that only one action is triggered at a time. When multiple actions are active at the same time, the game engine can only displays one of them on any given frame. To help resolve ambiguity, you can use the "Priority" field in the action actuator. Actions with lower numbers will override actions with higher numbers.

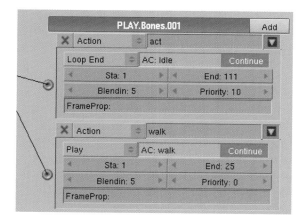

FLYING BUDDHA

A 3D MEMORY GAME

Carsten Wartmann

Flying Buddha Memory Game

"Flying Buddha" is a game designed by Freid Lachnowicz (artwork, models, textures) and me (Carsten Wartmann, Python and game logic). The goal of the game is to find pairs of gongs, like in the good old "Memory" game. Besides that, it also includes some action elements, like the dragonfly which will become angry (note the indicator on the top-right) if you jump too high. Also it requires some good timing for the controls of the Buddha. The Buddha's goal, reaching "Zen" is completed when he has found all pairs. For competitions the time needed to solve will be displayed on screen.

CONTROLS	DESCRIPTION
CURSOR KEYS	Movement, you can steer in the air and slow down your fall
SKEY	Select a gong

Load the game `Games/FlyingBuddha.blend` from the CDROM and have fun playing it!

Accessing game objects

Accessing individual objects from Blenders game engine is not trivial. In the "Flying Buddha" game, I needed a possibility of randomly shuffling the gongs at game start.

Generally speaking, it is a good thing to have as much game logic as possible contained on the object that needs that logic. This helps when re-using this object in the same or even different (Blender) scenes. So my first idea was to let the gongs choose a new position themselves. But this soon turned out to be too complicated, because of synchronizing problems and complex logic in the gongs.

I then decided to use an object to control the shuffling process, and have the information about the other objects including their positions gathered by a Near Sensor. This approach has many advantages. For example we can filter out whole groups of objects with the "Property:" field, we are not bound to a fixed number of objects etc.

Logic Bricks

Load the file `Tutorials/FlyingBuddha/FlyingBuddha_simple.blend` from the CDROM. It contains a simpler version of the "Flying Buddha" game, which does not contain all the intro scenes but is fully functional (press **CTRL**-**LEFT** for a full screen view). Use this file to explore the Game Logic.

The difference in the full game and this tutorial file are built-in debugging and testing logic. Most notably is that you can test the re-shuffling of the gongs every time by pressing **SPACE**. The logic for this is on the "Flamethrower" object (on layer 4).

Have a look at Figure "Logic Bricks for shuffling the gongs". The interesting parts in this context are the Sensors "mixitbaby" and "near". Both are connected to a Python Controller, which is then connected to a Message Actuator. Also note the "shuffle" Property, this controls the number of swapped pairs. The other Bricks are not related to the shuffling, they are needed for other game parts.

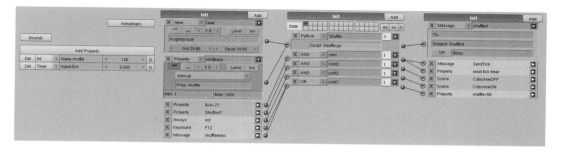

Logic Bricks for shuffling the gongs

As you can see, the Near Sensor only looks for objects carrying a Property with the name "num". Also make sure that the "Dist:" setting is high enough for the Near Sensor to cover all objects.

The Python Controller will be called every frame by the Property Sensor as long the Property "num" is in the range from 1 to 1000.

Shuffle Python script

Open a Text Window (**SHIFT**-**F11**) and choose the script "Shuffle.py" with the Menu Button.

Script to shuffle the gongs:

```python
1.    # Shuffle script, swaps positions of two gongs
2.
3.    import GameLogic
4.
5.    def ranint(min,max):
6.      return(int(GameLogic.getRandomFloat()*(max+1-min)+min))
7.
8.    contr = GameLogic.getCurrentController()
9.    owner = contr.getOwner()
10.   key   = contr.getSensor("mixitbaby")
11.   near  = contr.getSensor("near")
12.   mess  = contr.getActuator("shuffled")
13.
14.   # collects all gongs
15.   objs=near.getHitObjectList()
16.
17.   if key.isTriggered() and len(objs)==20:
18.     owner.shuffle = owner.shuffle - 1
19.     if owner.shuffle<0:
20.       GameLogic.addActiveActuator(mess,1)
```

```
21.      else:
22.          g1 = ranint(0,19)
23.          g2 = ranint(0,19)
24.
25.          pos1 = objs[g1].getPosition()
26.          pos2 = objs[g2].getPosition()
27.          objs[g1].setPosition(pos2)
28.          objs[g2].setPosition(pos1)
```

So lets have a look into the script. The lines 1 to 12 contain the usual initialization, and getting information about the Controller, Sensors, Actuators and the owner which is needed to access Properties. The definition of a new function in line 5 is used to make a random function which returns an integer number in a specified range. This will save us much typing later.

In line 15 the first important step is done, using the method getHitObjectList() of the "near" object, we collect all game objects within the Near Sensors range into the list "objs".

Line 17 tests if the Property Sensor ("key") is triggered and if all objects (the gongs) are collected in the "objs" list. This is necessary to avoid Python script errors due to uninitialized objects.

In line 18 we decrement the Property "shuffle" by one to keep track how many swaps we already did.

The if-block beginning in line 19 executes the Message Sensor connected to the Python Controller if the Property "shuffle" is less then zero, the message can then be used to start the game.

The else-block is executed when "owner.shuffle" is bigger than zero. This means that gongs need to be swapped.

In lines 22-23 we get two random numbers into the variables "g1" and "g2". The numbers will be in a range from 0 to 19 because we have 4x5=20 gongs. "g1" and "g2" are the indices of the gongs we want to swap in the next lines. Note that lists in python start with the element "0".

In the lines 25-26 the script reads the positions of the gong-objects using the random indices. The method used here is getPosition(). You can insert a print pos1,pos2 statement after line 26 to actually see the gong positions while running the game.

Python is an auto documenting language. Use a print dir(object) statement to find out what methods an object provides.

The final two lines then swap the positions of the two gongs. The first object indexed as objs[g1] is set to "pos2" which is the position of the first gong. Same for the other gong. You can see the shuffling process in the game itself by looking at the gongs from the backside.

In this tutorial I showed you how to use Python in the game engine to access and change objects in a scene. We used this approach to keep the game logic local on the objects. If you are used to non object-oriented programming languages or systems, this may appear strange to you at first. But this approach has many advantages. For example, you don't need to change the logic while editing your scenes or adding objects, the script will even work when adding objects while running the game. Also, re-using the logic in other scenes is much easier this way.

YO FRANKIE!

THE OPEN GAME PROJECT

Campbell Barton

After Orange and Peach, the Blender Institute did continue with a new open project: Apricot. This time it wasn't a movie but a 3D game! Starting february 1st 2008, a small team of again the best 3D artist and developers developed a game jointly with the on-line community. The main characters in the game are based on the short 3D animation open movie Big Buck Bunny .

Just like our previous Open Projects Orange and Peach, the game itself and all of the production files have been published under the Creative Commons, free to be reused and for everyone to learn from. More importantly, the team was challenging Blender and Crystal Space to the max, inspiring the entire development community

APRICOT

to prove an open source production pipeline is ready for industry quality 3D game creation.

Now the project is over and lead even to two games! It was planned to use the crystal space game engine, but during the project also the Blender game engine was used to make ant own game. This massive use of Blender for creating realtime content lead to a huge leap in Blender development, especially in the realtime part, just as the open movies "Elephants Dream" and "Big Buck Bunny" did.

In this book we will of course concentrate on the Blender game engine and just touch the surface of the game, on the "Yo Frankie!" DVD itself (available separately) you will find:

- A full functional prototype in the Blender Game Engine, running in Linux, Windows and OS X.
- A complete level in Crystal Space, with installer, running in Linux, Windows and OS X.
- All .blend files, models, textures, sound clips, game sources, and so on... all the material used to create the game.
- Documentation and video tutorials by the team members about all technical aspects the game; like how to re-use assets, animate characters, or add new levels.
- The Big Buck Bunny movie in various formats

Visit the http://apricot.blender.org blog for more information about this project.

Creative Commons

The Apricot open game project, the data we'll publish online and on the DVDs, and all of the contents on this website is licensed under the Creative Commons Attribution license 3.0. If any content on this site is not licensed as such, it will be clearly indicated. In short, this means you can freely reuse and distribute this content, also commercially, for as long you provide a proper attribution.

The attribution is: (c) copyright Blender Foundation - apricot.blender.org. Excluded from the Creative Commons is: all logos (including Blender logo, Apricot logo, Yo Frankie! logo, Creative Commons logo) and associated trademarks.

Yo Frankie! Blender Game Engine Logic

The game is separated into a number of blendfiles, characters, levels and props. The levels and props have almost no logic, only properties assigned to them that the characters use to define how to interact with them.

APRICOT

The levels contain mostly static scenery, linked in characters, props and effects as groups.

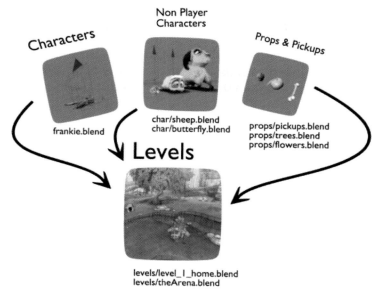

Characters

Non Player Characters

Props & Pickups

frankie.blend

char/sheep.blend
char/butterfly.blend

props/pickups.blend
props/trees.blend
props/flowers.blend

Levels

levels/level_1_home.blend
levels/theArena.blend

Having a character with its camera, animations, sounds and logic in an external blend file is extremely powerful, not only being able to link the one character into multiple levels, but also having multiple instances of that character in a level.

Logic Sharing

Once we had the logic for the sheep, we wanted to be able to add extra characters without having to redo the logic. This was made possible by the recent addition of group instances in the game engine, added especially for the Apricot project.

Character specific objects such as the armature, mesh and shadow mesh of each character are parented to a dummy mesh that runs the logic. All three groups share the logic objects but have unique armature and meshes.

sheep.blend character groups

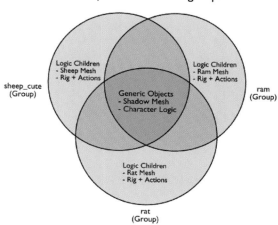

sheep_cute
(Group)

Logic Children
- Sheep Mesh
- Rig + Actions

Logic Children
- Ram Mesh
- Rig + Actions

ram
(Group)

Generic Objects
- Shadow Mesh
- Character Logic

Logic Children
- Rat Mesh
- Rig + Actions

rat
(Group)

To avoid each character behaving in the same way, a script runs when the character starts that sets a "type" property based on the children. The type property determines if the character can attack, get kicked, carried and how aggressive they are.

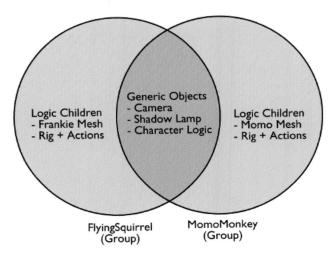

frankie.blend character groups

Logic Children
- Frankie Mesh
- Rig + Actions

Generic Objects
- Camera
- Shadow Lamp
- Character Logic

Logic Children
- Momo Mesh
- Rig + Actions

FlyingSquirrel
(Group)

MomoMonkey
(Group)

There are two playable characters (Frankie and Momo) which also share logic but have their own unique mesh and armature.

No changes in behavior are needed however they do need to use different key layouts and have their own section of the screen (splitscreen). As with the sheep this is done when the character starts, for the moment only one or two players are supported at once, but adding more would be trivial.

States

States are a new addition to blender added for the Apricot project, allowing us to group logic into states that can each be enabled and disabled (you could think of them as logic layers). States were used heavily with all complex gamelogic. Frankie for example has states such as idle, walking, running, falling, gliding, hanging, drowning and death. Each state has a number of sensors and actuators that will switch states under certain conditions.

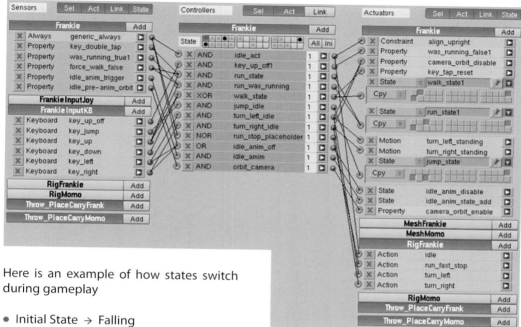

Here is an example of how states switch during gameplay

- Initial State → Falling
- Ground Collision → Idle State
- UpKey → Walk State
- No Ground Collision → Fall State
- Water Collision → Drown State

Logic Elements

Frankie's Camera

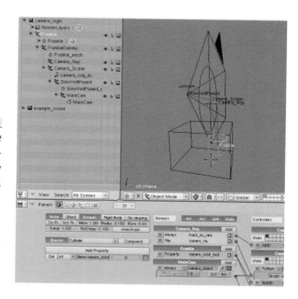

This file (**YoFrankie/tutorialfiles/bge_camera_example.blend**) shows how the Apricot camera works. Although a 3rd person camera facing forward is not overly complex there are are still various issues to overcome.

The initial problem we had with Blender's camera was that Frankie could become obscured by objects which made the game unplayable.

We started by parenting a camera to Frankie, using Blender's slow parent feature to dampen the cameras response to Frankie, avoiding jitter and jarring motion. To prevent trees and walls getting in the way of the camera, a ray sensor from Frankie points towards the camera and uses a python script to scale the camera parent based on the collision location.

Notes:

- There is a dummy character in this file to test movement, added so the camera has something to look at.
- The scene with the terrain and pillars is a 'Set Scene' called "example_scene".
- Keys for movement are Arrow Keys and Space for jump. Keys 1 and 2 set orbit on and off.

Objects and their use (matching frankie.blend)

- Frankie - Parent mesh with all player control and properties
- FrankieDummy - Mesh that shows Frankie (the rig and mesh) in frankie.blend
- Camera_Ray - An empty that tracks the camera from Frankie's position. This casts a ray to the camera and detects if anything is in the way of the view.
- Camera_Scaler - This is a parent to the camera so scaling it changes the camera distance from Frankie. The scale is controlled by a python script that uses the Camera_Ray hit position to set the scale. (this is the only script used by this camera setup). There is also an orbit mode that makes this object rotate about to see Frankie better from all sides while he is idle, drowning or dead.
- SlowVertParent - This is the parent of the camera, slow parent is used so changes in scale or Frankie turning are not applied instantly to the camera. We needed to use a vertex parent for the camera, because otherwise the camera would have scale applied to it which caused distotion of the 3D view.
- MainCam - The main camera tracks to the Camera_Ray

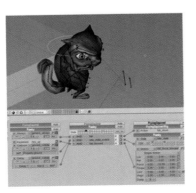

Frankie's States (Simplified)

This character logic example (**YoFrankie/tutorialfiles/bge_logic_state_example.blend**) is based on Frankie's logic and shows how you can use states to control behavior without setting any properties or running python scripts.

Python should be used to add more advanced functionality, but using states helps give scripts a limited context keeping them smaller.

Keys

- Up, Left, Right - Movement
- Space - Jump

Level Properties

- ground - used to detect the floor you can walk on
- kill - sends you to the death state

States

1. Idle state. Can jump, walk and turn from here.
2. Walk state. Can jump, idle and turn from here.
3. Jump State. Only ever enabled for one logic tick, adds upward force and goes into fall state immediately. This is because motion from other states (walk in this case) can interfere with the jump force.
4. Fall State. Can land from here. This state is enabled on startup (notice the black dot over the state) and is enabled whenever Frankie is not touching a 'ground' property object.
6. General State for turning, and checking if Frankie touches any 'kill' objects. This state is always enabled while Frankie is alive, having one of these states is useful for situations you want the character to react to regardless of his current behavior.
15. Death, this state turns off the general state, removing user input, waits for 4 seconds and ends the object.

Level Portals

This collection of blendfiles **YoFrankie/ tutorialfiles/portal_test.blend** show how a single character can be linked into any number of scenes and blendfiles, easily moving between them with portals.

The character is a group of objects with game logic and a camera. This group is then linked into many levels keeping the character logic in one place where it can be edited.

These examples focus on how we did portals, which can do the following.

- Move to another location in the level.
- Move to another scene in the blend file (object if its defined).
- Move to another blend file (scene and object if they are defined).
- Keep the properties of the character such as life and inventory between scenes and blendfiles.

To make a portal just add an object you can collide with and give it the property "portal", value "SomeObjectName" for e.g. On touching the portal you'll be transported to an object called "SomeObjectName".

If you want to move to another scene add the property "portal_scene", value "MyOtherScene" for example.

To go into another blend file add the property "portal_blend", value "//level_2.blend" for example. The value is a path to another blend file, the // prefix means it's in the same directory as the current blend file.

When using "portal_scene" or "portal_blend" properties, the "portal" property must be present, if you don't want to set an object location, its value should be an empty string.

The properties described work the same way as the Apricot levels, however character scripts were modified for the purpose of this example.

Take a look at the portals in this directory for examples.

Splashing

Here is an example YoFrankie/tutorial-files/bge_splash_example.blend showing how splashes are created for the water and lava levels.

Water objects need collision sensors linking to "splash_logic"'s controller. In this case there are two water objects, but there is no limit.

splash_logic runs a python script called "detect_splash" whenever there are collisions, t he "detect_splash" script moves "splash_logic" to each collision location and adds a splash object.

This way many splashes can happen at once.

It is up to the objects that land on the water to float, sink or be removed, they only need to collide with the water. In this example the cube's dynamics are suspended and it is removed after 200 logic ticks.

The empty objects above are there to create objects that make a splash however any object could be dropped.

The splash object itself must be in a disabled layer for the AddObject actuator to work. See layer 20.

Dual-player Split Screen

This file **YoFrankie/tutorialfiles/bge_splash_ example.blend** shows how two instances of the same character group can have their own keys and screen assigned on start.

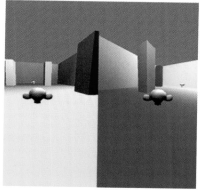

This is done by having a python init script for each character that assigns a unique ID, used to configure each differently.

Once the script runs, the state is changed to respond to user input only. The character objects in this scene are dupligroup instances. Change to the "character_group" scene to see their logic and see the "frank_init_2player" script to see how they are initialized.

Use the arrow keys for player one, WASD keys for player two.

Menu

This blendfile **YoFrankie/tutorialfiles/bge_menu_ example.blend** shows a simplified version of the Yo-Frankie start menu.

The menu has the following functionality:

- Input from mouse, keyboard or joystick.
- Menu items can load scenes, blendfiles or trigger your own actuators.

- Toggle and radio menu items can be used to set configuration options.
- Options can be saved an loaded to a file using new functionality in the game actuator.
- Logic is generic, reusable between multiple menus.

Implementation

The basis of the menu is quite simple, all objects starting with "item_" are alphabetically sorted and treated as menu items. Only one item can be active at a time by pressing up/down or passing the mouse over it. Pressing enter or clicking will execute the menu items action.

The "menu_select" script is where most of the menu logic is controlled. It runs on the "menu_logic" object, reacting to user input by scanning the scene for "item_" prefixed objects and adjusting their properties accordingly.

The "active" property is used by all items. When set to 1, the items sensor detects this and plays an animation. For YoFrankie we chose to use invisible items so we could attach animations to one or more objects, giving us a larger area for the mouse to activate as well.

Item Activation Type: Trigger

These items only need an extra "trigger" property. When the menu item is activated trigger is set to 1. The items own logic needs to check for the trigger value to act on it. Once executed the trigger value needs to be set back to zero. See the menu items "Quit", "Save Config" and "Load Config"

Item Activation Type: Portal

Using the same properties as in the levels, portals can load blendfiles, scenes and objects (to set the initial location).

The properties are

- **active** • described above.
- **portal** • object name
- **portal_scene** • scene name
- **portal_blend** • blendfile name

See the menu items "Open Blendfile", "Configure" and "Back" for examples of a portal.

Configuration

If you want to configure settings in a menu, you can use the python dictionary "GameLogic.globalDict" which is kept between loading files and can be saved and loaded to a file with the game actuator.

All game configuration is kept in a dictionary - GameLogic.globalDict['conf'].

There are currently two types of buttons that will automatically adjust the python dictionary when activated. Both use the "conf_key" property to specify which setting is changed.

Even through there are only a few buttons, many configuration buttons can be added without making any changes to the menus inner workings.

See the "init_options" script and menu items in the options scene to see how they work.

Toggle

This is fairly simple, the toggle button switches value in the configuration dictionary on and off.

- **active** • described above.
- **toggle** • 0 or 1, the menu item checks this to display a larger dot when enabled.
- **conf_key** • toggle this option, GameLogic.globalDict['conf'][conf_key] = True or False

Radio

Unlike the toggle button, multiple radio buttons share the same conf_key.

- **active** • described above.
- **radio** • the value of conf_key when the button is enabled. So for instance 3 buttons low/med/high would have "radio" values of 0,1,2.
- **enabled** • only 1 of the radio buttons sharing the same conf_key will ever be enabled at a time. This is used to play an animation making the enabled option stand out.

- **conf_key** • toggle this option, GameLogic.globalDict['conf'][conf_key] will be set to the "radio" value of the button thats enabled.

This example omits key binding configuration since it is fairly complicated and specific to YoFrankie.

Frankie's Logic

Frankie's behavior is made from a number of objects with an invisible parent that does almost all the logic. The logic bricks are divided into manageable states (walk, run, fall, idle etc) so each state can be edited without dealing with the logic from other states.

There are two main exceptions to this rule, status (15) and action (16) so Frankie can execute actions and his life is maintained throughout gameplay.

Sensor logic bricks detect

- user input (keyboard or joystick)
- collisions with special level elements (eg. lava, water, bounce, portal).
- property changes to health and inventory.

Actuators are used to

- play animations and sounds
- enter new states
- set properties for health, carrying and timers.
- apply physics forces (eg. jumping and running)
- constrain orientation (eg. walk - upright, run - ground parallel, glide - limit pitch).

Scripts are needed for advanced functionality like

- gliding, where Frankie's pitch influences speed and descent.
- hanging off a ledge, where rays are cast to detect the top of the ledge setting Frankie's vertical position.
- Context sensitive actions that test surroundings for enemies, what Frankie's carrying and his inventory.

Frankie's States

- idle (1) state is the default state when Frankie is on the ground and not doing anything.
- walk (2) when holding forward or backwards.
- servo motion actuator to maintain constant speed.
- run (3) when holding down action key and forward.
- linear velocity is only used to move Frankie forward.

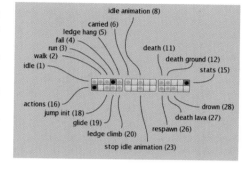

- a distance constraint actuator with the rotation option enabled is used to keep Frankie running parallel to the surface of the ground (making loop-the-loops possible)
- run speed is controlled from a the "frank_run_speed" script, that adjusts the run speed based on the "boosted" property and Frankie's pitch (to accelerate around a loop-the-loop).
- fall (4) state is set when Frankie is not colliding with any ground objects and immediately after jumping.
- Frankie is constrained to being upright while falling using an orientation constraint actuator.
- From this state Frankie can also bounce or change states by landing on another player to be carried, grab onto a ledge or glide by holding down jump.
- ledge hang (5) state continuously keeps Frankie attached to an edge where Frankie can shimmy from side to side, drop off or climb if there is ground above the ledge.
- This is one of the few states where actions are disabled (state 16)
- dynamics are not suspended, the python script keeps Frankie attached to the edge.
- carried (6) when Frankie's "carried" property is non-zero, this state is set, almost all functionality is disabled and Frankie can only throw objects.
- idle animation (8) when idle for a while this state is added, using the "frank_random_anim" script to play a random animation actuator.
- This state differs from others because it's added on top of another state. Since this state only plays an animation it doesn't matter if it's disabled by another state being set, such as walking or falling.
- death (11) is set when Frankie's life is zero, this state will immediately switch to state 12 or 27 if there is lava collision.
- death ground (12) plays the death animation then sets respawn state 26. This state is set exclusively, disabling all player input.
- stats (15) updates Frankie's health, reacts to being hit, touching water, collects pickups, activates portals and sends messages to the heads up display (HUD)

overlay scene.

- This state will run most of the time, in all other states where Frankie has free movement - (not death, drown or respawn).
- actions (16) state detects input and performs actions - a combination of playing animations and performing action logic. The logic for catching and checking if Frankie is on the ground or not is also done in this state.
- the "frank_action_all" script senses key input, checks what there is to kick or throw then sets the "action_name" property and plays the animation. This keeps the script running while "action_name" is set. Running the logic on keypress would be simple but not very convincing, so the script has a frame set for each action to execute logic, after the frame in the armature animation and the "action_done" property is set.
- You can add your own actions by adding a key sensor, action actuator and following the conventions in "frank_action_all" script.
- this state also runs along side most other states (as with state 15), however it's disabled during ledge grab and ledge climb.
- jump init (18) state plays a sound, sets the linear velocity and resets the "jump_timer" and "grounded" property.
- After setting the properties we immediately switch to the fall state. This is done because having all jump actuators attached to controllers in idle, walk and run states would be hard to maintain.
- glide (19) state is enabled by holding jump while falling. All of the glide logic is performed in the "frank_glide" script which deals with the dynamics of speed and pitch to enable swooping and remaining airborne for a short time.
- ledge climb (20) is used when pressing forward while hanging on a ledge. An animation plays while Frankie moves up onto the ledge above.
- Servo motion actuators move Frankie up and forward at a fixed speed without having to suspend dynamics.
- The motion actuators are synchronized with the animation using delay sensors to time the change in motion from upward to forward.
- stop idle animation (23) resets the idle animation timer and disables camera orbit, then disables the animation state and its own state.
- respawn (26) resets Frankie's location and restores almost all his properties to their original values.
- death lava (27) is the same as death ground, except a different animation and sound play.
- drown (28) state is similar to the death states, except instead of respawning, the "frank_drown_revive" script moves Frankie to the second last location where he was touching the ground.

Frankie's Properties

- **id** This is a unique player ID integer for each player, 0 and 1 for players 1 and 2. This is used when initializing the player to set key keyboard preferences and splitscreen. When you throw an object, your "id" is assigned to its "projectile_id" so we know who last threw the object. Starting as -1, correctly initialized in the script "frank_init"
- **grounded** is used by a lot of Frankie's logic bricks and scripts to know if he is on the ground or not. This value is managed by the "frank_ground_test" script (State 16) where a "ground" collision and -Z ray sensor are used to detect if the ground state changes. This property could be removed and be replaced with ground collision sensors everywhere, however a collision sensor alone can jitter on bumpy terrain, the combination of ground + ray gives better results.
- **predator** is used by sheep, ram and rat logic to tell you're an enemy and to attack or run away from you.

Type		Name		Value		D
Int	⇕	Name:id	◄	-1	►	D
Int	⇕	Name:grounded	◄	0	►	D
Bool	⇕	Name:predator	True	False		D
Bool	⇕	Name:kickable	True	False		D
Int	⇕	Name:hit	◄	0	►	D
String	⇕	Name:orig_pos				D
String	⇕	Name:ground_pos				D
String	⇕	ame:ground_pos_old				D
Timer	⇕	me:water_touch_time	◄	1.000	►	D
Int	⇕	Name:camera_orbit	◄	0	►	D
Timer	⇕	ame:idle_anim_timer	◄	-8.000	►	D
Int	⇕	Name:carrying	◄	0	►	D
Int	⇕	Name:carried	◄	0	►	D
Timer	⇕	Name:force_walk	◄	0.000	►	D
String	⇕	Name:action_name				D
Int	⇕	Name:action_done	◄	0	►	D
String	⇕	Name:throw_item				D
Int	⇕	Name:life	◄	13	►	D
Int	⇕	Name:life_max	◄	13	►	D
Timer	⇕	Name:revive_time	◄	1.000	►	D
Timer	⇕	Name:jump_time	◄	0.000	►	D
Int	⇕	Name:double_jump	◄	2	►	D
Float	⇕	Name:glide_z_init	◄	0.000	►	D
Timer	⇕	Name:wall_run_timer	◄	1000.000	►	D
Timer	⇕	Name:boosted	◄	0.000	►	D
Int	⇕	Name:can_climb	◄	0	►	D
Timer	⇕	e:ledge_regrip_timer	◄	100.000	►	D

- **kickable** is used for 2 player mode to allow you to kick each other. Sheep and rats also have this property.
- **hit** is set by other objects logic when you're attacked (rats, rams or a second player). When this is set, Frankie's life property will have the hit value subtracted and the hit value set back to zero. The "frank_health" script responds to non-zero hit values. Using this method makes adding in your own enemies easier, all they need to do is set the "hit" value of the object they are attacking.
- **orig_pos** stores Frankie's initial location when entering the level. When Frankie dies this position is used for respawning. This value is initialized in the "frank_init" script. It is used in "frank_respawn" and as a fallback location in "frank_revive" scripts.
- **ground_pos** and **ground_pos_old** properties are updated every second, storing the last instance Frankie was on the ground. At the moment this is only used for reviving after drowning, where Frankie is revived at the (2nd) last point where he touched the ground. ground_pos_old is always a second older than ground_pos

to make sure the ground location used isn't too close to the water and set imme-diately before drowning. These values are set in frank_ground_pos

- water_touch_time Simply drowning when Frankie touches the water doesn't work well, especially when jumping off drowning sheep. This timer is used to make sure Frankie is touching the water for a short period before switching to the drowning state. (see water_timer sensors and controller in State 15)
- camera_orbit is an integer used to set the camera orbiting around Frankie when he plays idle animations, drowns or falls in lava. The "Camera_Scaler" object has a sensor that checks this property, running a motion actuator when it is nonzero and plays an ipo when it is false to set the rotation back. See "Camera_scalers" orbit_on and orbit_off controllers.
- idle_anim_trigger This timer is used to play idle animations when Frankie has been inactive for a while. It is initialized to a negative number and will orbit the camera, then add the idle animation state around 0.0 See logic bricks in State 1 with the idle_anim prefix
- carrying integer is set to 1 when Frankie is carrying something. Many scripts use this to check if Frankie can do actions like collect items, tailwhip, double jump and run. The main logic setting this value is the "frank_carry" script which runs when-ever an object with the "carried" property touches Frankie. See State 16 frank_car-ry controller.
- carried defines this as an object that can be carried (player 1 can carry player 2 for example). Its value is used by scripts and logic bricks to know if you are being car-ried. When this is nonzero state 6 is set where dynamics are suspended and Frankie can't do very much (except throw anything he's already carrying).
- force_walk timer is used when we want to stop Frankie from running, when the timer is below zero the run state will switch immediately back to walk. This is set to always be negative when carrying an object, and used to force walking for a short time when Frankie is hit, throwing, kicking and tail-whipping.
- action_name is used when Frankie performs an action - currently its value will be either "throw_carry", "throw", "kick" or "tailwhip". This means we know what action is currently running and also stops multiple actions from running at once. Once finished the value will be set to an empty string. See state 16 where the "frank_ac-tion_all" script is used to control all the actions
- action_done is used by the "frank_action_all" script to check if the function asso-ciated with an action has run yet. Without this, actions could not take place in the middle of an animation. See state 16 also
- throw_item stores the item Frankie will throw next. If there were more collectible items that had different purposes, this could be used to cycle through active items. See "frank_sense_pickup" script in state 15 where the last collected item sets the "throw_item" and "frank_action_all" in State 16 where the "throw_item" defines the item to throw next
- life for storing Frankie's current health and for updating the HUD meter. See the "frank_health" script in State 15
- life_max Frankie's maximum health value to limit how much life Frankie can pick

up. See "frankie_scene_pickup" in State 15

- revive_time is set to zero when Frankie is hit, another hit won't be applied until "revive_time" is over 1.0. See "frank_health" script from state 15
- jump_time timer is set to 0.0 upon jumping, where it is used to ignore any ground collisions for a short time and then to detect if it's too late to do a double jump. jump time is also re-used for timing the glide duration. See "frank_ground_test" on State 16 and State 18 where the jump values are set
- double_jump is used to check if Frankie has double-jumped (since you can only double-jump once) See "frank_fall" script in State 4.
- glide_z_init is set to Frankie's Z axis when he starts gliding, its used to make sure he can never glide to a higher level then when he starts. See the "frank_glide" script in State 19
- run_wall_timer is used so Frankie can flip off a wall when he runs into any wall with the "slip" property. See "frank_wall_run" script in State 3
- boosted is set set when Frankie catches a butterfly (touches a pickup with a "boost" property), making his colour flash run a lot faster. See "frank_run_speed" script in State 3, "frank_sense_pickup" where the boost value is set
- can_climb is set when hanging by casting a ray above the ledge to detect if there is any ground for Frankie to climb onto. If this is not zero, pressing up while hanging will make Frankie climb up onto the ledge. See "frank_ledge_hang" script in State 5
- ledge_regrip_timer is used when dropping from a ledge (down key while hanging) to stop Frankie from grabbing the ledge immediately after dropping. See the "frank_ledge_collide" script in State 4

Building a simple test level

Most of the game on the DVD uses Blenders GLSL materials, so it is needed to use a decent graphics card to get the full look and performance. On the "Yo Frankie! DVD" there is also a (graphically) simple game.

Level Design Physics/Logic

Setting up a level to run with Frankie's logic is easy to start with, just make sure any area you want to stand on has the "ground" property.

From here you can play the level, you'll probably notice glitches but these can be dealt with by fine tuning the level (see notes below).

Physics Objects

The current method of defining ground and barriers is limited in that it requires you to have separate objects for each.

For the "Yo Frankie!" levels it was easier to remove collisions from the scenery and add invisible physics objects.

Physics can be disabled for scenery in the game logic buttons. Physics only objects can have their render option turned off in the outliner so they are initialized invisible (saves adding UV's and using the invisible option).

Materials

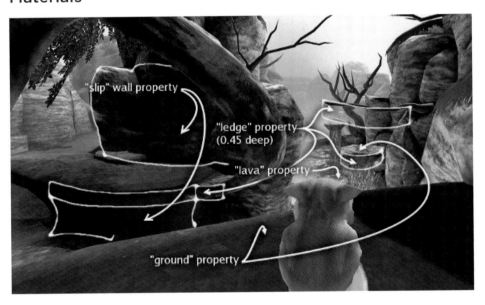

Walls and other vertical surfaces you dont want to run up should have a material with no friction (see the materials DYN button).

Properties

These properties are checked for in Frankie and other entities logic, so the characters interact correctly with the level.

- ground property is used to define anything Frankie can stand on. These surfaces don't have to be flat (a loop-the-loop for instance has the "ground" property). However make sure this isn't assigned to walls and barriers.

Platforms you jump up onto should be surrounded by a barrier that doesn't have the "ground" property, The top should be outset about 0.05 so collision with the top of the barrier won't also collide with the ground, otherwise Frankie will start walking before he is on top of the platform.

- slip wall property makes back-flips off walls possible when run directly into. Running at the wall from an angle will cause Frankie to run parallel to the wall. This isn't necessary for gameplay to work but makes running around a level feel smoother. The value of this property isn't used.
- ledge property is used to define areas that Frankie can hang.on. The value of this property isn't used. o These should be vertical strips 0.45 deep. The Ghost collision option can be used if you want to be able to ungrip and fall through the ledge-grab geometry (with branches for example).
- bounce property will make the object bounce Frankie back up in the air when he falls onto it. The value of this property isn't used.
- kill property will make Frankie lose as many lives as the kill value which must be an integer.
- water property should be applied to the surface of a river so Frankie drowns when touching it for a short time. *This object should be a ghost. The value of this property isn't used.*
- Lava is similar to water, just plays a different animation for Frankie.
- liquid this property should be applied to water or lava objects so pickups will disappear when touching them. The value of this property isn't used.

Starting A New Level Using Linked Groups

This tutorial will take you through linking groups from external blendfiles, into your own scene, using the "Yo Frankie!" characters and other assets for your own level.

Set Blender to the default scene. Now scale the Cube down to a flat ground and make it also bigger. Change to the Logic Buttons **F4** and add a Property "ground" to our ground cube. This will tell the player characters (Frankie, Momo, the sheeps etc.) where to walk on.

Now use the menu "File → Append or Link" or **SHIFT**-**F1** and browse to the CDROM, look for the folder and file **YoFrankie/chars/frankie.blend** . Click it with **LMB** and you will enter the file itself. Here you can browse all elements in that file. Now click

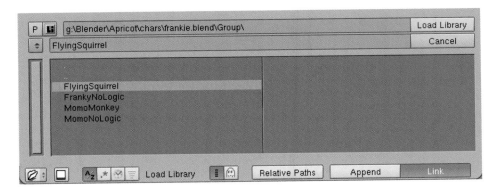

on "Group", you will see some groups, containing Frankie the main character and also Momo.

Look at the header, right now the "Append" button is active. This will append the group into our scene. We should use this option when we want to change the imported object or character later. However, it is better to copy the needed things from the original location into an own location and use the power of library linking.

Now activate "Link", for this quick test we will just use the characters as they are supposed to be used in the "Yo Frankie!" game. So select "FlyingSquirrel" with **LMB** and use the "Load Library" button.

Remember that when you use "Linking" you always have to put the CDROM into the drive when you try to load your new level. For starting a real new game or a level which will integrate into the game you should copy the CDROM contents to a place on your harddisk.

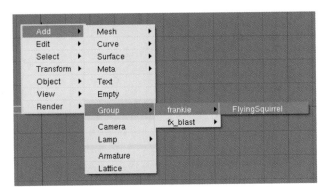

Right now nothing appeared in our scene, no wonder, because we linked a group. Place the 3D Cursor where you want to add the character and use the Toolbox with **SPACE** → Add → Group → frankie → FlyingSquirrel to add a dupligroup intance.

You should now be able to run the game by pressing **P**, however the scene will be without textures. So stop the game engine with **ESC** and choose "Blender GLSL

Materials" from the "Game"-menu and switch to the textured viewmode by pressing **ALT**-**Z**.

You should now also see a shadow on the ground, if not you need to assign a material to the ground. It is best to keep the main characters on layer 1 and also put there the ground and all elements on which the characters shadow should fall.

You already noticed that the screen splits into two views, even if there is no second player. This is because we need some initialization for the main characters. Split the big 3D view and change one window to a Text Editor using **SHIFT**-**F11**. Now use **ALT**-**O** to open the script **YoFrankie/tutorialfiles/ init_options.py** .

Init the main characters:

```
5.      '''
6.      Setup default configuration options
7.      use GameLogic.globalDict which is stored between loading blend
         files
8.      '''
9.      import GameKeys
10.
11.     def main():
12.       try:   conf = GameLogic.globalDict['CONFIG']
13.       except:   conf = GameLogic.globalDict['CONFIG'] = {}
14.
15.       def confdef(opt, value):
16.           if not conf.has_key(opt):
17.               conf[opt] = value
18.
19.       confdef('PLAYER_COUNT', 1)
20.       confdef('GRAPHICS_DETAIL', 2) # 2 == high
21.       confdef('GRAPHICS_GLSL', 1) # toggle
22.
23.       # Keys
24.
25.       # P1
26.       confdef('KEY_UP_P1', GameKeys.UPARROWKEY)
27.       confdef('KEY_DOWN_P1', GameKeys.DOWNARROWKEY)
28.       confdef('KEY_LEFT_P1', GameKeys.LEFTARROWKEY)
```

```
29.      confdef('KEY_RIGHT_P1', GameKeys.RIGHTARROWKEY)
30.
31.      # P2
32.      confdef('KEY_UP_P2', GameKeys.WKEY)
33.      confdef('KEY_DOWN_P2', GameKeys.SKEY)
34.      confdef('KEY_LEFT_P2', GameKeys.AKEY)
35.      confdef('KEY_RIGHT_P2', GameKeys.DKEY)
36.
37.      # P1
38.      confdef('KEY_JUMP_P1', GameKeys.MKEY)
39.      confdef('KEY_THROW_P1', GameKeys.SPACEKEY)
40.      confdef('KEY_ACTION_P1', GameKeys.NKEY)
41.
42.      # P2
43.      confdef('KEY_JUMP_P2', GameKeys.GKEY)
44.      confdef('KEY_THROW_P2', GameKeys.JKEY)
45.      confdef('KEY_ACTION_P2', GameKeys.HKEY)
46.
47.      #
48.      import Rasterizer
49.      Rasterizer.showMouse(True)
50.
51.   main()
52.
```

Now add an Empty and use an Always Sensor to just call this script one time. To do so you need to switch off the pulse button.

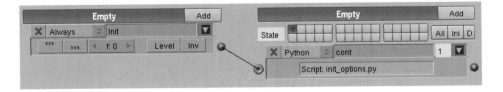

We can now add more elements. First try to add some water, for now it is not important to make good looking water, so we can just add a plane and give it a blueish color. Give it a Property "water" and make it "Ghost" in the Logic Buttons **F4**. As soon as a character touches the water it will drown.

Similarly working are game objects with the "kill" Property. When touching them character will loose life energy until he dies.

You can now start adding more objects and maybe sheep, rats or whatever and start to design your own "Yo Frankie!" Level.

Modify Apricot Files

If you like to make a new game or at least to change vital parts of "Yo Frankie!" then it is recommended to copy the whole folder tree to your disk and work in there. Save changes to the files into a new file, so that your changes don't interfere with the original levels.

My goal is to make a special butterfly level, where Frankie only has to collect butterflies.

First I loaded the butterfly **YoFrankie/chars/butterfly1.blend** and saved it under a new name. First thing we have to do is to switch of (set to "False") the Property "pickup". We will handle our things ourself here. Now locate the Keyboard Sensor and change it to a Collision Sensor. Enter "predator" in the Property field, so it will only react on collsions with a main character.

In the Ray Sensor "above_anything" we can now lower the Range value, so that Franky can reach a flying butterfly with a normal jump.

Beside that I am sending a message with the subject "Butterfly", so we can count the score.

For a mean effect I also added a detached butterfly-wing and will add it to the scene when the butterfly is catched.

Next I modified **Frankie.blend** . I don't want to use the (quite complex) HUD overlay which comes with Frankie. So I simply deleted the name "hud" in the Scene Actuator. This one is a bit hidden in the complex logic of Frankie. It is on the object "Main Cam" and you need to make the logic bricks visible by clicking on the name "Main Cam".

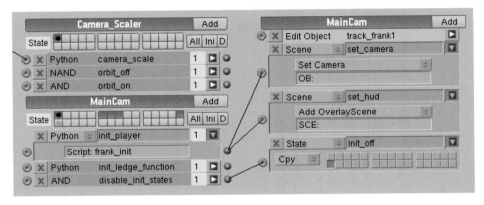

We are now ready to test our modified files. Make a simple level, don't forget to add the "ground" Properties to the ground objects and use the **init_options.py** script to initialize the player. Now add a main Character and some butterflies. You should now be able to catch the butterflies.

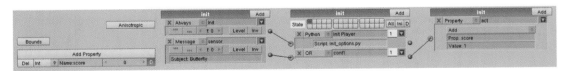

With a simple logic you are now able to count the score when the option "Show Debug Properties" in the "Game"-menu is activated.

I also added an own HUD (see **YoFrankie/tutorialfiles/Butterflylevel.blend**) for displaying my "kill count" and dropped in some props from the game. This was all done in a couple of hours, sure I am not the greatest level designer, but however, without the help of all the production data I could have never made such a visually appealing game in such a short time. It takes much longer to make a level playable or fun, but with the latest developments we unlock Blender for the artists more and more, you don't need to be a developer anymore for this kind of stuff.

You can see that it needs some exploration and coming with that a deeper under-standing of the complex coherences of the "Yo Frankie!" files, but the reward is high, you look behind the scenes of a professionally done game. Be sure to check out all the other files and tutorials on the "Yo Frankie!" DVD.

CHAPTER 13

A
REFERENCE
TO THE BLENDER GAME ENGINE

Carsten Wartmann

The reference section will be your guide to exploring the Blender 3D game engine further after following the tutorials. To learn modeling and linear animation refer to the books mentioned in the appendix.

Real-time Materials

There are different options on how to use materials for real time-content in Blender. All different kinds have specific advantages and disadvantages. The material system in Blender is now nearly completely usable in the game engine, however these materials need a good graphics cards.

Because of the deep impact on the speed of your game you probably need to make a decision what kind of material you want. In the Game menu you will find options to switch between the materials.

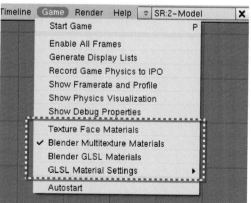

Game menu material options

The following sections will explain the material options in the Game-menu.

Texture Face Materials

Texture Face Materials are the most basic materials in the game engine. Basically they only provide basic Materials (color) or one texture.

Features like lighting, specularity, hardness are working on vertex level so for low poly objects you will see artifacts in the lighting or in the specularity spot.

For a basic material, add a new one in the Material Buttons **F5** or choose an existing one. Then change colors or other attributes. The object will be lit according to the lights (see also BGE Lamps) in the same layer.

To add a texture we have to use UV texturing, see UV Texturing. The texture will be mixed with the material color (only in the game engine not in the 3D view). To get vertex lighting we need to set the faces to "Light" in the Texture Face Panel in the Edit Buttons **F9**. Use the "Copy"-button to copy the Active Face Mode from the active to all selected faces. Beside the mixing with the plain material color it is also possible to use vertex-colors, see Vertex Paint.

Blender Multitexture Materials

With these materials it is possible to have more than one (3) texture on an object. These textures can mix in different kind of ways. This makes it possible to have simple pre rendered light maps or faked reflections (using EnvMaps). Especially helpfull is the possibility to bake the render into the texture, this can be done in the "Render"-menu.

Lighting, specularity, hardnes for Blender Multitexture Materials is calculated on vertex level.

You need to add a material with more than one texture channel. Then assign two or three textures to it, set the texture blending mode to one of the supported modes:

Add, Multiply, Substract, Divide or Mix. For Mix you need to adjust the Col: slider too.

Be sure to uncheck "UseAlpha" in the texture or the mixing will not produce the correct results!

The texture coordinates should come from one ore more UV Textures, which you can add and manage in the Edit Buttons **F9**, "Mesh"-panel.

The Mesh Panel

Examples:

- **Multitexture.blend**   (supported mixing modes)

GLSL Materials

Blenders GLSL Materials are the newest development for real time 3D and interactive display in the 3D Views. In the game engine you exactly get what you see in the 3D Views and it even almost looks like rendered. The purpose of this system is to stick closely to the material system as in Blender's internal renderer. Only a subset of the material options are supported, with hopefully more in the future, but the ones that are supported should give nearly identical results. Some advanced features like ray tracing are not likely to be added given that graphics card don't support them efficiently yet.

The main supported features are:

- All material diffuse and specular shaders.
- Diffuse and specular ramps.
- All nodes, except for the dynamic node and limited support for material node.
- Image textures only with few options.
- A subset of the texture mapping options.
- All lamp types except area, and basic support for shadow buffers.
- Unlike Multitexture materials, most material and light settings are currently not

animateable with GLSL materials.

The limitations:

- All objects will compute the lighting for all lamps, even if they are far away or on another layer. Hence it is important to keep the number of lamps as low as possible. For example for outdoor scenes, two sun or hemi lamps can illuminate the whole scene already.
- The game engine supports maximum two UV layers and no compatible Orco texture coordinates.

GLSL Materials Performance Tips

Since Blender's materials system was designed for off line rendering and the GLSL materials attempt to be compatible with the internal render, they may not render as fast as more optimized game engines. Therefore it is important to optimize the material and light settings for best performance:

- If some settings are set to values like 0.001 or 0.98, the visual difference with settings 0.0 or 1.0 may be very small, but it makes it harder for Blender to optimize the shader. Therefore it is advised to set such settings to 0.0 or 1.0 so that the effect can be completely disabled and does not need to be computed at all.
- Various material shaders are supported, but may perform very slow. Lambert and Phong are fastest, so if possible those should be used. Note that for specularity Cook Torr is the default, which can in many cases be switched to Phong without much difference.
- Additionally it helps to disable specularity if it is not needed. Not only can the Spec value be set to 0.0 in materials, but it also helps to enable No Specular on lamps, so only one lamp affects specularity for example.
- If an image does not have alpha, it can help to disable Use Alpha in the texture buttons.
- Avoid slow texture or ramp blending modes, mix/add/subtract/multiply are the fastest, hue/saturation/value/color are very slow.
- Alpha blending needs to be avoided if possible, and Clip Alpha is a faster alternative, see the game engine alpha blending for more information.
- For shadows, it is more efficient to bake them for the whole scene, and use an OnlyShadow spot lamp for the character. On this spot lamp it is best to set the shadow buffer size low, enable No Specular, set SpotBl to 0.0. Also then the Layer option for shadow can be enabled so that the lamp only casts the shadow of the character.

Graphics Card Support

This implementation takes advantage of the OpenGL Shading Language (GLSL), and requires a graphics card and drivers that support it. The game engine already supported such GLSL shaders, though they had to be manually written. The following cards typically support it, though the earlier ones have restrictions on the complexity of materials and the number of lights. Be sure to install the latest graphics card drivers as they might fix bugs and improve performance.

- ATI Radeon 9x00, Xx00, X1x00, HD2x00 and HD3x00 series and newer.
- NVidia Geforce FX, 6x00, 7x00, 8x00, 9x00 and GTX 2x0 and newer.

Intel or VIA graphics cards, ATI Radeon cards older then the Xx00 series, and Nvidia Geforce cards older than the 6x00 series are unlikely to support this functionality well, unless through a slow software fall back. The game menu provides settings to disable things such as lights, advanced shaders or shadows which can help on older graphics cards or complicated scenes.

Game Engine Alpha Blending

Transprarent faces are always expensive in a real time environment. Therefor there are different modes which all have their limitations but differ in rendering speed.

For clarity, here is an overview of alpha sorting in the game engine, there are four transparency types in the game engine:

- Opaque: solid, no transparency at all.
- Alpha: transparency with values between 0-1, blends with faces behind it.
- Add: like Alpha, but adds color rather than blends.
- Clip Alpha: otherwise known as binary alpha, each pixel renders either completely opaque (when alpha > 0.5) or completely transparent (alpha <= 0.5).

Ideally one would not have to deal with such settings, but for good performance it is important to pick the right ones, since rendering with Alpha isn't as fast as Opaque. In many cases Clip Alpha can be used instead of Alpha while still being nearly as fast as Solid. For example for leaves one usually does not need partial transparency.

These settings can be set per face in the Texture Face panel. Note that for GLSL materials, the ZTransp setting must be used to enable any alpha, consistent with the internal render engine. The Alpha/Add/Clip Alpha settings can then be used to specify the exact blending type.

One important thing to know is that for rendering faces with Alpha and Add correct, the faces must be sorted before rendering in every frame. This is only supported in the game engine, not in the Blender viewport, which means that faces with alpha will draw incorrect in some cases there. Clip Alpha does not require sorting, which is useful since sorting objects with many polygons is slow.

Sorting has to be enabled with the Sort option in the Texture Face panel. The reason alpha sorting has to be set separately is because of the performance hit, and some objects might still render OK without sorting, so it is not enabled by default.

Lamps in the game engine

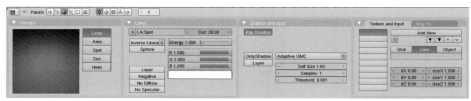

Lamps are created with the Toolbox (**SPACE** → Add Lamp) you can then choose the type of the lamp.

For a selected lamp you can switch to the Lamp Buttons **F5** to change the properties of that lamp. These properties are the type of the lamp, the color, the energy, etc. Due to the fact that the game engine is fully integrated in Blender, there are some buttons which are only useful for linear animation.

Common settings for all lamp types are the energy, and the color (adjustable with the RGB sliders).

To allow a face to receive real-time lighting in Blenders game engine, the face has to be set to "Light" in the "Texture Face"-panel. With the layer settings for lamps and objects (Edit Buttons, **F9**) you can control the lighting very precisely. Lamps only affect faces on the same layer(s) as the lamp. Per Layer you can use eight lamps (OpenGL limitation) for real-time lighting.

Lamp types for the game engine

Lamp • Lamp is a point light source.

Spot • This lamp is restricted to a conical space. In the 3DView the shape of the spotlight is shown with broken lines. Use the SpotSi slider to set the angle of the beam.

Sun • The "Sun" lamp type is a directional light. The distance has no effect on the intensity. Change the direction of the light (shown as a broken line) by rotating the lamp.

Hemi • Only supported with GLSL Materials! A "Hemi" lamp is a 180° constant light source. Great for fill light.

The "Lamp" and "Spot" lights are sensitive to distance. Choose a method for this in the "Falloff" menu.

GLSL Shadows

Dynamic shadows (moving objects or lamps) in the game engine are possible with GLSL Materials and Spot Lamps. Static shadows can be realized using light mapping techniques.

First enable GLSL Materials in the Game menu. Then assign a Blender Material to all the shadow receiving objects. Enter the Textured Mode with **ALT**-**Z**.

Use a Spot with "Buffer Shadow" enabled as lamp. Set the size of the spot (SpotSi) according to your scene. Note that shadow lamps can easily decrease the speed of your game. If your shadow is too jagged like in the image, then you might increase the ShadowBufferSize. Try to keep both values as low as possible.

Bias • If the shadow is only partially visible or parts of your object don't cast a shadow on the object itself, then decrease the "Bias:" value.

Only Shadow • In some situations it is nice to have a shadow but avoid illumination caused by the lights source itself. Examples are character shadows where the shadow gives a visual hint how high a character is while jumping for example.

Different
ShadowBufferSize
settings

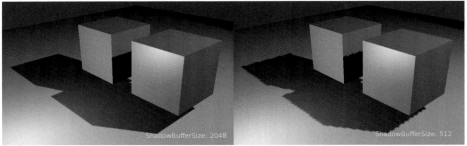

Use the "Layer" option (see below) in the "Shadow and Spot" Panel to avoid that other objects interfere with the characters shadow. If your character needs to rotate use Vertex Parenting to attach the lamp.

Layer Buttons:

- Layer in the "Lamp"-panel: This lamp only shines on objects in the same layer(s) as the lamp. Also shadows are only received from this lamp if the object shares the layer with the lamp.
- Layer in the "Shadow and Spot"-panel: Only Objects in the same layer cast shadow from this lamp.

Examples:

- GLSL_Lamps.blend
- GLSL_LayerLamps.blend
- GLSL_Lamps_Bias.blend
- GLSL_Lamps_OnlyShadow.blend

UV Texturing

The UV editor is fully integrated into Blender and allows you to uv-map textures onto the faces of your models. Each face can have individual texture coordinates and an individual image assigned. This can be combined with vertex colors to darken or lighten the texture or to tint it.

UV Mapping is the art of mapping a 2D image around a 3D object with as few distortions as possible!

With GLSL Materials now nearly the whole material system is available in the game engine. However this also needs some attention with textures. For now it is not so simple as with the old Texture Face Materials to get two images on different faces on one object. With GLSL we need multi-materials for that.

For UV mapping you enter Edit Mode for your object (only mesh objects supported). It is recommended to use the Face Select Mode in the Edit Mode, however it is perfectly ok to select faces by selecting 3 or 4 vertices or 3 or four edges. All the powers of EditMode are usable (i.e. Border Select, Circle Select, see also the Select-menu).

We now need UV coordinates for the object. This can be achieved in some ways depending on the way you work or what you prefer:

- select faces, then assign or load an image in the UV/Image Editor
- use "New" in the "Mesh"-panel in the Edit Buttons **F9** to make a new UV Texture
- unwrap the object using **U**

CTRL-**F** calls the "Face Specials"-menu

Important functions for UV mapping here:

- Face Mode Set/Clear: setting the face modes, like Tex, Tiles, Light, Invisible, Collision etc. This can also be done in the "Texture Face"-panel in the Edit Buttons
- UV Rotate/Mirror: Rotate/mirror the texture-coordinates

In the "Texture Face"-Panel of the Edit Buttons **F9** you will find these functions also, and more.

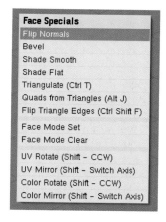

The Face Specials Menu

Face modes

The Texture Face Panel

Tex • This enables the use of textures. To use objects without textures, disable "Tex", then the material color will be used or paint the faces with Vertex-Paint.

Tiles • This indicates and sets the use of the tile mode for the texture, see Section Tiles.

Light • Enables real-time lighting on faces. Lamps only affect faces of objects that are in the same layer as the lamp. Lamps can also be placed on more than one layer, which makes it possible to create complex real-time lighting situations. See also Section Lamps in the Game Engine

Invisible • Makes faces invisible. These faces are still calculated for collisions, so this gives you an option to build invisible barriers, etc.

Collision • The faces with this option are evaluated by the game engine. If that is not needed, switch off this option to save resources.

Shared • With this option vertex colors are blended across faces if they share vertices.

Twoside • Faces with this attribute are rendered two sided in the game engine.

ObColor • Faces can have color that can be animated by using the ColR, ColG, ColB and ColA Ipos. Choosing this option replaces the vertex colors.

Halo • Faces with this attribute are rendered with the negative X-axis always pointing towards the active view or camera.

Billboard • Faces with this attribute are pointing in the direction of the active view with the negative X-axis. It is different to "Halo" in that the faces are only rotated around the Z-axis.

Shadow • Faces with this attribute are projected onto the ground along the Z-axis of the object. This way they can be used to suggest the shadow of the object without using expensive real-time shadows.

Text • Faces with this attribute are used for displaying bitmap text in the game engine, see Section Bitmap Text.

Sort • Enable sorting of faces for correct alpha drawing. Note this is slow, use Clip Alpha whenever possible!

Opaque • Normal opaque rendered faces. The color of the texture is rendered as color.

Add • Faces are rendered transparent. The color of the face is added to what has already been drawn. Black areas in the texture are transparent, white are fully bright. Use this option to achieve light beam effects, glows or halos around lights. For real transparency use the next option "Alpha".

Alpha • The transparency depends on the alpha channel of the texture.

Clip Alpha • The transparency depends on the clipped alpha channel of the texture. (See also Alpha Blending).

The "Copy" buttons will always copy the Face Modes from the active face (dotted highlight) to the selected (pink highlight) faces. "CopyUV", "CopyTex" and "CopyColor" are copying UVs, texture and color from the active face to the selected faces.

In the "Copy Face Selected" menu called by **CTRL**-**C** you find more helpful functions to copy face properties.

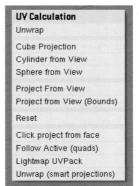

Copy Face Selected
Active Material
Active Image
Active UV Coords
Active Mode
Active Transp
Active Vertex Colors
TexFace UVs from layer
TexFace Images from layer
TexFace All from layer
Vertex Colors from layer

The Copy Face Selected Menu

Unwrapping

Unwrapping helps you to find a mapping from the 2D image to your 3D Object. A plane or a cube are easy to map, but with more organic and round objects like bottles, spheres or faces you need help in unwrapping. Usually the automatic unwrapping is the base and the artist then optimizes the result.

The UV Calculation menu is called out of Edit Mode with **U**, all selected faces are taken into calculation.

UV Calculation
Unwrap
Cube Projection
Cylinder from View
Sphere from View
Project From View
Project from View (Bounds)
Reset
Click project from face
Follow Active (quads)
Lightmap UVPack
Unwrap (smart projections)

The UV Calculation Menu

Unwrap • Unwraps the object taking seams into account

Cube Projection • Cubic projection (good base for walls, houses, technical devices)

Cylinder from View • Cylindrical projection (bottles, tires)

Sphere from View • Spherical projection (planets, marbles)

Project from View • The UV coordinates are calculated using the projection of the 3DWindow (good base for manually tweaking the result)

Project from View (Bounds) • The UV coordinates are calculated using the projection of the 3DWindow and then scaled to fit into the image dimensions.

Reset • Resets the UV coordinates of the selected faces

Click project from face • With three mouse clicks you can interactively set the uv coordinates in the 3DView

Follow Active (quads) • The quads of an object are unwrapped. Good for complex rectangular buildings. With the option "Loop Average" the face areas will be taken into account.

Lightmap UVPack • Method to unpack complex objects to use the map for light maps.

Unwrap (smart projections) • Powerfull unwrap method for mechanical and architectural objects.

The UV Calucation Panel

In the "UV Calculation"-panel of the Edit Buttons **F9** you can fine tune some parameters for unwrapping.

Image Aspect • Scales the unwrapping to the texture aspect

Transform Correction • With this option, the UV stays intact during an edge slide

Cube Size and Cyl Radius • Adjusts the size or radius for cubic or cylindrical unwrapping

Unwrapper (Conformal/Angle Based) • Unwrapping method

Fill Holes • Fill holes to prevent overlaps inside the unwrap

View Aligns Face/Top/Obj • Align the sperical/cylindrical unwrapping to the equator, pole or to the object align itself

Polar ZX/ZY • Polar 0 is X or Y for cylindrical or spherical unwrap

Seams

Seams are important for a good unwrapping. They define the edges where the unwrap algorithm is "cutting" the mesh apart. Place seams so that they are not noticeable or at a place where the material or texture changes much. Try to match the face areas in the projection with the faces of the 3D object.

Select the edges you want the seam to be and do **CTRL**-**E** → Mark Seam. To clear a seam use **CTRL**-**E** → Clear Seam.

UV/Image Editor

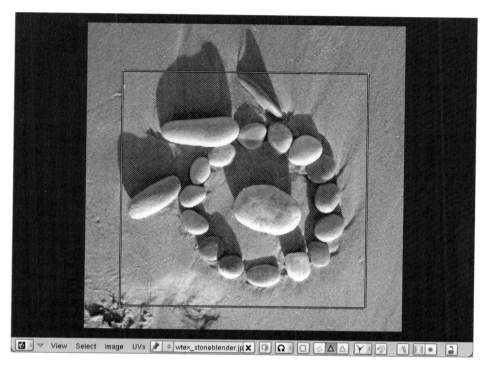

Anatomy of the UV/Image Window:

View menu

Basic functions for the window, including zoom, maximize etc.

In the View Properties panel you can find nice functions to help you while working with UVs. Deactivate the "Face"-button to switch off the display of faces which can occlude your sight on the object and the image. "Repeat Image" helps you with tiling the image on the objects faces. "UV Stretch" will give you a visual hint how much your image gets distorted. Also note the possibility to set and read the position of the 2D Cursor.

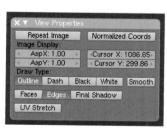

The View Properties Panel

Image menu

Basic image functions for load, save, pack etc. Also place for Python helper scripts.

The UVs Menu

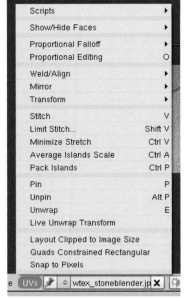

Select menu (only avaible when the mesh is in EditMode)

This menu contains special selection methods.

UVs menu

This menu contains many useful functions for working with UVs. It is beyond the scope of this chapter to explain everything here.

Working with UV Coordinates

As soon as you have a UV Texture on your object, you can work with it in the UV/Image Editor. UV vertices are represented with yellow (selected) or pink (unselected) points, connected by lines , just like in EditMode.

There are almost the same tools to work with the UV vertices as you are used to from the EditMode. Grab with **G**, rotate with **R**, scale with **S** etc.

Unlike in meshes all UV faces (triangle or quad) have their own vertices, there is no sharing between vertices, because we need to be able to move any faces where ever we want. However, because it is often needed to move vertices together, an option is enabled by default to stick vertices together for easy editing. You can choose this behavior in the UV/Image Editor header:

The Sticky UV Selection Menu

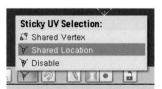

Shared Vertex • This will stick 3D vertices which are shared by faces in the mesh. Usually you don't want to separate such vertices in the UV coordinates, because this will generate seams in the texture on the object.

Shared Location (default) • Vertices in the UV coordinates will be moved together when they share the same place (in a 5 pixel range)

Disable • Move vertices freely

Texture Tiles

Texture Tiles can be used to have more textures in one image an still be able to re-peat textures on the objects. This is quite useful to save texture memory on older systems. The other use is to have simple animated textures.

Load a tiled texture into the UV/Image Editor, unwrap your object and assign the texture. Open the "Real-time Properties"-panel in the View-menu.

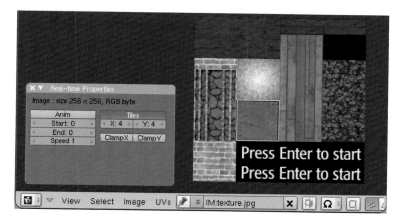

The Real-time
Properties Panel

Now set "X:" and "Y:" according to the number of tiles in your texture and activate "Tiles". In Edit Mode you can now select the tile you want to use with **SHIFT**-**LMB** from the texture. It is now possible to use the normal UV editing tools and so for example scale up to have the tile repeated on your object.

For a simple texture animation you load a tiled texture on your object, then also set "X:" and "Y:" according to the number of tiles in your texture, no need to activate "Tiles" this time. Instead activate "Anim" and set the "Sta:" and "End:" to the desired values (End = X * Y). Finally set the speed (in frames per second) of the animation with "Speed:". You should now see a texture animation in your game. For a GLSL Material you also need a Blender Material and a Texture with your animation, then you could for example animate a Nor map to get real ripples on your water object.

Texture Tiling Animation only works for Texture Face Materials and GLSL Materials.

Examples:

- **TextureTiling.blend**
- **TileAnim.blend**
- **TileAnimGLSL.blend**

Bitmap Text

Blender has the ability to draw text in the game engine using special bitmap fonts textures. These bitmap fonts can be created from a TrueType or a Postscript outline font. See **http://www.ashsid.sk/wp/?p=21&lang=en-us** for how to make your own. On the CDROM are some textures with bitmap fonts to try.

To get bitmap text or numbers displayed on a single face you need a special bitmap with the font rendered onto it. UV map the first character ("@") of the text-bitmap onto your text object (usually a plane). In the "Texture Face"-panel in the Edit Buttons **F9** activate "Text" for all faces of your text object.

UV-Mapping "@"

Then create a property named "Text" for your object. The property can be any type, so a Boolean Property will also be rendered as "True" or "False". For testing use a String-property and enter some text. Then start the game engine to see the results.

Vertex Paint

To start VertexPaint press **V** or select the VertexPaint mode in the 3D View Header.

The selected object will now be drawn solid. You can therefore now draw on the vertices of the object while holding **LMB**, the size of the brush is visualized by a circle while drawing. **RMB** will sample the color under the mouse pointer.

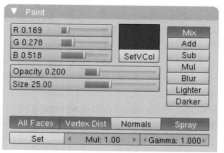

The Vertex Paint Panel

Enter the Edit Buttons **F9** to see the "VertexPaint"-panel. Here you can also find more options to control VertexPaint.

R, G, B • The active color used for painting. Can also be set by using the Color Picker called by a **LMB** -click into the color field (see below)

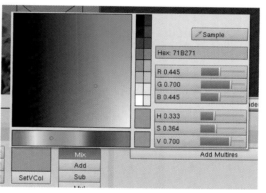

The Color Picker

Opacity • The extent to which the vertex color changes while you are painting.

Size • The size of the brush, which is drawn as a circle during painting.

Paint Modes

The manner in which the new color replaces the old when painting.

Mix • the colors are mixed.

Add • The colors are added.

Sub • The paint color is subtracted from the vertex color.

Mul • The paint color is multiplied by the vertex color.

Blur • Blurs the color according to the surrounding colors

Lighter • Paint over darker areas only

Darker • Paint over lighter areas only

Color field • A **LMB** click calls the color picker

SetVCol • Sets all vertices to the chosen color

All Faces • Paint on all faces inside the brush

VertexDist • This specifies that the extent to which the vertices lie within the brush also determines the brush's effect.

Normals • The vertex normal (helps) determine the extent of painting. This causes an effect as tough you were painting with light.

Spray • Continues to add color while holding **LMB** and moving the mouse

Set • The "Mul" and "Gamma" factors are applied to the vertex colors of the Mesh.

Mul • The number by which the vertex colors are multiplied when "Set" is pressed.

Gamma • The number by which the clarity (Gamma value) of the vertex colors are changed when "Set" is pressed.

You can choose on which faces you like to paint with the Painting Mask, called by **F** or the icon **▣** in the 3D View header. You can now select faces with the **RMB**, **SHIFT** -**RMB**, Border- or Circle-Select. Painting will now only occur on the selected faces.

When the Painting Mask is active, you can choose with the Buttons "Faces", "Edges" and "Hidden Edges" how the faces or edges should be displayed while painting. This especially helps while staring to paint on a solid colored object.

Texture Paint

To start Texture Paint select the Texture Paint Mode in the 3D Window header or out of the UV/Image Editor. Depending from where you activated Texture Paint you are now ready for painting either in the 3D View on your objects, or in the UV/Image Editor on your texture.

Texture Paint needs a UV textured object to work. You also need to unpack a packed texture first.

In the UV/Image Editor you paint like in a 2D paint application, in the 3D View you actually painting on the 3D object depending on how the faces are oriented in 3D space.

You can now paint holding the **LMB**. **RMB** will sample the color located under the mouse pointer.

REFERENCE

In the 3D View you can call the "Paint Properties"-panel with **N**. Here you can adjust the color. Using the **F** you can switch on a paint mask, meaning you can only paint on the selected faces. Faces are selected like in Edit Mode, **RMB** selects, **SHIFT** **RMB** adds, you can also use Border Select or Circle Select.

The Paint Properties Panel

In the "Paint"-panel in the Edit Buttons **F9**, you can also choose between different paint modes and mix modes. Further you can adjust the opacity, size, falloff and spacing of you brush strokes. It is also possible to add or recall brush settings or to paint using a different texture.

The Paint Panel

The "Image Paint"-panel has similar options. But aside of that you can also clone draw a different texture onto your texture.

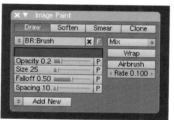

The Image Paint Panel

Resource Handling

For publishing and easier handling of Blender's files, you can include all resources into the saved file. Normally textures, samples and fonts are not included in a file while saving. This keeps them on your disk and makes it possible to change them and share them between files. But if you want to distribute a file it is possible to pack these resources into the Blendfile, so you only need to distribute one file, preventing missing resources.

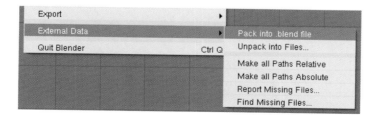

The External Data Menu

The functions for packing and unpacking are summarized in the "External Data"-menu. You can see if a file is packed if there is a little "parcel" icon to the right in the menu bar. After you packed a file, all new added resources are automatically packed (AutoPack).

When working with textures, sounds or fonts you will notice a pack-icon near the File- or Datablock-Browse. This icon allows you to pack/unpack the file independently.

External Data menu entries

Pack into .blend file • This packs all resources into the Blendfile. The next save will write the packed file to disk.

Unpack File options

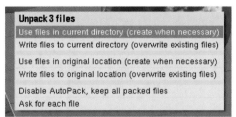

Unpack into Files • This unpacks all resources to the current directory. For textures a directory "textures" is created, for sounds a "samples" directory and fonts are unpacked to "fonts".

A menu will request further options. Be careful with the options overwriting files.

Use files in current directory • This unpacks only files which are not present in the current directory. It creates files when necessary.

Write files to current directory • This unpacks the files to the current directory. It overwrites existing files!

Use files in original location • This uses files from their original location (path on disk). It creates files when necessary.

Write files to original location • This writes the files to their original location (path on disk). It overwrites existing files!

Disable AutoPack, keep all packed files • This disables AutoPack, so new inserted resources are not packed into the Blendfile.

Ask for each file • This asks the user for the unpack options of each file.

Make all Paths Relative • This option changes all file paths so that they address the file in a relative way. So you can move your scene between different computers without caring for drives letters or such.

Make all Paths Absolute • This makes all paths absolute.

Report Missing Files • Reports missing files. A text buffer "missing_files.log" is created and contains informations about the missing files.

Find Missing Files • With this option you can point Blender to a directory containing the missing files.

Blender's Game Engine

Technically speaking the Blender game engine is a framework with a collection of modules for interactive purposes like physics, graphics, logic, sound and networking. Functionally the game engine processes virtual reality, consisting of content (the world, its buildings) and behaviors (like physics, animation and logic). Elements in this world - also called GameObjects - behave autonomously by having a set of tools called Logic Bricks, and Properties. For comparison, the Properties act as the memory, the Sensors are the senses, the Controllers are the brain and the Actuators allow for actions in the outside world (i.e. muscles).

At the moment, the Controllers can be scripted using Python, or simple expressions. The idea is that the creation of logical behavior can be edited in a more visual way in the future, so the set of controllers expands with AI state machines, etc. Controllers could be split in control centers, like an audio visual center, motion center, etc.

The Blender game engine contains two physics systems. One is the older and depreciated "Sumo", which is still integrated inside Blender to enable older games to run. The new and very advanced physics system is called "Bullet" (Author Erwin Coumans also known as one of the original authors of Blender's game engine, see **www.bulletphysics.com**) which calculates the physical behaviors of the objects, like falling, forces and collisions.

Options for the game engine

Start Game • Starts the game, shortcut is **P**. If there is more than one 3D View the cursor changes into a question mark and you can now choose the view the game should be started in.

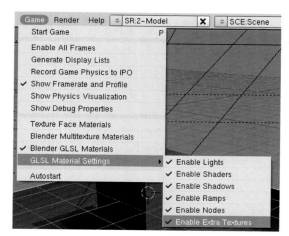

Game Engine Options

Enable All Frames • Normally the game engine will try to play the game in 60 frames per second (fps), if the CPU or graphics power is not high enough the engine will start dropping frames to maintain the overall speed of objects. This can cause stutter in the play-back or even cause errors in collisions. With "Enable All Frames" the movement of the objects will slow down, but no frame will be dropped. This option is also very useful when using the game physics for linear animation.

Generate Display Lists • This option can improve the performance of the game (esp. in big and complex levels) quite a lot. However on older graphics cards this can lead to errors.

Record Game Physics to IPO • The movements of game objects will be recorded into Ipo animations. Very helpful for complex physics based animations (rolling, fall-ing, jumping, collisions etc.)

Show Framerate and Profile • This will display statistical informations during game play. Good for optimizing your game.

Show Physics Visualization • This option draws objects bounds and also shows the status of physical objects. Good for debugging and testing physics.

Show Debug Properties • This option enables the display of properties with the debug "D" button set in textured views. Wireframe and solid shaded views always display debug properties.

Texture Face Materials • Most basic material and texture system in Blender. See Realtime Materials.

Blender Multitexture Materials • Advanced use of multiple textures for games. See Realtime Materials.

Blender GLSL Matrials • Up to date material system. Requires modern graphics cards. See Realtime Materials.

GLSL Material Settings • In the sub menu you can enable/disable features of the GLSL material system for performance reasons or compatibility with graphics cards.

Autostart • A .blend-file with this option will autostart the game after loading. To edit such a .blend you can prevent autostart with a command line option.

Other Game Engine Options: In the User Preferences window you will find some more options:

Mipmaps • Mip-mapping is a texture filter to avoid flickering in textures and to en-hance performance, especially when viewed from distance or a flat angle. In some cases this filtering can be unwanted or can even cause a performance drop, so this can be disabled here.

Disable Game Sound • Disable game sound, helpful to avoid errors on computers without sound hardware.

GL Texture Clamp • With these options you can force textures to a specific size. This can help to enhance the performance on slow computers or older graphics cards.

Logic Buttons

The Logic Buttons are meant for making interactive 3D worlds in Blender. Blender is a complete development tool for interactive worlds including a game engine to play the worlds. All this is done without compiling the game or interactive world. Just press **P** and it runs in real-time. The main window for working with the Blender game engine are the Logic Buttons **F4** (⊙). Here you define your Logic Bricks, which add the behavior to your objects.

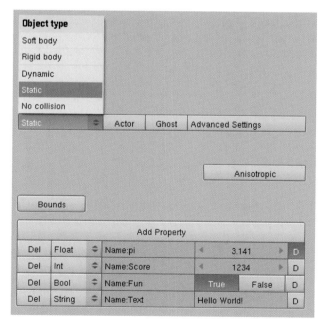

Logic Buttons, left part

The word "games" is here used for all kinds of interactive 3D-content; Blender is not limited to making and playing games, you can also, for example, create scientific visualizations or interactive 3D-manuals.

The Logic Buttons can logically be separated in two parts. The left part contains global settings for GameObjects.

This includes settings for general physics, like the damping or mass. Here you also define wether an object should be calculated with the built-in physics, as an actor or should be handled as an object forming the level (like props on a stage).

Settings for GameObjects:

With the menu button defaulting to **Static** you can choose how the physics engine should thread your object:

No collision • No collision detection for the whole object. Use this for objects which can never be touched by any dynamic object to save performance.

Static • This object acts as surrounding for a level or as a prop (like on a stage). These objects are still movable with Logic Bricks or Ipos, dynamic objects will react on collision with them.

Dynamic • These objects will follow the laws of physics, like falling, bouncing and colliding

Rigid body • This option enables the use of advanced physics by the game engine. This makes it possible that spheres roll automatically when they make contact with other objects and the friction between the materials is non-zero. Other shapes will tip over, tumble etc.

Soft Body • This makes an object a soft body.

If you only see few buttons, one labeled "Physics" you need to create a world in the Shading Context **F5***, World Buttons which also creates a physics environment.*

The "Advanced" button will call a pop up which covers advanced settings for the chosen object type.

Depending on the object type other buttons will appear:

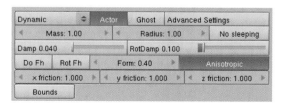

Actor • This makes Static objects detectable for Near and Radar sensors. Dynamic and Rigid Body objects are always an actor.

Ghost • Ghost objects don't restitute to collisions, but still trigger a collision sensor.

Advanced Settings • Clicking on this button will call a pop-oup menu containing advanced settings for the choosen object type. For dynamic objects it will contain:

> **Margin** • Each physics object has a collision margin in which collisions are detected. This margin leads to a much more stable simulation. However, for small objects or special cases you might want to decrease this margin to avoid gaps between resting objects.

No sleeping • Disable auto (de)activation for dynamic objects. Usually a object will be deactivated until it gets moved or hit by another object to save performance. For character objects this behavior can be unwanted.

Mass • The mass of a dynamic actor has an effect on how the actor reacts when forces are applied to it. You need a bigger force to move a heavier object. Note that heavier objects don't fall faster! It is the air drag that causes a difference in the falling speed in our environment (without air, e.g. on the moon, a feather and a hammer fall at the same speed). Use the "Damp" value to simulate air drag.

Radius • The size of the bounding sphere for sphere bound objects. The bounding sphere determines the area with which collisions can occur.

Damp • General (movement) damping for the object. Use this value for simulating the damping an object receives from air or water. In a space scene you might want to use very low or zero damping, air needs a higher damping, use a very high damping to simulate water.

RotDamp • Same as "Damp" but for rotations of the object.

Do FH • The FH system allows floating and hovering objects. Use together with the FH settings in the DYN Materials section.

Rot FH • Uses the face normal of the ground object to rotate the object.

Anisotropic • Anisotropic friction. This enables different friction along the axes of an object. Great for sliding/skiing etc.

For the advanced settings for soft body objects please look in the soft body section.

With the "Bounds"-button you can activate other bounds types than the default bounding-sphere:

Box • Bounding box extends around the objects.

Bounds types

Sphere • or default (no Bounds button activated): Spherical bounds, visualized by a dotted circle in the 3D View. The Radius can be changed in the "Radius:" field.

Cylinder • Cylindrical bounds, good for wheels, bottles, cans etc.

Cone • Cone shaped bounds.

Convex Hull • Convex (outward bulging surface) hull around the actual shape of the object. No holes or inward bulges are calculated.

Triangle Mesh • This makes concave objects possible, for performance it is still recommended to use compound objects

Compound • Adds dynamic children (parented with **CTRL**-**P** to the main object) to the physics calculation

Properties

Below the object settings you define the Properties of a GameObject. These Properties can carry values, which describe attributes of the object like variables in a programming language. Use "ADD property" to add properties.

Properties carry information bound to the object, similar to a local variable in programming languages. No other object can normally access these properties, but it is possible to copy Properties with the Property (Copy) Actuator (see Property Actuator) or send them to other objects using messages (see Message Body).

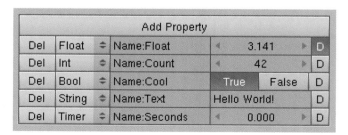

The big "ADD property" button adds a new Property. By default a Property of the float type is added. Delete a Property with its "Del" button. The Menu Button defines the type of the Property. Click and hold it with the left mouse button and choose from the pop up menu. The "Name:" text field can be edited by clicking it with the left mouse button. **SHIFT**-**BACKSPACE** clears the name.

Property names are case sensitive. So "Benoit" is not equal to "benoit".

The next field is different for each of the Property types. For the Boolean type there are two radio-buttons; choose between "True" and "False". The string-type accepts a string; enter a string by clicking in the field with the left mouse. The other types use a Number Button to define the default value. Use **SHIFT**-**LMB** for editing it with the keyboard, click and drag to change the value with the mouse.

Property types:

Boolean (Bool) • This Property type stores a binary value, meaning it can be "TRUE" or "FALSE". Be sure to write it all in capitals when using these values in Property Sensors or Expressions.

Integer (Int) • Stores a number like 1,2,3,4,... in the range from -2147483647 to 2147483647.

Float • Stores a floating point number like 3.14159265.

String • Stores a text string.

Timer • This Property type is updated with the actual game time in seconds, starting from zero. On newly created objects the timer starts when the object is "born".

Example of some Logic

The right part of the Logic Buttons is the command center for adding logic to your objects and worlds. The logic consists of the Sensors, Controllers and Actuators.

Sensors are like the senses of a life form; they react on key presses, collisions, contact with materials (touch), timer events or values of properties.

The Controllers are collecting events from the sensors and are able to calculate them to a result. These are similar to the mind or brain of a life form. Simple Controllers just do an AND on the inputs. An example is to test if a key is pressed AND a certain time has passed. There are also OR Controllers and you can also use Python scripting and expressions in the Expression Controller to create more complex behavior.

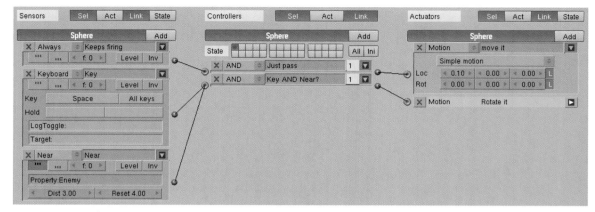

Logic Bricks The Actuator actually performs actions on objects. A Motion Actuator for example is like a muscle. This muscle can apply forces to objects to move or rotate them. There are also Actuators for playing predefined animations (via Ipos), which can be compared to a reflex.

The logic is connected (wired) by click and hold **LMB** on an outlet (sphere) then dragging the mouse to the inlet and release. Sensors to Controllers and Controllers to Actuators. After wiring you are immediately able to play the game! If you discover something in the game you don't like, just stop the game engine, edit your 3D world and restart. This way you can drastically cut down your development time!

The Blender Laws of Physics

All objects in Blender with the "Dynamic" or "Rigid Body" option set are evaluated using the physics laws as defined by the physics engine and the user.

The key property for a dynamic object is its mass. Gravity, forces, and impulses (collision bounce) only work on objects with a mass. Also, only dynamic objects can experience drag, or velocity damping (a crude way to mimic air/water resistance).

Note that for dynamic objects using dLoc and dRot may not have the desired result. Since the velocity of a dynamic object is controlled by the forces and impulses, any explicit change of position or orientation of an object may not correspond with the velocity. For dynamic objects it's better to use the linV and angV for explicitly defining the motion.

As soon we have defined a mass for our dynamic object, it will be affected by gravity, causing it to fall until it hits another object with its bounding. The gravity has a value of 9.81 by default, if you use one Blender unit as 1m and the mass of 1.0 as one Kilogram your objects will almost react as in the real world. You can change the gravitation in the World Buttons with the "Grav" slider. A gravity of zero is very useful for space games or simulations.

Damping can be used to simulate air drag. Damping decreases the velocity in percent (%) per second. Damping is useful to achieve a maximum speed. The larger the speed the greater the absolute decrease of speed due to drag. The maximum speed is attained when the acceleration due to forces equals the deceleration due to drag. Damping is also useful for damping out unwanted oscillations due to springs.

RotDamp does the same as Damp, but for rotational movements. Use the "Damp:" and "RotDamp:" settings to suggest the drag of air or other environments. Don't use it to simulate friction. Friction can be simulated by using the dynamic material settings.

Do Fh and Rot Fh are a special way to simulate floating behaivior. Together with the dynamic settings in the Material this can be used to make boats or hovercrafts.

For some objects you need to have different friction in different directions. For instance a skateboard will experience relatively little friction when moving it forward and backward, but a lot of friction when moving it side to side. This is called anisotropic friction. Selecting the "Anisotropic" button in the Logic Buttons **F4** will enable anisotropic friction. After selecting this button, three sliders will appear in which the relative coefficient for each of the local axes can be set. A relative coefficient of zero denotes that along the corresponding axis no friction is experienced. A relative coefficient of one denotes that the full friction applies along the corresponding axis.

Dynamic Settings in the Material

Some physical attributes can be defined with the material settings of Blender. The Material Buttons can be accessed via the icon in the header of the Buttons Window or by pressing **F5**. Create a new material or choose an existing one with the Menu Button in the header.

In the Material Buttons you then need then to activate the "DYN" button to see the dynamic settings.

Restitute • Objects will bounce on a collision. To control the amount of bounce add a material to the objects and set the Restitute value in the DYN section of the material to near zero for a soft material and near 1.0 for a very elastic material. Note that a very elastic ball will not bounce on a very soft material, so tune both materials.

A Material's Dynamic settings

Friction • Friction is a force tangential to the contact surface. The friction force has a maximum that is linear to the normal, i.e., the force that presses the objects against each other, (the weight of the object). The friction value denotes the Coulomb friction coefficient, i.e. the ratio of the maximum friction force and the normal force. A larger friction value will allow for a larger maximum friction. For a sliding object the friction force will always be the maximum friction force. For a stationary object the friction force will cancel out any tangent force that is less than the maximum friction. If the tangent force is larger than the maximum friction then the object will start sliding.

Fh Force • In conjunction with the "Do Fh" and/or "Rot Fh" in the Logic Buttons F4 you make an object float above a surface. "Fh Force" controls the force that keeps the object above the floor.

Fh Dist • "Fh Dist" controls the size of the Fh area. When the object enters this area the Fh mechanism starts to work.

Fh Damp • Controls the damping inside the Fh area. Values above 0.0 will damp the object movement inside the Fh area.

Fh Norm • With this button activated the object also gets a force in the direction of the face normal on slopes. This will cause an object to slide down a slope.

Examples:

- **FhDemo.blend**
- Another way to have floating behavior is the Force Field Consraint, see **Force-FieldConstraint.blend**

Soft Bodies by Erwin Coumans

From Blender 2.48 onwards, the game engine features Bullet soft body simulation.

Soft Body Features
- Flat cloth or volumetric soft bodies
- Control over mass, friction, stiffness, shape matching and collision detection settings
- Collision detection beween soft bodies as well as rigid bodies and static collision bounds of all types.
- Attaching soft bodies against rigid bodies or using fixed pinning
- Physics Debug Visualization of the dynamic soft body structures
- Dynamically create new soft bodies using the Add Object Actuator

Creating a Bullet Soft Body
- Choose "Soft Body" in the Logic Buttons **F4**
- Choose a collision shape bounds for soft bodies, the bounds types for soft bodies are automatically restricted to convex hull or triangle mesh bounds.

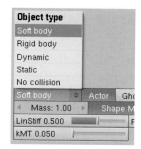

Choosing a Soft
Body Object Type

Basic Soft Body Setting

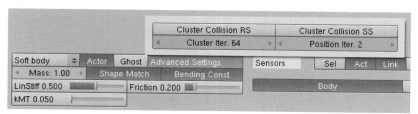

LinStiff • Linear Stiffness, lower values create very flexible soft bodies, and larger values (1) more stiffness. Note that the shape matching feature and bending constraints will still keep extreme flexible bodies in shape.

Shape Match • when this option is enabled, Bullet will remember the original shape of each soft body, and tries to match the shape of a soft body, no matter how large the deformation has been.

kMT • Shape matching coefficient, how strong the soft body will return to its original shape. This only appear when the "Shape Match" option is enabled.

Friction • allows to control the dynamic friction for soft bodies, in the range "[0..1]". 0.0 means no friction, soft bodies will slide.

Advanced Settings

Cluster Collision RS/SS • collision clusters can improve the collision detection, and it can avoid soft bodies passing through triangle meshes. Instead of colliding between individual vertices/nodes and faces, deformable convex clusters can be used. You can choose to use clusters between soft bodies (SS), or between soft body and rigid body (RS).

Cluster Iter • Higher values will create more detailed collision clusters. If you choose 1 it will use a single cluster using all vertices. This setting is only used if Clusters RB / SS is enabled.

Position Iter • position solver iterations. Use a higher value to improve the quality of position correction for soft bodies.

Pinning or attaching Soft Bodies

You can use the Rigid Body Joint to attach a rigid body to a soft body. Similar to rigid body constraints, you can also pin/fix a soft body to make a vertex non-movable: just don't provide a second attachment object, or attach to a static object.

Right now, vertex groups are not supported, so you have to use Rigid Body Joint constraints.

- Select a single soft body, or both a soft body and rigid body, using the "Add Constraint"-button in the Object Context **F7**, Object Buttons, "Constraints"-panel.
- Enable the Show Pivot to see where the soft body will be pinned (px/py/pz frame). Bullet will automatically take the closest vertex/node to this pivot point.
- You can use multiple constraints to pin/attach multiple parts of the soft body.
- Python constraints can be used to create soft body constraints while the game is running. However, currently you cannot remove those constraints on-the-fly.

General soft body tips and some known issues
- Blender 2.48 performs no collisions between soft bodies that have Clusters enabled, and soft bodies that have Clusters disabled. This will be fixed in future versions.
- Subdivide the soft body triangle mesh to allow some more deformation: go into Edit Mode, select all vertices (**A** or **A-A**) and hit subdivide.
- UV Sphere meshes are not compatible with soft bodies, so use a Ico sphere instead.
- If the mesh is too detailed, simplify the mesh using mesh

decimation-modifier
- Use Show Physics Visualization to debug is-sues with soft bodies, collision shapes etc. Enable the setting in the game menu.
- When running the game with Show Physics Visualization enabled, you will notice the complex dynamic structures for soft bod-ies:
- Don't use scaled meshes. Instead, use the Apply Scaling feature, or Apply Scale and Rotation by selecting the soft body object and pressing **CTRL**-**A**

Debugging
Visualization

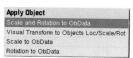

Applying Scaling

Bullet Game Engine Features

The physics engine in Blender is called "Bullet" (author Erwin Coumans, also known as one of the original authors of the Blender game engine) calculates the physical behaviors of the objects, like falling, forces and collisions. Bullet is a 3D Collision De-tection and Rigid Body Dynamics Library for games. Open Source, ZLib license, free for commercial use, including Playstation 3.

The Bullet engine is used to drive many aspects of a game like GameLogic (Ray-, Near-, Collision Sensors), Constraints (Point, Hinge, Generic), it also contains a ve-hicle setup (only accessible via Python)

Bullet Physics Tips and FAQ

Avoid Scaling
Don't scale your objects. Apply scale using **CTRL**-**A**. If you use Sphere-bounds, make sure the radius fits the sphere.

Keep masses for dynamic objects similar
If an object of 100 kg rests on an object of 0.1 kg, the simulation will have difficul-ties. In order to avoid large mass ratios, keep mass of objects similar (in the order of a few kg)

Assign the right bounds type
For a cylinder, choose cylinder, even for non-moving ob-jects. Similar for a box etc. Convex Hull can approximate meshes for moving objects and static objects.

Choosing the
Bounds type

Don't use too many vertices in Convex Hull meshes

About 4 to 32 vertices should be fine. For more complex objects use simple proxy objects for the collision margin

Leave the center of the object in the middle of the mesh

The center (where the axis are) needs to be inside the mesh, not near to the boundary or outside!

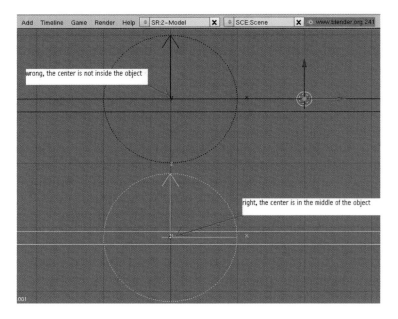

Leave the gravity to 10, don't make it too large

The physics simulation works better with smaller gravity, so if possible don't use large gravity.

Avoid very small dynamic objects (< 0.2 units)

Don't make dynamic objects smaller then 0.2 units if possible. For the default gravity, 1 unit equals 1 meter, so any 'side' of the objects should be bigger then that.

No large objects

Don't use large objects, or large triangles.

Don't use degenerate triangles

Triangles that are have extreme long sides as well as extreme short sides can lead to problems.

After a few seconds, the object doesn't move anymore. It doesn't

interact with moving platforms etc.

You can manually activate an object, using python command ‚object.restoreDy-
namics'.

Or use the ‚no sleeping' button. But don't use the, no sleeping' button too much, perhaps just for the main character/car etc.

How to setup a vehicle

Use the PhysicsConstraints module in Python, and create a special constraint on a rigid body.

- For collision Bounds it is best to use Convex Hull Polytope. Remember to switch on collision for the chassis polygons!
- Don't use box, because shifting the center of the box doesn't work.
- Give the vehicle enough space to move: too narrow roads, too sharp corners and high street curbs and other obstacles that are difficult to avoid are very frequent mistakes which makes driving frustrating, rather then fun.

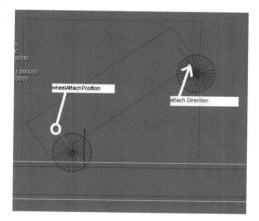

This constraint allows to add wheels, set tire friction, suspension, steering and so on.

There is a demo **vehicle3_Steering fix.blend** in the physics demos.

See the Python Vehicle Script for the code.

- To improve (vehicle) simulation quality add this line to the python scrips:
  `PhysicsConstraints.setNumTimeSubSteps(2)`
- don't set friction of track and ground to zero, better lower the friction of car chassis This way you can add traffic cones and other interesting dynamic objects. Ground friction of 0 means bad physics quality.
- Try to tweak the form factor (under No sleeping button) a little bit, but keep it close to 0.4. For example 0.45
- For debugging to see that the ray cast for each wheel has correct position and direction use:

```
#draw the raycast lines
PhysicsConstraints.setDebugMode(1)
```
- Make sure you don't use overlays scenes and other camera effects (split screen/viewports) during debugging. The debug lines will not properly show up.

There is a small gap between the ground and my object
Except for boxes and sphere, there is indeed a tiny gap (0.06 by default) between objects. This gap allows the simulation to run smoother and more stable.

It is not recommended, but you can reduce the gap with the "Margin" parameter in the Logic Buttons or using Python:

```
controller = GameLogic.getCurrentController()
owner = controller.getOwner()
owner.setCollisionMargin(0.01)
```

You can also consider using margin of zero for static/non moving objects, and leave the default margin for dynamics objects.

I want higher quality simulation or create IPO key frames for animation
If you are on high performance machines or just rendering / creating key frames, and don't worry about real time you can increase the sub steps to improve quality of simulation, using a python script

```
import PhysicsConstraints
PhysicsConstraints.setNumTimeSubSteps(2)
```

default is 1, while 2 or more make simulation more accurate.

Rigid Body Joints

The Constraints Panel

Rigid Body Joints can be added in the Object Buttons **F7**, "Constraints"-panel. Add a "Rigid Body Constraint" with the "Add Constraint" button. Constraints will keep a Object in a defined location or restrict the rotation around defined axes. However be careful, it is possible to break a constraint/joint using dLoc or dRot movements.

In common for all rigid body constraints are the position and rotation of the Pivot point (visualize with "ShowPivot"). Enter the name of the object to constrain into the field "toObject:".

The "No Col." button disables the collision detection between the two linked bodies. Often the bodies are (almost) overlapping, and collision detection conflicts with the other constraints.

Always remember that you add constraints to the parent object, not the constrained object (child)!

For debugging and visualizing a constraint it is very helpful to use the "Show Physics Visualization" from the Game-menu.

With the "Rigid Body Constraint" chosen from the "Constraints"-panel you can specify different types of constraints:

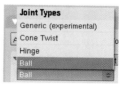

The different Constraint types

Ball • Point to point constraint, also known as ball socket joint, limits the translation so that the local pivot points of two rigid bodies match in world space. A chain of rigid bodies can be connected using this constraint.

Hinge • Hinge constraint, or revolute joint, restricts two additional angular degrees of freedom, so the body can only rotate around one axis, the hinge axis. This can be useful to represent doors or wheels rotating around one axis. The user can specify limits and motor for the hinge.

Cone Twist • To create rag dolls, the cone twist constraint is very useful for limbs like the upper arm. It is a special point to point constraint that adds cone and twist axis limits.

Generic • A generic D6 constraint. This generic constraint can emulate a variety of standard constraints, by configuring each of the 6 degrees of freedom (dof). The first 3 dof axis are linear axis, which represent translation of rigid bodies, and the latter 3 dof axis represent the angular motion. For each axis:

- Lowerlimit == Upperlimit → axis is locked.
- Lowerlimit > Upperlimit → axis is free
- Lowerlimit < Upperlimit → axis it limited in that range

Examples:

- **RigidBodyJointTypes.blend**
- **ConstraintHinge.blend**

Sound Buttons

The Sound Buttons are used for loading and managing sounds for the Blender game engine. Currently only WAV files are supported.

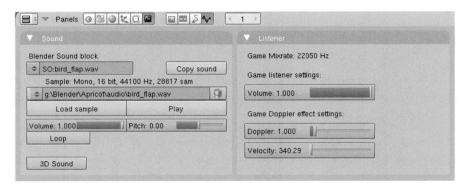

In the "Sound"-panel you can see the name of the Sound Object (here " **SO:bird_ flap.wav** "). This name is set to the name of the sound sample by default, you can always rename it. With the Menu Button next to the "SO:" you can browse existing Sound Objects and load new Sound Objects. "Copy sound" makes a duplicate of the sound.

Below the "SO:" block you can assign already loaded samples to the Sound Object. So the Sound Object name doesn't have to be the name of the sample. For example you can use a Sound Object "SO:explosion" and then use "explosion_nuke.wav" later. You load samples using the "Load Sample" button. Using the Menu Button to the left of the file location, you can browse samples already loaded and assign one to the Sound Object.

Above the sample location, Blender gives you some basic information about the loaded sample, like the sample frequency, 8 or 16bit and if the sample is stereo or mono.

When the pack/unpack button (parcel) is pressed, the sample is packed into the *.blend file, which is especially important when distributing files.

The "Play" button plays the sound, you can stop a playing sound with **ESC**. The "Vol:" slider sets the volume of the sample. With the "Pitch:" value you can change the frequency of the sound. Currently there's support for values between half the pitch (-12 semitones) and double the pitch (+12 semitones). Or in Hertz if your sample has a frequency of 1000 Hz, the bottom value is 500 and the top 2000 Hz.

The "Loop" button sets the looping for the sample on or off. Depending on the play-mode in the Sound Actuator this setting can be overridden. "Ping Pong" plays the sound forwards, then backwards in a loop, great for engine sounds.

The "3D Sound" button activates the calculation of 3D sound for this Sound Object. This means the volume of the sound depends on the distance and position (stereo effect) between the sound source and the listener. The listener is the currently active camera.

The "Scale:" slider sets the sound attenuation. In a 3D world you want to scale the relationship between gain and distance. For example, if a sound passes by the camera you want to set the scaling factor that determines how much the sound will gain if it comes towards you and how much it will diminish if it goes away from you. The scaling factor can be set between 0.0, all positions get multiplied by zero, no matter where the source is, it will always sound as if it is playing in front of you (no 3D sound), 1.0 (a neutral state, all positions get multiplied by 1) and 5.0 which over accentuates the gain/distance relationship.

The "Listener"-panel in the Sound Buttons defines global settings for the listener. The listener is the current active camera. The "Volume:" slider sets the global volume of all sounds. The settings for the Doppler effect are currently not supported.

Performance and design issues

Computers get faster every month, nowadays nearly every new computer has a hardware accelerated graphics card. But still there are some performance issues to think about. This is not only a good design and programming style but also essential for the platform compatibility Blender provides. So to make a well-designed game for various platforms, keep these rules in mind:

1. Don't use properties in combination with AND/OR/Expression controller as scripting language. Use the Python Controller for all more complex things
2. Use as few inter-object Logic Brick connections as possible.
3. Use **ALT**-**D** (instanced mesh for new object) when replicating meshes, this is better than **SHIFT**-**D** (copies the mesh).
4. Alpha mapped polygons, especially sorted, are expensive, so use with care.
5. Switching off the collision flag for polygons is good for performance. The use of "Ghost" is also cheaper then a regular physics object.
6. Keep the polygon count as low as possible. It's quite easy to add polygons to models, but very hard to remove them without screwing up the model. The detail should be made with textures.
7. Keep your texture-resolution as low as possible. You can work with hi-res versions and then later reduce them to publish the game.
8. Polygons set to "Light" are expensive. Use with care or use lightning baked into

textures.

9. Instead of real-time lighting use VertexPaint to lighten, darken or tint faces to suggest lighting situations.
10. Use simpler geometry for bounding and collision-bounds of objects
11. Separate real time shadows to layers
12. Use GLSL Materials with care, not all graphics cards will provide them (or fall back to a slow software rendering).

Game Logic Bricks

The game logic in Blenders game engine is assembled in the Realtime Buttons. Here you wire the different Logic Bricks together. The following is a brief description of all the Logic Bricks currently available.

Sensors

Sensors act like real senses; they can detect collisions, feel (Touch), smell (Near), view (Ray, Radar).

Always Sensor

Always Sensor with common elements for Sensors

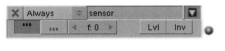

The most basic Sensor is the Always Sensor. It is also a good example for the common buttons every sensor has.

The button labeled "X" deletes the Sensor from the game logic. This happens without a confirmation, so be careful. The Menu Button to the right of the delete button (here labeled "Always") allows you to choose the type of Sensor. Click and hold it with the left mouse button to get the pop up menu. Next is a Text Button, which holds the name of the Sensor. Blender assigns the name automatically on creation. Click the name with the left mouse button to change the name with the keyboard.

Name your Logic Bricks and Blender objects to keep track of your scenes. A graphical logic scheme can become very complex.

With the small arrow button you can hide the contents of the Logic Brick, so it only shows the top bar. This is very handy in complex scenes. Together with the State system (see State-system) this helps to keep track of complex logics.

The next row of buttons is used to determine how and at which frequency a Sensor is "firing". This topic is a bit complex, so we will give examples in more than one part of this documentation.

General things on sensors

The internal state of a sensor can only take two values: true or false. This state value is updated at each frame based on the external conditions that the sensor monitors: keyboard key press/release for the keyboard sensor, mouse movement for the mouse sensor, etc. At the start of each frame, the BGE runs through all the enabled sensors and updates their internal state. The sensor state remains unchanged through the rest of the frame processing. Transition between true/false states is the primary cause for triggering controllers. The Lvl and Pulse buttons can be used to generate more triggers but this is discussed in a later section. The Inv button inverts the internal state: when the external condition is true, the internal state is false and vice-versa.

The direction of the transition (false/true or true/false) does not matter for triggering the controllers: either way, the controller is executed. Note that the controller is not executed immediately, but only when all enabled sensors have been updated. Regardless if multiple sensors are triggering the same controller, each triggered controller is executed only once. The internal state transition of a sensor triggers all the active controllers that are attached to it.

A controller that is executed will usually check the internal state of the sensors and take appropriate action. The logic controllers (AND, OR, XOR…) evaluate a formula using the state of all the sensors connected to them as input values; they do not use the transition information. The Python controller runs a user provided script and it is up to the script writer to check the state of the sensors using the Sensors "isPositive()" function. Note that the transition information is available through the "isTriggered()" function: the script writer can find out which of the sensor triggered the controller.

Pulse Modes and Lvl

The Lvl and Pulse buttons can be used to generate more triggers than just state transition.

Pulse Mode Buttons

There are two pulse buttons: one for the true state (left) and for the false state (right). When either button is selected, the frequency parameter "f:" determines at which frame interval the triggers are generated. A trigger is generated every frequency+1 frame. If the frequency parameter is 0, a trigger is generated on every frame. If the false(true) state pulse button is selected, the repeated triggers are produced when the sensor internal state is false(true). The pulse triggers are synchronized with the state transition: the first pulse trigger will arrive frequency+1 frame after the state transition. If both buttons are selected, repeated pulses are produced all the time but are still synchronized with the state transitions.

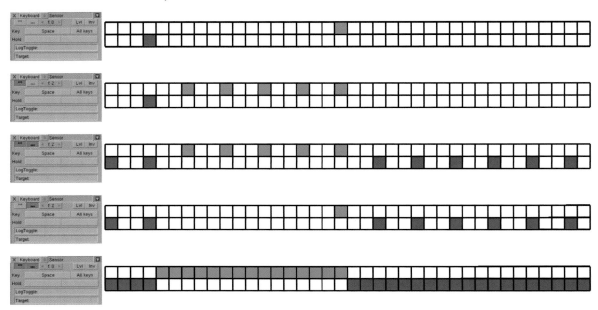

Different Pulse Mode Settings on a Keyboard Sensor

Before activating any pulse mode in the Sensor, try first without, this can save much performance, this is especially important with the Always Sensor. If you still need a pulse mode, think if you can raise the f: (frequency) setting, this can also save much performance.

If none of the mode buttons are activated the Always Sensor fires exactly one time. This is very useful for initializing stuff at the start of a game.

Lvl button: This button has only an effect when entering a state (when the state to which the sensor is connected is being activated due to a state actuator). Normally, a sensor generates an event (activates the controller) only when there is a transition in its internal state. When the Lvl button is selected, the sensor will always generate an initial event, whether positive or negative, based on the current sensor state. Example: you have a keyboard sensor that controls a motion actuator; you want the motion actuator to be immediately activated even if the key is already pressed when entering the state, so select the Lvl button.

Limitation: for the time being, this works reliably only if the sensor is connected to a single state. In a future version, it will work even if the sensor is used by multiple states.

Examples:

- **PulseModesDiagramm.blend** (visualizes the Pulses and their values)
- **MoveCertainDist.blend** (different uses of Pulse-Modes with the Motion Actuator)

Common Sensor Python Functions

RETURNS	FUNCTION	EXPLANATION
integer	getFrequency()	The frequency for mode sensors
bool	getInvert()	True if this sensor activates on negative events.
bool	getUseNegMode()	True if the sensor is in negative mode.
bool	getUsePosMode()	True if the sensor is in positive mode.
bool	isPositive()	True if this sensor brick has been activated.
	setFrequency(freq)	Sets the frequency for mode sensors.
	setInvert(invert)	Sets if this sensor activates on positive (true) or negative events.
	setUseNegMode()	Sets negative mode.
	setUsePosMode()	Sets positive mode.
bool	getLevel()	Returns whether this sensor is a level detector or an edge detector.
bool	isPositive()	True if this sensor brick is in a positive state.
bool	isTriggered()	True if this sensor brick has triggered the current controller.
	reset()	Reset sensor internal state, effect depends on the type of sensor and settings.
	setLevel(level)	Set whether to detect level or edge transition when entering a state.
bool	isA()	Allows to check if a python object is of a certain type. For example, if you get an object from the scene's object list, you can check if this object is of type lamp: if ob.isA("KX_LightObject"): ...

All Sensors provide these functions.

Delay Sensor

The Delay sensor generates positive and negative triggers at precise time, expressed in number of frames. The delay parameter defines the length of the initial OFF period. A positive trigger is generated at the end of this period. The duration parameter defines the length of the ON period following the OFF period. There is a negative trigger at the end of the ON period. If duration is 0, the sensor stays ON and there is no negative trigger. The sensor runs the OFF-ON cycle once unless the repeat option is set, then the OFF-ON cycle repeats indefinitely (or the OFF cycle if duration is 0).

Delay Sensor Python Functions

RETURNS	FUNCTION	EXPLANATION
	setDelay(delay)	Set the initial delay (in frames) before the positive trigger.
	setDuration(duration)	Set the duration (in frames) of the ON pulse after initial delay and the generation of the positive trigger events.
	setRepeat(repeat)	Set the sensors repeat mode.
integer	getDelay()	Return the delay parameter value.
bool	getDuration()	Return the duration parameter value.
bool	getRepeat()	Return the repeat parameter value.

Keyboard Sensor

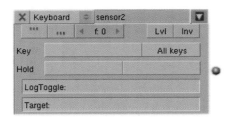

The Keyboard Sensor is one of the most often used Sensors because it provides the interface between Blender and the user.

The mode buttons are common for every Sensor so they have the same functionality as described for the Always Sensor.

By activating the "All keys" Button, the Sensor will react to every key. In the "Hold" fields you can put in modifier keys, which need to be held while pressing the main key.

The Keyboard Sensor can be used for simple text input. To do so, fill in the Property which should hold the typed text (you can use Backspace to delete chars) into the "Target:" field. The input will be active as long the Property in "LogToggle:" is "TRUE".

Keyboard Sensor Python Functions

RETURNS	FUNCTION	EXPLANATION
integer	getKey()	Returns the key code this sensor is looking for.
	setKey(keycode)	Set the key this sensor should listen for.
list of key status. [[keycode, status]]	getPressedKeys()	Get a list of keys that have either been pressed, or just released this frame (when the Sensor is triggered)
list of key status. [[keycode, status]]	getCurrently-PressedKeys()	Get a list of currently pressed keys that have either been pressed, or just released. With this function you will get all pressed keys even if the Sensor is not triggered anymore.

Import the GameKeys module (see GameKeys Module) to have symbolic names for the keys.

Mouse Sensor

Currently, the Sensor is able to watch for mouse clicks, mouse movement or a mouse over. To get the position of the mouse cursor as well you need to use a Python-script.

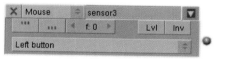

To get the coordinates of the mouse it is necessary to use Python, see the examples.

Common Mouse Sensor Python Functions

RETURNS	FUNCTION	EXPLANATION
integer	getXPosition( )	Gets the mouse's X-position.
integer	getYPosition( )	Gets the mouse's Y-position.

Use the Menu Button to choose between the Mouse Sensor types :

Left/Middle/Right Button • The sensor gives out an event when the correlated mouse button is pressed.

Mouse Sensor Types

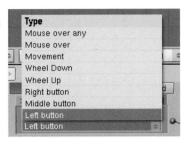

Wheel up/down • The sensor gives an event when the mouse wheel is moved up or down.

Movement • The sensor sends out an event when the mouse is moved.

The following two mouse over modes are working as follows: a ray is fired from the mouse pointer into the scene (see examples section below on how to make the mouse pointer visible in a game). The results of the ray to object collision can be used in several ways, this reflects in the python functions for the mouse over modes.

Mouse over • The Sensor sends an event when the mouse pointer is over the object which carries the Sensor. To make mouse over work as expected, ensure to start the game in a Camera view!

Mouse over any • The Sensor sends an event when the mouse pointer is over any object (with collision faces). To make mouse over any work as expected, ensure to start the game in a Camera view!

Mouse Over Any Sensor Python Functions

RETURNS	FUNCTION	EXPLANATION
list [x, y, z]	getHitNormal()	Returns the normal of the detected face.
KX_GameObject	getHitObject()	Returns game object the mouse is over.
list [x, y, z]	getHitPosition()	Position in space where the ray hits the object.
list [x, y, z]	getRayDirection()	Where the ray points to.
list [x, y, z]	getRayTarget()	Returns the end point of the sensor ray.
list [x, y, z]	getRaySource()	Returns the start point of the sensor ray.

Examples:

- **Blends/Reference/Trackball.blend** (Trackball View, Blender style, uses MMB)
- **Blends/Reference/ShowMouse.blend** (making the mouse pointer visible)
- **Blends/Reference/MouseOverAdd.blend** (adding objects at the mouse cursor)
- **Blends/Reference/GetHitNormal.blend** (use of getHitNormal())

Touch Sensor

The Touch Sensor gives an event when the
object it is assigned to, touches a material.
If you enter a material name into the "MA:"
text field it only reacts to this material otherwise it reacts to all touches.

The Touch Sensor inherits from the Collision Sensor, so it provides the same methods, hence the method names. See also Collision Sensor.

Touch Sensor Python Functions

RETURNS	FUNCTION	EXPLANATION
	setProperty(name)	Argument is a string containing the property or material name to collide with.
string	getProperty()	Returns the property or material to collide with.
KX_GameObject	getHitObject()	Returns the last object hit by this touch sensor.
list [KX_GameObject]	getHitObjectList()	Returns a list of all objects hit in the last frame.
bool	getTouchMaterial()	Returns true if this sensor looks for a specific material, false if it looks for a specific property.
	setTouchMaterial(flag)	Set flag to true to switch on positive pulse mode, false to switch off positive pulse mode.

Collision Sensor

The Collision Sensor is a general Sensor
used to detect contact between objects.
Besides reacting to materials it is also ca-
pable of detecting Properties of an object. Therefore you can switch the input field
from Material to Property by clicking on the "M/P" button.

Collision Sensor Python Functions

RETURNS	FUNCTION	EXPLANATION
	setProperty(name)	Argument is a string containing the property or material name to collide with.
string	getProperty()	Returns the property or material to collide with.
KX_GameObject	getHitObject()	Returns the last object hit by this touch sensor.
list [KX_GameObject]	getHitObjectList()	Returns a list of all objects hit in the last frame.
bool	getTouchMaterial()	Returns true if this sensor looks for a specific material, false if it looks for a specific property.
	setTouchMaterial(flag)	Set flag to true to switch on positive pulse mode, false to switch off positive pulse mode.

Near Sensor

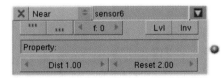

The near sensor reacts to actors near the object with the sensor.

The near sensor only senses objects of the type "Actor" (a dynamic object is also an actor).

If the "Property:" field is empty, the near sensor reacts to all actors in its range. If filled with a property name, the sensor only reacts to actors carrying a property with that name.

You can set the spherical range of the near sensor with the "Dist" Number Button. The "Reset" value defines at what distance the near sensor is reset again.

The Near Sensor is a special case of a touch sensor, see Touch Sensor for the Python methods and functions.

Radar Sensor

The Radar Sensor acts like a real radar.

It looks for an object along the axis indicated with the axis pop up.

If a property name is entered into the "Prop:" field, it only reacts to objects with this property.

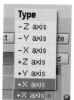

The Axis Pop up

In the "Ang:" field you can enter an opening angle for the radar. This equals the angle of view for a camera. The "Dist:" setting determines how far the Radar Sensor can see.

Objects can't block the line of sight for the Radar Sensor. This is different for the Ray Sensor (see Ray). You can combine them for making a radar that is not able to look through walls.

Radar sensor is a near sensor with a conical sensor object. Please look at Near for the common Python methods.

Radar Sensor Python Functions

RETURNS	FUNCTION	EXPLANATION
list [x, y, z]	getConeOrigin()	Returns the origin of the cone with which to test.
list [x, y, z]	getConeTarget()	Returns the center of the bottom face of the cone with which to test.
float	getConeHeight()	Returns the height of the cone with which to test.

Examples:

- **Radar.blend**

Property Sensor

The Property Sensor senses Properties attached to the object carrying the Property Sensor.

You can change the type with the pop up menu to Equal, Not Equal, Interval and Changed.

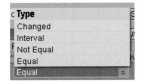

The "Equal" type Property Sensor checks for equality of the property given in the "Prop:" field and the value in "Value:". If the condition is true, it fires events according to the pulse mode settings.

The "Not Equal" Property Sensor checks for inequality and then fires its events.

The "Interval" type property sensor fires its event if the value of property is inside the interval defined by "Min:" and "Max:". This sensor type is especially helpful for checking float values, for which you can't depend on reaching a value exactly. This is most common with the "Timer" Property.

The "Changed" Property Sensor gives out events every time a Property is changed. This can, for example, happen through a Property Actuator, a Python script or an Expression.

Property Sensor Python Functions

RETURNS	FUNCTION	EXPLANATION
	getType()	Gets when to activate this sensor.
	setType(checktype)	Set the type of check to perform.
string	getProperty()	Return the property with which the sensor operates.
	setProperty(name)	Sets the property with which to operate.
string	getValue()	Return the value with which the sensor compares to the value of the property.
	setValue(value)	Set the value with which the sensor operates.

Random Sensor

The Random Sensor fires a pulse randomly according to the pulse settings (50/50 pick). The Random is a so called "pseudo random", that means with the same seed the same sequence of numbers will be generated. This can be used to achieve "random" behavior that is the same on every game start. For more complex random functions see Random Actuator.

With a seed of zero the Random Sensor works like an Always Sensor, which means it fires a pulse every time.

Random Sensor Python Functions

RETURNS	FUNCTION	EXPLANATION
	setSeed(seed)	Sets the seed of the random number generator.
integer	getSeed()	Returns the initial seed of the generator.
bool	getLastDraw()	Returns the last random number generated.

Ray Sensor

The Ray Sensor casts a ray for the distance set into the Number Button "Range". If the ray hits an object with the right Property or the right Material the Sensor fires its event.

Other objects block the ray, so that it can't see through walls. See Radar, as well.

Without a material or property name filled in, the Ray Sensor reacts to all objects.

Ray Sensor Python Functions

RETURNS	FUNCTION	EXPLANATION
KX_GameObject	getHitObject()	Returns the game object that was hit by this ray.
list [x, y, z]	getHitPosition()	Returns the position (in world coordinates) where the object was hit by this ray.
list [nx, ny, nz]	getHitNormal()	Returns the normal (in world coordinates) of the object at the location where the object was hit by this ray.
list [dx, dy, dz]	getRayDirection()	Returns the direction of the ray (in world coordinates).

Message Sensor

The Message Sensor fires its event when a Message arrives. The "Subject:" field can be used to filter messages matching the given subject.

Message Sensor Python Functions

RETURNS	FUNCTION	EXPLANATION
	setSubjectFilterText(subject)	Change the message subject text that this sensor is listening to.
integer	getFrameMessageCount()	Get the number of messages received since the last frame.
list	getBodies()	Gets the list of message bodies.
string	getSubject()	Gets the message subject this sensor is listening for from the Subject: field.
list	getSubjects()	Gets the list of message subjects received.

See in section Message Body on how to get the message body.

Joystick Sensor

With the Joystick Sensor you can access joysticks, game pads and other gear connected to the computer. With logic bricks it is only possible to use buttons and to check if a joystick axis is moved a certain amount. To get the values of analog devices it is necessary to use a Python script, see the examples below.

With the type menu of the joystick sensor you can choose what the sensor should sense.

Common for all Joystick Sensor types is "Index:", which tells Blender which joystick to use. The "All" button selects that all events for this type should trigger the sensor, especially usefull for Python scripts.

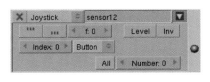

Button • The number button "Number: 0" selects the joystick button to use.

Axis • With "Number: 1" you choose which axis pair to use. With the menu right to the "Number: 1" Button you choose in which direction the stick needs to be moved for the sensor to fire an event. With "Threshold: 0" you can choose a value how much the stick needs to be moved to let the sensor fire. This is mostly used if an analog stick is used.

Hat • Some joysticks and game pads have a hat-controller, mostly used to change the view direction. With the "Number: 1" button you choose which head-controller to use. Hat-controllers can sense usually 8 directions, up, up+right, right, right+down, etc. The "Direction:" field gives the direction in a binary manner:

DIRECTION	VALUE
up	1
right	2
down	4
left	8

If you like to check for up and right you simply add the values, 1+2=3. Normally you can't press up and down at the same time on conventional sticks, but of course this way we are very flexible and have a 4 bit digital input we could use also for other things (robotic experiments, other types of input devices...).

Joystick Sensor Python Functions

RETURNS	FUNCTION	EXPLANATION
list	getAxis()	Returns the current axis this sensor reacts to.
list	getAxisValue()	Returns a list of the values for the current state of each axis.
integer	getButton()	Returns the current button this sensor is checking.
list	getButtonValue()	Returns a list containing the indicies of the current pressed state of each button.
list	getHat()	Returns the current direction of the hat.
integer	getIndex()	Returns the joystick index to use.
integer	getNumAxes()	Returns the number of axes.
integer	getNumButtons()	Returns the number of buttons.
integer	getNumHats()	Returns the number of hats.
integer	getThreshold()	Returns the threshold of the axis.
bool	isConnected()	Returns True if a joystick is connected at this joysticks index.
	setAxis()	Sets the current axis this sensor reacts to.

RETURNS	FUNCTION	EXPLANATION
	setButton()	Sets the button the sensor reacts to.
	setHat()	Sets the hat the sensor reacts to.
	setIndex()	Sets the joystick index to use.

Examples:

- **AnalogInput.blend** (get analog input from a joystick)

Actuator Sensor

 The actuator sensor detects when a certain actuator on the same object is triggered, useful for reducing the number of controllers and wires because you don't need to pass this information with properties anymore.

The sensor generates a positive when the corresponding sensor is activated and a negative when it is deactivated (the contrary if the Inv option is selected).

Actuator Sensor Python Functions

RETURNS	FUNCTION	EXPLANATION
string	getActuator()	Return the Actuator with which the sensor operates.
	setActuator(name)	Sets the Actuator with which to operate.

Notes:

- Actuators are disabled at the start of the game; if you want to detect the On-Off transition of an actuator after it has been activated at least once, unselect the Lvl and Inv options and use a NAND controller.
- Some actuators deactivate themselves immediately after being activated. The sensor detects this situation as an On-Off transition.

Examples:

- See Pinnball tutorial (detection of a completely played Ipo)
- This Actuator is also very useful to detect the loss of contact of the distance Constraint Actuator

Controllers

Controllers act as the brain for your game logic. This reaches from very simple decisions like connecting two or more inputs, simple expressions, to complex Python scripts which can carry artificial intelligence.

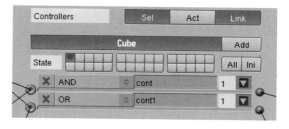

Common Controller Python Functions

RETURNS	FUNCTION	EXPLANATION
list [SCA_ISensor]	getSensors()	Gets a list of all sensors attached to this controller.
SCA_ISensor	getSensor(name)	Gets the named linked sensor.
list [SCA_IActuator]	getActuators()	Gets a list of all actuators linked to this controller.
SCA_IActuator	getActuator(name)	Gets the named and linked actuator.
integer	getExecutePriority()	Returns the priority for this actuator.
	setExecutePriority(priority)	Sets the priority for this actuator.
string	getName()	Get the given name.
KX_GameObject	getOwner()	Gets the owner of the Controller.
string	getScript()	Get the name of the Python script.
	setScript(scriptname)	Set the name of the Python script.
integer	getState()	Get the current state of the Controller.
bool	isA()	Allows to check if a python object is of a certain type. For example, if you get an object from the scene's object list, you can check if this object is of type lamp: if ob.isA("KX_LightObject"): ...

Simple Logical Controllers

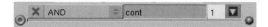

The **AND** controller only passes an event if all inputs are true.

The **OR** controller passes an event if any number of the inputs is true.

The **NAND** controller is an inverted AND controller: the output is true if any of the inputs is false.

The **NOR** controller is an inverted OR controller: the output is false if any of the inputs is true.

The **XOR** controller is an exclusive OR: the output is true if and only if one input is true and all the other inputs are false.

The **XNOR** controller is an inverted XOR: the output is false if and only if one input is false and all the other inputs are true.

The NAND, NOR and XNOR controllers are very useful to create complementary outputs to start and stop actuators synchronously.

Expression Controller

With the Expression Controller you can create slightly complex game logic with a single line of "code". You can access the output of sensors attached to the controller and access the properties of the object.

The expression mechanism prints out errors to the console, so have a look there if anything fails.

Expressions

Expressions can be used in the Expression Controller and the Property Actuator.

Valid expressions

EXPRESSION TYPE	EXAMPLE
Integer numbers	15
Float number	12.23224
Booleans	TRUE, FALSE
Strings	"I am a string!"
Properties	propname
Sensornames	sensorname (as named in the sensor Logic Brick)

Arithmetic expressions

EXPRESSION	EXAMPLE
EXPR1 + EXPR2	Addition, 12+3, propname+21
EXPR1 - EXPR2	Subtraction, 12-3, propname-21
EXPR1 * EXPR2	Multiplication, 12*3, propname*21
EXPR1 / EXPR2	Division, 12/3, propname/21
EXPR1 > EXPR2	EXPR1 greater than EXPR2
EXPR1 >= EXPR2	EXPR1 greater or equal EXPR2
EXPR1 < EXPR2	EXPR1 less than EXPR2

Boolean operations

OPERATION	EXAMPLE
NOT EXPR	Not EXPR
EXPR1 OR EXPR2	logical OR
EXPR1 AND EXPR2	logical AND
EXPR1 == EXPR2	EXPR1 equals EXPR2
Conditional statement: IF(Test, ValueTrue, ValueFalse)	

Expression examples

EXPRESSION	RESULT	EXPLANATION
12+12	24	Addition
property == "Carsten"	TRUE or FALSE	String comparison between a Property and a string
"Erwin" > "Carsten"	FALSE	A string comparison is done

Python Controller

 The Python controller is the most powerful controller in the game engine. You can attach a Python script to it, which allows you to control your GameObjects, ranging from simple movement up to complex game-play and artificial intelligence.

Enter the name of the script you want to attach to the Python Controller into the "Script:" field. The script needs to exist in the file or Blender will ignore the name you type.

Remember that Blender treats names as case sensitive! So the script "player" is not the same as "Player".

Python for the game engine is covered in BGE Python

Python Controller Functions

RETURNS	FUNCTION	EXPLANATION
string	getScript()	Gets the Python script this controller executes.
	setScript(script)	Sets the Python script this controller executes.

State System

States are a way to achieve complex logics without cluttering your Logic Buttons and having to redo already existing Logic Bricks. States are a group of Logic Bricks which get executed at a certain time or state (hence the name) of the game.

Imagine a character wandering around. There may be different materials for the ground (e.g. ice and sand), a different control method in water or air, etc. Without states you would now start to use Properties, Property-Sensors and Actuators to control what state the actor has. With the state system probably only one Logic Brick changes the state and you are done.

State internals (by Benoit Bolsee)

The state system is object based. The current state mask is stored in the object as a 32 bit value; each bit set in the mask is an active state. The controllers have a state mask too, but only one bit can be set: a controller belongs to a single state. The game engine will only execute controllers that belong to active states. Sensors and actuators don't have a state mask but are effectively attached to states via their links to the controllers.

Sensors and actuators can be connected to more than one state. When a controller becomes inactive because of a state change, its links to sensors and actuators are temporarily broken (until the state becomes active again). If an actuator gets isolated, i.e. all the links to controllers are broken, it is automatically disabled. If a sensor gets isolated, the game engine will stop calling it to save CPU power. It will also reset the sensor internal state so that it can react as if the game just started when it gets reconnected to an active controller. For example, an Always sensor in no mode that is connected to a single state (i.e. connected to one or more controllers of a single state) will generate an event each time the state becomes active. This feature is not available on all sensors, see the notes below.

State GUI

This system system is fully configurable through the GUI: the object state mask is visible under the object bar in the controller's colum as an array of buttons just like the 3D view layer mask. Click on a state bit to only display the controllers of that state. You can select more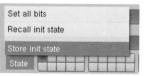
The State Menu

than one state with **SHIFT**-**LMB**. The "All" button sets all the bits so that you can see all the controllers of the object. The "Ini" button sets the state mask back to the objects default state. You can change the default state of objects by first selecting the desired state mask and storing using the menu under the "State" button.

If you define a default state mask, it will be loaded into the object state make when you load the blend file or when you run the game under the Blenderplayer. However, when you run the game with Blender, the current selected state mask will be used as the startup state for the object. This allows you to test specific state during the game design.

The controller displays the state it belongs to with a new button in the controller header. When you add a new controller, it is added by default in the lowest enabled state. You can change the controller state by clicking on the button and selecting another state. If more than one state is enabled in the object state mask, controllers are grouped by state for more readability.

The new "Sta" button in the sensor and actuator column header allows you to display only the sensors and actuators that are linked to visible controllers.

A new state actuator is available to modify the state during the game. It defines a bit mask and the operation to apply on the current object state mask:

Cpy • the bit mask is copied to the object state mask.

Add • the bits that are set in the bit mask will be turned on in the object state mask.

Sub • the bits that are set in the bit mask will be turned off in the object state mask.

Inv • the bits that are set in the bit mask will be inverted in the object state mask.

Things to note:

- Although states have no name, a simple convention consists of using the name of the first controller of the state as the state name. The GUI will support that convention by displaying as a hint the name of the first controller of the state when you move the mouse over a state bit of the object state mask or of the state actuator bit mask.
- Each object has a state mask and each object can have a state engine but if several objects are part of a logical group, it is recommended to put the state engine only in the main object and to link the controllers of that object to the sensors and actuators of the different objects.
- When loading an old blend file, the state mask of all objects and controllers are initialized to 1 so that all the controllers belong to this single state. This ensures backward compatibility with existing games.
- When the state actuator is activated at the same time as other actuators, these actuators are guaranteed to execute before being eventually disabled due to the state change. This is useful for example to send a message or update a property at the time of changing the state.
- Sensors that depend on underlying resource won't reset fully when they are isolated. By the time they are activated again, they will behave as follows:

  Keyboard sensor • keys already pressed won't be detected. The keyboard sensor is only sensitive to new key presses.

  Collision sensor • objects already colliding won't be detected. Only new collisions are detected.

Near and radar sensor • same as collision sensor.

Actuators

Actuators are the executing Logic Bricks. They can be compared with muscles or glands in a life form.

Depending on the type or purpose of an Actuator, an Actuator can act differently on a pulse. Some inputs are more like keys (the get released when no pulse arrives) some act more like a switch (needs to be switched off by a pulse carrying a negative value). This is especially important for the Motion Actuator.

Common Actuator Python Functions

RETURNS	FUNCTION	EXPLANATION
integer	getExecutePrior-ity()	Returns the priority for this actuator.
	setExecutePriority (priority)	Sets the priority for this actuator.
string	getName()	Get the given name.
KX_GameObject	getOwner()	Get the owner object.
bool	isA()	Allows to check if a python object is of a certain type. For example, if you get an object from the scene's object list, you can check if this object is of type lamp: if ob.isA("KX_LightObject"): ...

(Shape) Action Actuator

The Shape Action Actuator will play Actions or Shape Key animations in the game engine. If you add it to a mesh, it will add a Shape Action Actuator, if added to an Armature it will be an Action Actuator. Have a look at the examples below and the Character Animation tutorial.

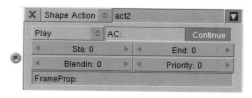

Fill in the start and end frame of your action into the "Sta:" and "End:" fields.

Action play modes

Play • Plays the Action from "Sta" to "End" at every positive pulse the Actuator gets. Other pulses while playing are discarded.

Flipper • Plays the Action from "Sta" to "End" on activation. When the activation ends it plays backwards from the current position. When a new activation reaches the Actuator the Action will be played from the current position onwards.

Loop Stop • Plays the Action in a loop as long as the pulse is positive. It stops at the current position when the pulse turns negative.

Loop End • This plays the Action repeatedly as long as there is a positive pulse. When the pulse stops it continues to play the Action to the end and then stops.

Property • Plays the Action for exactly the frame indicated in the property entered in the field "Prop:".

Enter the name of your (Shape) Action into the field "AC:". Blender will blank the input if the entered name does not exist.

If you switch states the "Continue"-button becomes important. In case the "Continue"-button is pressed, upon deactivation of the Actuator, the last played frame of the action will be stored and restored when the Actuator is enabled (because of a state switch) again.

In case you have more than one Action on your Object, "Blendin:" allows you to blend between the Actions. "Blendin:" is measured in numbers of frames.

Actions with lower "Priority:" will override Actions with higher priority. Keep in mind that the overriding Actions need to be lower in the Actuators stack.

Enter a Property name into the "FrameProp:" field to get the actual frame number of the played action. This is very handy to synchronize the game with specific actions.

Action Actuator Python Functions

RETURNS	FUNCTION	EXPLANATION
	setAction(action, reset=True)	Sets the current action.
	setStart(start)	Specifies the starting frame of the animation.

RETURNS	FUNCTION	EXPLANATION
	setEnd(end)	Specifies the ending frame of the animation.
	setBlendin(blendin)	Specifies the number of frames of animation to generate when making transitions between actions.
	setPriority(priority)	Sets the priority of this actuator.
	setFrame(frame)	Sets the current frame for the animation.
	setProperty(prop)	Sets the property to be used in FromProp playback mode.
	setBlendtime (blendtime)	Sets the internal frame timer.
	setType(mode)	Sets the operation mode of the actuator.
	setContinue(cont)	Set the actions continue option True or False.
integer	getType()	Returns the operation mode of the actuator.
bool	getContinue()	When True, the action will always play from where last left off, otherwise negative events to this actuator will reset it to its start frame.
string	getAction()	Returns the name of the action associated with this actuator.
float	getStart()	Returns the starting frame of the action.
float	getEnd()	Returns the last frame of the action.
float	getBlendin()	Returns the number of interpolation animation frames to be generated when this actuator is triggered.
float	getFrame()	Returns the current frame number.
string	getProperty()	Returns the name of the property to be used in FromProp mode.
	setChannel (channel, matrix, mode=False)	Sets the channel to use.

RETURNS	FUNCTION	EXPLANATION
	setAction(action, reset=True)	Sets the current action. action (string): The name of the action to set as the current action. reset: Optional parameter indicating whether to reset the blend timer or not. A value of 1 indicates that the timer should be reset. A value of 0 will leave it unchanged. If reset is not specified, the timer will be reset.
	setStart(start)	Specifies the starting frame of the animation. Parameters: start (float) the starting frame of the animation.

Examples:

- **ShapeAction.blend** (Shape and Armature Action playing in the game engine)

Motion Actuator

The motion actuator is meant to move objects. Depending if you have a non-dynamic (so not evaluated by the physics engine) or dynamic object (see BGE Physics) it changes its appearence a bit. So for non-dynamic objects the Simple Motion Actuator would look like:

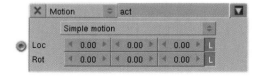

Because we operate in a 3D environment all parameters are for all three axis, so the numbers below are meant from left to right as X, Y and Z value of a parameter.

Loc • X, Y and Z values by which the object should be moved upon activation of the Actuator.

Rot • Rotation around X, Y and Z axis when the Actuator is activated. Normally you can look at this value as rotation speed. However if you need to rotate a certain amount of degrees you can use this formula to calculate the value for the Rot-parameter: Rot = Degrees / 50

With activated (default) "L"-buttons (L for local) all rotations and movements will be along the objects axes. With a deactivated "L"-button the movement or rotation will be along the world coordinates.

REFERENCE

The Motion Actuator needs a negative event to deactivate, see "examples/MoveCertain-Dist.blend"

For dynamic Objects there are many more options:

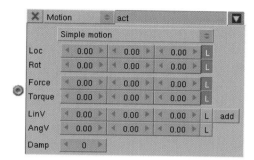

Loc • X, Y and Z value the object should be moved upon activation of the Actuator.

Rot • Rotation around X, Y and Z axis when the Actuator is activated. Normally you can look at this value as rotation speed. However if you need to rotate a certain amount of degrees you can use this formula to calculate the value for the Rot-parameter: Rot = Degrees / 50

The movement and orientation of dynamic Objects is usually evaluated by the physics engine to simulate natural behaviors of the objects, e.g. falling and colliding with other objects. Using Loc/Rot for dynamic objects is not recommended unless you know what you are doing or you want to achieve a special effect.

Force • Dynamic objects have a mass, and you need a force to move them. This force can be set here for X, Y and Z axes.

Torque • Same as for Force but here a force to rotate the object.

LinV • Sets a linear velocity of the object. This can be used to set a starting speed of an object, but it should not be used to actually move the object. When the "Add"-button is pressed the velocity will be added to the existing object velocity.

AngV • Same as Linv but for rotational speed.

Damp • Damp works only for LinV and AngV (linear and angular Velocity). It defines the time constant, in frames, to get to the specified velocity.

With activated (default for Loc/Rot/Force/Torque) "L"-buttons (L for local) all rotations and movements will be along the objects axes. With a deactivated "L"-button the movement or rotation will be along the world coordinates.

To avoid problems with objects getting faster and faster, or to allow more control over your game-physics there is another type of Motion Actuator, the Servo Control Actuator. You choose this type with the "Motion Type"-menu:

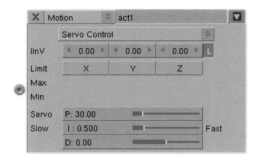

This variant of the motion actuator allows to control speed with force. The control is technically of the type "PID" (Propotional, Integral, Derivate): the force is automatically adapted to achieve the target speed. All the parameters of the Servo Actuator are configurable. The result is a great variety of motion style: anisotropic friction, flying, sliding, pseudo Dloc, etc. This actuator should be used in preference to Dloc and LinV as it produces more fluid movements, avoids the collision problems with Dloc and interacts correctly with gravity unlike linV.

LinV • target speed as (X,Y,Z) vector in local or world coordinates (mostly useful in local coordinates).

Limit • the force can be limited along each axis (in the same coordinates of LinV). No limitation means that the force will grow as large as necessary to achieve the target speed along that axis. Set a max value to limit the acceleration along an axis (slow start) and set a min value (negative) to limit the brake force.

P • Proportional coefficient of servo controller, don't set directly unless you know what you're doing.

I • Integral coefficient of servo controller. Use low value (<0.1) for slow reaction (sliding), high values (>0.5) for hard control. The P coefficient will be automatically set to 60 times the I coefficient (a reasonable value).

D • Derivate coefficient. Leave to 0 unless you know what you're doing. High values create instability.

Notes:

- The servo motion actuator applies forces, it is therefore not compatible with other actuators that sets the force too, i.e a simple motion force actuator or another servo motion. Although it is possible to combine two servo motion actuators that works on different axes.
- This actuator is compatible with a simple Drot motion actuator but not with LinV and Dloc motion.
- This actuator works perfectly in a zero friction environment: the PID controller will simulate friction by applying force as needed.
- (0,0,0) is a valid target speed.

Motion Actuator Python Functions

RETURNS	FUNCTION	EXPLANATION
list [x,y,z,local]	getAngularVelocity()	Gets the angular Velocity (AngV) set in the Actuator.
list [x,y,z,local]	getDLoc()	Gets the Loc set in the Actuator.
list [x,y,z,local]	getDRot()	Gets the Rot set in the Actuator.
integer	getDamping()	Gets the Damp set in the Actuator.
list [x,y,z,local]	getForce()	Gets the Force set in the Actuator.
list [min,max,active]	getForceLimitX()	Gets the force limit X as set in the Actuator (Servo Control).
list [min,max,active]	getForceLimitY()	Gets the force limit Y as set in the Actuator (Servo Control).
list [min,max,active]	getForceLimitZ()	Gets the force limit Z as set in the Actuator (Servo Control).
	setForceLimitX()	Sets the force limit for the x-axis.
	setForceLimitY()	Sets the force limit for the y-axis.
	setForceLimitZ()	Sets the force limit for the z-axis.
list [x,y,z,local]	getLinearVelocity()	Gets the linear velocity set in the Actuator.
list [x,y,z,local]	getTorque()	Gets the torque set in the Actuator.
	setAngularVelocity()	Sets the torque value.
list [x,y,z]	setDLoc(x,y,z,local)	Set the values for the DLoc row, use local=0 to move along global axes.
list [x,y,z]	setDRot(x,y,z,local)	Set the values for the DRot row, use local=0 to rotate around global axes.
	setDamping (damping)	Damping for the linV/linRot.

RETURNS	FUNCTION	EXPLANATION
	setForce(x,y,z,local)	Set the values for the Force row, use local=0 to move along global axes.
	setLinearVelocity (x,y,z,local)	Set the values for the linV row, use local=0 to move along global axes.
	setTorque(x,y,z,local)	Set the values for the Torque row, use local=0 to rotate around global axes.

Constraint Actuator

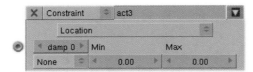

The Constraint Actuator offers different ways to constraint or inhibit a movement or degree of freedom. Use the "Constraint Type"-menu to choose between Location, Orientation and Distance.

Location

With the Constraint Actuator of the type "Location" you can constrain the location of an object in the 3D-space.

First choose a axis over which you want to limit the movement. If you need to constrain an object on more axes, use more Constraint Actuators.

With the values under "Min" and "Max" you adjust the limits of the movement. The values are in Blender units.

"damp" controls how fast/hard (low values) or slow/soft (high values) the Actuator reacts on a position change of the object.

Notes:

- for dynamic objects this Controller is of limited use because it will not define a hard border, instead have a look at Bullet-Constraints
- for dynamic objects try to use the Servo-Control Motion Actuator

Examples:

- See the "Flying Buddha" demo (Buddha main character)

Distance

This variant of the constraint actuator allows to set the distance and orientation relative to a surface. The controller uses a ray to detect the surface (or any object) and adapt the distance and orientation parallel to the surface.

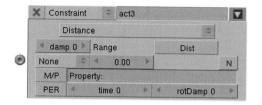

Damp • Time constant (in numbers of frames) of distance and orientation control.

Dist • Select to enable distance control and set target distance. The object will be positioned at the given distance of surface along the ray direction.

Direction • choose a local axis as the ray direction.

Range • length of ray. Objects within this distance will be detected.

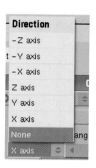

N • Select to enable orientation control. The actuator will change the orientation and the location of the object so that it is parallel to the surface at the vertical of the point of contact of the ray.

M/P • Select to enable material detection. Default is property detection.

Property/Material • name of property/material that the target of the ray must have to be detected. If not set, property/material filter is disabled and any colliding object within range will be detected.

PER • Select to enable persistent operation. Normally the actuator disables itself automatically if the ray does not reach a valid target.

time • Maximum activation time of actuator. Zero means unlimited, values above zero meaning number of frames before automatic deactivation.

rotDamp • Time constant (in numbers of frame) of orientation control. Zero: use Damp parameter. Above zero: use a different time constant for orientation.

Notes:

- If neither N nor Dist options are set, the actuator does not change the position and orientation of the object; it works as a ray sensor.

- The ray has no "X-ray" capability: if the first object hit does not have the required property/material, it returns no hit and the actuator disables itself unless PER option is enabled.
- This actuator changes the position and orientation but not the speed of the object. This has an important implication in a gravity environment: the gravity will cause the speed to increase although the object seems to stay still (it is repositioned at each frame). The gravity must be compensated in one way or another. the new servo control motion actuator is the simplest way: set the target speed along the ray axis to 0 and the servo control will automatically compensate the gravity.
- This actuator changes the orientation of the object and will conflict with Drot motion unless it is placed BEFORE the Drot motion actuator (the order of actuators is important)
- All parameters are accessible through Python.

Orientation

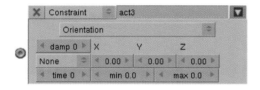

This variant of the constraint actuator allows to align an object axis along a global direction.

Damp • Time constant (in numbers of frames) of orientation control.

X, Y, Z • Global coordinates of reference direction.

time • Maximum activation time of actuator. Zero means unlimited, values above zero mean number of frames before automatic deactivation.

Direction • choose a local axis as the ray direction.

Notes:

- (X,Y,Z) = (0,0,0) is not a valid direction
- This actuator changes the orientation of the object and will conflict with Drot motion unless it is placed BEFORE the Drot motion actuator (the order of actuators is important). - This actuator doesn't change the location and speed. It is compatible with gravity.
- All parameters are accessible through Python.

Force Field

This variant of the constraint actuator provides a very similar service to the Fh material feature but with some specificities:

- It is defined at the object level: each object can have different settings and you don't need to use materials.
- It can be applied in all 6 directions and not just -Z.
- It can be enabled/disabled easily (it's an actuator).
- You can have multiple force fields active at the same time on the same object in different direction (think of a space ship in a tunnel with a repulsive force field on each wall).
- You can have a different damping for the rotation.

Besides that it provides the same dynamic behavior and the parameters are self explanatory. It works by adapting the linear and angular velocity: the dynamic is independent of the mass. It is compatible with all other motion actuators.

Note: linear and anisotropic friction is not yet implemented, the only friction will come from the object damping parameters. Support for friction will be added in a future revision.

Constraint Actuator Python Functions

RETURNS	FUNCTION	EXPLANATION
integer	getDamp()	Returns the damping parameter.
3-tuple	getDirection()	Returns the reference direction of the orientation constraint as a 3-tuple.
float	getDistance()	Returns the distance parameter.
integer	getLimit()	Returns the type of constraint.
float	getMax()	Returns the upper value of the interval to which the value is clipped.
float	getMin()	Returns the lower value of the interval to which the value is clipped.
integer	getOption()	Returns the option parameter.
string	getProperty()	Returns the property parameter.
float	getRayLength()	Returns the length of the ray.
integer	getRotDamp()	Returns the damping time for application of the constraint.
integer	getTime()	Returns the time parameter.

RETURNS	FUNCTION	EXPLANATION
	setDamp(duration)	Sets the time constant of the orientation and distance constraint. If the duration is negative, it is set to 0.
	setDirection(vector)	Sets the reference direction in world co-ordinates for the orientation constraint.
	setDistance(distance)	Sets the target distance in distance con-straint.
	setLimit(type)	type: integer 1 : LocX 2 : LocY 3 : LocZ 7 : Distance along +X axis 8 : Distance along +Y axis 9 : Distance along +Z axis 10 : Dis-tance along -X axis 11 : Distance along -Y axis 12 : Distance along -Z axis 13 : Align X axis 14 : Align Y axis 15 : Align Z axis Sets the type of constraint.
	setMax(upper_bound)	Sets the upper value of the interval to which the value is clipped.
	setMin(lower_bound)	Sets the lower value of the interval to which the value is clipped.
	setOption(option)	Several options of the distance con-straint. Binary combination of the fol-lowing values: 64 : Activate alignment to surface 128 : Detect material rather than property 256 : No deactivation if ray does not hit target 512 : Activate dis-tance control.
	setProperty(property)	Sets the name of the property or mate-rial for the ray detection of the distance constraint. If empty, the ray will detect any colliding object.
	setRayLength(length)	Sets the maximum ray length of the dis-tance constraint.
	setRotDamp(duration)	Sets the time constant of the orientation constraint. If the duration is negative, it is set to 0.
	setTime(duration)	Sets the activation time of the actua-tor. The actuator disables itself after this many frames. If set to 0 or negative, the actuator is not limited in time.

Ipo Actuator

The Ipo Actuator can play the Ipo-curves for the object that owns the Actuator. If the object has a child with an Ipo (in a parenting chain) and you activate "Child" in the Actuator, the Ipo for the child is also played.

The animation is played from "Sta:" to "End:" (in frames). If you enter a valid Property name in the "FrameProp:" field this Property will be updated with the current frame number of the Ipo played. Be carefull with the float Property type, this can hold non whole numbers, which should be checked with the "Interval"-Propery Sensor.

The Ipo in the game engine will be played with the speed indicated as "FPS:" (frames per second) in the Display Buttons F12 in the "Format"-panel.

The "Force" Button will convert the "Loc" Ipo curves into forces for dynamic objects. When pressed, the "L" Button appears which cares for applying the forces locally to the objects coordinate system. This can be used for a nice jumping action or similar.

The Add button, mutually exclusive with Force button. When selected, it activates the Add mode that consists in adding the Ipo curve to the current object situation in world coordinates, or parent coordinates if the object has a parent.

Scale Ipo curves are multiplied instead of added to the object current scale. If the local flag is selected, the Ipo curve is added (multiplied) in the object's local coordinates.

Delta Ipo curves are handled identically to normal Ipo curves and there is no need to work with Delta Ipo curves provided that you make sure that the Ipo curve starts from origin. Origin means location 0 for Location Ipo curves, rotation 0 for Rotation Ipo curves and scale 1 for Scale Ipo curves.

"Current object situation" means the object's location, rotation and scale at the start of the Ipo curve. For Loop Stop and Loop End Ipo actuators, this means at the start of each loop. This initial state is used as a base during the execution of the Ipo Curve but when the Ipo curve is restarted (later or immediately in case of Loop mode), the current object situation at that time is used as the new base.

For reference, here is the exact operation of the Add mode for each type of Ipo curve (oLoc, oRot, oScale, oMat: object's loc/rot/scale and orientation matrix at the start of the curve; iLoc, iRot, iScale, iMat: Ipo curve loc/rot/scale and orientation matrix resulting from the rotation).

LOCAL	OPERATION
LOCATION	
false	newLoc = oLoc+iLoc
true	newLoc = oLoc+oScale*(oMat*iLoc)
ROTATION	
false	newMat = iMat*oMat
true	newMat = oMat*iMat
SCALE	
false	newScale = oScale*iScale
true	newScale = oScale*iScale

Add+Local mode is very useful to have dynamic objects executing complex movement relative to their current location/orientation. Of course, dynamics should be disabled during the execution of the curve.

Ipo play modes

Play • Plays the Ipo from "Sta" to "End" at every positive pulse the Actuator gets. Other pulses received while playing are discarded.

Ping Pong • Plays the Ipo from "Sta" to "End" on the first positive pulse, then backwards from "End" to "Sta" when the second positive pulse is received.

Flipper • Plays the Ipo for as long as the pulse is positive. When the pulse changes to negative the Ipo is played from the current frame to "Sta".

Loop Stop • Plays the Ipo in a loop for as long as the pulse is positive. It stops at the current position when the pulse turns negative.

Loop End • This plays the Ipo repeatedly for as long as there is a positive pulse. When the pulse stops it continues to play the Ipo to the end and then stops.

Property • Plays the Ipo for exactly the frame indicated by the property named in the field "Prop:".

Ipo Actuator Python Functions

RETURNS	FUNCTION	EXPLANATION
integer	getEnd()	Returns the frame at which the ipo stops playing.
bool	getForceIpoActsLocal()	Return whether to apply the force in the object's local coordinates rather than the world global coordinates.
bool	getIpoAsAdd()	Returns whether to interpret the ipo as additive rather than absolute.
bool	getIpoAsForce()	Returns whether to interpret the ipo as a force rather than a displacement.
integer	getStart()	Returns the frame from which the ipo starts playing.
integer	getType()	Returns the operation mode of the actuator.
	set(type, startframe, endframe, mode?)	type: Play, PingPong, Flipper, LoopStop, LoopEnd or FromProp (string) startframe: first frame to use (int) endframe : last frame to use (int) mode? : special mode (0=normal, 1=interpret location as force, 2=additive) Set the properties of the actuator.
	setEnd(frame)	Set the frame at which the ipo stops playing.
	setForceIpoActsLocal (local)	Set whether to apply the force in the object's local coordinates rather than the world global coordinates.
	setIpoAdd(add)	Set whether to interpret the ipo as additive rather than absolute.
	setIpoAsForce(force)	Set whether to interpret the ipo as a force rather than a displacement.
	setProperty(propname)	Set the property to be used in FromProp mode.
	setStart(frame)	Set the frame from which the ipo starts playing.
	setType(mode)	mode: Play, PingPong, Flipper, LoopStop, LoopEnd or FromProp (string) Set the operation mode of the actuator.

Examples:

- **AddIpo.blend**
- **Jump.blend**
- **IpoFrameProperty.blend**

Camera Actuator

 The Camera Actuator tries to mimic a real cameraman. It keeps the actor in the field of view and tries to stay at a certain distance from the object. The motion is soft and there is some delay in the reaction to the motion of the object.

Enter the name of the object that should be followed by the camera (you can also use the Camera Actuator for non-camera objects) into the "OB:" field. The field "Height:" determines the height above the object the camera stays at. "Min:" and "Max:" are the bounds of distance from the object within which the camera is allowed to move. The "X" and "Y" buttons specify which axis of the object the camera tries to stay behind.

Camera Actuator Python Functions

RETURNS	FUNCTION	EXPLANATION
float	getHeight()	Returns the height value set in the Height: field.
float	getMax()	Returns the maximum value set in the Max: field.
float	getMin()	Returns the minimum value set in the Min: field.
object or string	getObject (name_only = 1)	name_only - optional arg, when true will return the KX_GameObject rather than its name. Returns the object this sensor reacts to.
bool	getXY()	Gets the axis the camera tries to get behind. True = X, False = Y
	setHeight()	Sets the height value.
	setMax()	Sets the maximum value.
	setMin()	Sets the minimum value.
	setObject(object)	object: KX_GameObject, string or None Sets the object this sensor reacts to.

RETURNS	FUNCTION	EXPLANATION
	setXY()	Sets axis the camera tries to get behind. 1=X, 0=Y

Sound Actuator

The Sound Actuator plays a Sound Object loaded using the Sound Buttons (see Section Sound Butttons). Use the Menu Button to browse and choose between the Sound Objects in the scene.

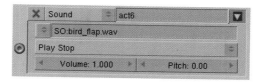

Sound play modes (Menu Button)

Play Stop • Plays the sound for as long as there is a positive event from the controller

Play End • Plays the sound to the end, when a positive event is sent from the controller

Loop Stop • Plays and repeats the sound, as long as the controller sends a positive event

Loop End • Plays the sound repeatedly, as long as the controller sends a positive event. When the events stops the sound is played to its end.

Sound Actuator Python Functions

RETURNS	FUNCTION	EXPLANATION
string	getFilename()	Gets the name of the sound block we play.
float	getGain()	Gets the gain (volume) of the sound.
integer	getLooping()	Returns the current loop mode of the actuator.
float	getPitch()	Returns the pitch of the sound.
float	getRollOffFactor()	Returns the roll off factor (scale for distance) for the sound.
integer	getType()	Returns the operation mode of the actuator.
	pauseSound()	Pause the sound.

RETURNS	FUNCTION	EXPLANATION
	setFilename(string)	Set the name of the sound block.
	setGain()	Sets the gain (volume) of the sound.
	setLooping()	Sets the loop mode of the actuator.
	setPitch()	Sets the pitch of the sound.
	setRollOffFactor()	Sets the roll off factor for the sounds.
	setType()	Sets the operation mode of the actuator.
	startSound()	(re)Starts the sound.
	stopSound()	Stops the sound.

Property Actuator

The Property Actuator is meant to assign values to properties or even calculate with properties. See the Chapter about Expressions.

With the mode-menu you can switch between the three modes of this Actuator.

Assign • Assigns a value or Expression (given in the "Value" field) to a Property. For example with an Expression like "Proppy + 1" the "Assign" works like an "Add". To assign strings you need to add quotes to the string ("...").

Add • Adds the value or result of an expression to a property. To subtract simply give a negative number in the "Value:" field.

Copy • This copies a Property named "Count" from the Object "Cube" into the Property "Proppy" on the actual object. This is an easy and safe way to pass information between objects. You cannot pass information between scenes with this Actuator!

This Actuator provides Python functions to get and set the values and Property-names. However, from Python it is much easier to access Properties directly.

Property Actuator Python Functions

RETURNS	FUNCTION	EXPLANATION
string	getProperty(name)	Return the property on which the actuator operates.
depends	getValue()	Returns the value with which the actuator operates.
	setProperty(name)	Set the property on which to operate. If there is no property of this name, the call is ignored.
	setValue(value)	Set the value with which the actuator operates. If the value is not compatible with the type of the property, the subsequent action is ignored.

Edit Object Actuator

This actuator performs actions on Objects itself, like adding new objects, deleting objects, etc. By default the type of this Actuator is set to "Add Object". With the type-menu you can switch between following types:

Add Object

With this Actuator type you can add new objects to the scene. This can be new enemies, bullets, particles (numerous small objects, not Blender Particles) etc.

The Add Object actuator adds an object to the scene. The new object is oriented along the X-axis of the creating object.

Keep the object you'd like to add on a separate and hidden layer. You will see an error message on the console or debug output when not following this rule and no object will appear.

Enter the name of the Object to add in the "OB:" field, if the entered Object does not exist in the scene Blender will blank the input field. The "Time:" field determines how long (in frames) the object should exist. The value "0" denotes it will exist forever. Be careful not to slow down the game engine by generating too many objects! If the time an object should exist is not predictable, you can also use other events (collisions, properties, etc.) to trigger an "End Object" for the added object using Logic Bricks.

With the "linV" buttons it is possible to assign an initial velocity to the added object. This velocity is given in X, Y and Z components. The "L" button stands for local. When it is pressed the velocity is interpreted as local to the axes of the added object.

Add Object Actuator Python Functions

RETURNS	FUNCTION	EXPLANATION
list [vx,vy,vz]	GetAngularVelocity()	Returns the angular velocity that will be assigned to the created object.
KX_Game-Object	getLastCreatedObject()	Get the object handle to the last created object. This way you can manipulate dynamically added objects.
list [vx,vy,vz]	getLinearVelocity()	Returns the linear velocity that will be assigned to the created object.
depends	getObject (name_only = 1)	Returns the name of the object that will be added. name_only - optional arg, when true will return the KX_GameObject rather than its name.
integer	getTime()	Returns the lifetime of the object that will be added.
	instantAddObject()	Immediately add object without delay.
	setAngularVelocity(vx, vy, vz)	Assign an angular velocity to the created object.
	setLinearVelocity(vx, vy, vz)	Assign a linear velocity to the created object.
	setObject(object)	Sets the object that will be added. There has to be an object of this name. If not, this function does nothing.
	setTime(duration)	Sets the lifetime of the object that will be added, in frames. If the duration is negative, it is set to 0. Zero means unlimited lifetime

Examples:

- **AddObject.blend**

End Object

This type of the Edit Object Actuator simply ends or kills the current Object.
This is very useful for ending a bullet's life after a collision or something similar.

Replace Mesh

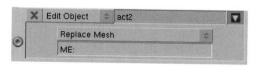

This type of the Edit Object Actuator replaces the mesh of the object by another mesh with the given name in
the "ME:" field.. The other mesh must be existent in the scene of course. Use a "Fake User" to ensure that you can't loose the mesh when working with Logic Bricks.

Replace Mesh Actuator Python Functions

RETURNS	FUNCTION	EXPLANATION
string	getMesh()	Returns the name of the mesh to be substituted.
	instantReplaceMesh()	Immediately replace mesh without delay.
	setMesh(name)	String or None set the mesh that will be substituted for the current one.

Track To

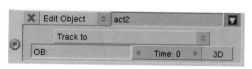

The "Track to" type, rotates the object in such a way that the Y-axis points to the target specified in the "OB:" field.
Normally this happens only in the X/Y plane of the object (indicated by the "3D" button not being pressed). With "3D" pressed the tracking is done in 3D. The "Time:" parameter sets how fast the tracking is done. Zero means immediately, values above zero produce a delay (are slower) in tracking.

Track To Actuator Python Functions

RETURNS	FUNCTION	EXPLANATION
KX_GameObject or string	getObject(name_only = 1)	Returns the object to track with the parent of this actuator.

RETURNS	FUNCTION	EXPLANATION
integer	getTime()	Return the time in frames with which the tracking motion is delayed.
bool	getUse3D()	Returns 1 if the motion is allowed to extend in the z-direction.
	setObject(object)	Set the object to track with the parent of this actuator.
	setTime(time)	Set the time in frames with which to delay the tracking motion.
	setUse3D(value)	Set to 1 to allow the tracking motion to extend in the z-direction, set to 0 to lock the tracking motion to the x-y plane.

Dynamics

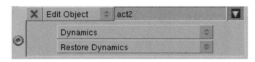

Using this type of the EditObject Actuator you can switch on and off the physical evaluation of the object carrying the Actuator. This can become handy to speed up things, e.g. disable dynamics for inactive enemies for example.

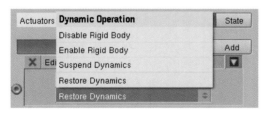

Enable/Disable Dynamics • switch on/off the whole physical behavior of the object.

Enable/Disable Rigid Body • switch on/off the rolling or tumbling physics for the object.

Dynamics Edit Object Actuator Python Functions

RETURNS	FUNCTION	EXPLANATION
integer	getOperation()	Returns the operation type of this actuator.
	setOperation (operation?)	operation? : type of dynamic operation 0 = restore dynamics 1 = disable dynamics 2 = enable rigid body 3 = disable rigid body Change the dynamic status of the parent object.

Scene Actuator

The Scene Actuator is meant for switching Scenes and Cameras in the game engine or add overlay or background scenes.

Choose the desired action with the Menu Button and enter an existing camera or scene name into the text field. If the name does not exist, the button will be blanked!

Reset • Simply restarts and resets the scene. It has the same effect as stopping the game with **ESC** and restarting with **P**.

Set Scene • Switch to the scene indicated into the text field. Switching will reset the actual scene!

Set Camera • Switch to the Camera indicated in the "OB:" text field.

Add OverlayScene • Adds the overlay scene indicated in the text field "SCE:", which is rendered on top of all other (existing) scenes.

Add BackgroundScene • Adds a background scene which will be rendered behind all other scenes.

Added Scenes with own lights will add to the light of the base scenes as well. If this is not wanted, remove the lights from the added scenes or use layered lighting.

Remove Scene • Removes a scene.

Suspend Scene • Suspends named ("SCE:") scene until "Resume Scene" is called. Be careful not to suspend the actual scene if there is no other scene to resume!

Resume Scene • Resumes a suspended Scene.

Scene Actuator Python Functions

RETURNS	FUNCTION	EXPLANATION
string	getCamera()	Return the name of the camera to switch to.
bool	getScene()	Return the name of the scene the actuator wants to switch to.

RETURNS	FUNCTION	EXPLANATION
bool	getUseRestart()	Return whether the scene will be restarted.
	setCamera(camera)	Set the camera to switch to.
	setExecutePriority()	None
	setScene(scene)	Set the name of scene the actuator will switch to.
	setUseRestart(flag)	Set flag to 1 to restart the scene.

Random Actuator

An often-needed function for games is a random value to get more variation in movements or enemy behavior.

The "Seed"-parameter is the value fed into the random generator as a start value for the random number generation. Because computer generated random numbers are only "pseudo" random (they will repeat after a (long) while) you can get the same random numbers again if you choose the same Seed.

A seed of zero means no random at all!

Enter the name of the property you want to be filled with the random number into the "Property:" field.

Random Actuators types

Boolean Constant • This is not a random function at all, use this type to test your game logic with a TRUE or FALSE value.

Boolean Uniform • This is the classic random 50-50 pick. It results in TRUE or FALSE with an equal chance. This is like an (ideal) flip of a coin.

Boolean Bernoulli • This random function results in a boolean value of TRUE or FALSE, but instead of having the same chance for both values you can control the chance of having a TRUE pick with the "Chance" parameter. A chance of 0.5 will be the same as "Bool Uniform". A chance of 0.1 will result in 1 out of 10 cases in a TRUE (on average).

Integer Constant • For testing your logic with a value given in the "Value:" field

Integer Uniform • This random type randomly produces an integer value between (and including) "Min:" and "Max:". The classical use for it is to simulate a dice pick with "Min: 1" and "Max: 6".

Integer Poisson • The random numbers are distributed in such a way that an average of "Mean:" is reached with an infinite number of picks.

Float Constant • For debugging your game logic with a given value.

Float Uniform • This returns a random floating point value between "Min:" and "Max:".

Float Normal • Returns a weighted random number around "Mean:" and with a standard deviation of "SD:".

Float Negative Exponential • Returns a random number which is well suited to describe natural processes like radioactive decay or lifetimes of bacteria. The "Half-life time:" sets the average value of this distribution.

Random Actuator Python Functions

RETURNS	FUNCTION	EXPLANATION
integer	getDistribution()	Returns the type of the active distribution.
depends	getPara1()	Returns the first parameter of the active distribution. Refer to the documentation of the generator types for the meaning of this value.
depends	getPara2()	Returns the first parameter of the active distribution. Refer to the documentation of the generator types for the meaning of this value.
string	getProperty(name)	Return the property to which the random value is assigned. If the generator and property types do not match, the assignment is ignored.
integer	getSeed()	Returns the initial seed of the generator. Equal seeds produce equal series.
	setBoolBernouilli(value)	Return false value * 100% of the time.
	setBoolConst(value)	Set this generator to produce a constant boolean value.

RETURNS	FUNCTION	EXPLANATION
	setBoolUniform()	Set this generator to produce true and false, each with 50% chance of occuring.
	setFloatConst(value)	Always return value.
	setFloatNegative Exponential(half_life)	Return negative-exponentially distributed numbers. The half-life ‚time' is characterized by half_life.
	setFloatNormal(mean, standard_deviation)	Return normal-distributed numbers. The average is mean, and the deviation from the mean is characterized by standard_deviation.
	setFloatUniform(lower_bound, upper_bound)	Return a random integer between lower_bound and upper_bound.
	setIntConst(value)	Always return value.
	setIntPoisson(value)	Return a Poisson-distributed number. This performs a series of Bernouilli tests with parameter value. It returns the number of tries needed to achieve success.
	setIntUniform(lower_bound, upper_bound)	Return a random integer between lower_bound and upper_bound. The boundaries are included.
	setProperty(name)	Set the property to which the random value is assigned. If the generator and property types do not match, the assignment is ignored.
	setSeed(seed)	Set the initial seed of the generator. Equal seeds produce equal series. If the seed is 0, the generator will produce the same value on every call.

Examples:

- **RandomActuator.blend**

Message Actuator

This Logic Brick sends out a message, which can be received and processed by the Message Sensor.

REFERENCE

The "To:" field indicates that the message should only be sent to objects with the given name.

The subject of the message is indicated in the "Subject:" field. With these two possibilities you can control the messaging very effectively.

The body (content) of the message can either be a text ("Body:") string or the content of a Property when "T/P" is activated ("Propname:"). See Section MessageBody on how to read the body of a message with a simple Python.script.

Message Actuator Python Functions

FUNCTION	EXPLANATION
setBody()	Sets the body of the message.
setBodyType()	Sets whether the body should be text or a Property name.
setSubject()	Sets the subject of the message.
setToPropName()	Sets the property name the message should be send to.

Game Actuator

With the Game Actuator you can load new levels from disk, quit or restart a game.

Start • Blender, the Blenderplayer or a Blender executable will load the named file from disk and start it. To pass information between the actual and loaded level see BGE Python Global Dict.

Restart • Restarts the current scene. All information is reset!

Quit • Quits a game. Inside Blender you will be back in the editing of the scene, in Blenderplayer or in executables you will return to operating system level. The quit function is especially important if you redefined the ESC key!

Load/Save GameLogic.globalDict • Loads/Saves the global directory to save game states. See BGE Python Global Dict.

Game Actuator Python Functions

RETURNS	FUNCTION	EXPLANATION
string	getFile()	Get the name of the file to start.

RETURNS	FUNCTION	EXPLANATION
	setFile(name)	Set the name of the file to start.

Visibility Actuator

This actuator allows you to make an object visible or invisible. Visible/invisible Recursive will make all child objects visible/invisible.

To change visibility from a Python script use the function setVisibility() *from the game object (*controller.getOwner().setVisible(visible,recursive)*).*

2D Filter Actuator

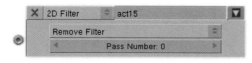

The 2D Filter Actuator is somehow special, because it works on the whole game. You can add it to any object and the whole image (real time)-rendered will be affected.

Currently there are some simple 2d filters and the possibility to add your own shader scripts.

Built-in Filters: Motion Blur, Blur, Sharpen, Dilation, Erosion, Laplacian, Sobel, Prewitt, Gray Scale, Sepia and Invert.

Custom Filters

Custom filters give you the ability to define your own 2d filter using GLSL. Its usage is the same as built-in filters, but you must select "Custom Filter" in 2D Filter actuator, then write a shader program into the Blender Text Editor and enter the shader script name.

For more information on the OpenGL Shading Language (GLSL) see GLSL specification on opengl.org.

You can also use these uniform variables in your shader program:

VARIABLE	USAGE
bgl_RenderedTexture	`uniform sampler2D bgl_RenderedTexture;`
bgl_TextureCoordinateOffset	`uniform vec2 bgl_TextureCoordinateOffset[9];`
bgl_TextureWidth	`uniform float bgl_TextureWidth;`
bgl_TextureHeight	`uniform float bgl_TextureHeight;`

Example Shader Program: Blue Sepia

```
1.    uniform sampler2D bgl_RenderedTexture;
2.    void main(void)
3.    {
4.        vec4 texcolor = texture2D(bgl_RenderedTexture,gl_TexCoord[0].
      st);
5.        float gray = dot(texcolor.rgb,vec3(0.299, 0.587, 0.114));
6.        gl_FragColor = vec4(gray * vec3(0.8, 1.0, 1.2),texcolor.a);
7.    }
```

Parent Actuator

The Parent Actuator sets or removes a parent relationship between two objects. The logic must be in the child object.

Set Parent • Sets a parent relationship between the object carrying the Actuator and the object named in the "OB:"-field which is then the parent (controlling object)..

Remove Parent • Removes the parent relation

Parent Actuator Python Functions

RETURNS	FUNCTION	EXPLANATION
KX_GameObject or string	getObject(name_only = 1)	Returns the object that is set as parent.
	setObject(object)	Sets the object to set as parent.

Examples:

- **ParentActuator.blend**

State Actuator

The State Actuator allows to set states (see BGE States).

Cpy • Copies the selected states from the Actuator to the general state. This will overwrite all states with the ones set in the Actuator.

Add • Add the selected states to the general state

Sub • Subtract the selected states from the general state

Inv • Inverting the selected states bitwise. See Examples

State Actuator Python Functions

FUNCTION	EXPLANATION
setMask(mask)	Set the value that defines the bits that will be modified by the operation. The bits that are 1 in the value will be updated in the object state, the bits that are 0 are will be left unmodified except for the Copy operation which copies the value to the object state.
setOperation(op)	op : bit operation (0=Copy, 1=Set, 2=Clear, 3=Negate) Set the type of bit operation to be applied on object state mask. Use setMask() to specify the bits that will be modified.

Examples:

- **InvStateActuator.blend**
- **StateDebug.blend**

Game Engine Python

Python is an interpreted, interactive, object-oriented programming language.

Python combines remarkable power with very clear syntax. It has modules, classes, exceptions, very high level dynamic data types, and dynamic typing. Python is also usable as an extension language for applications that need a programmable interface.

Beside this use as an extension language, the Python implementation is portable to (at least) all platforms that Blender runs on.

Python is copyrighted but freely usable and distributable, even for commercial use.

In Blender there are two incarnations of the Python integration: Blender Python meant for extending Blender and its modeling and animation tools and the BGE Python meant to be used with real time content.

Text Window

The Text Window is a simple but useful text editor, fully integrated into Blender. Its main purpose is to write Python scripts, but it is also very useful for writing comments in the Blendfile or to explain the purpose of the scene to other users.

```
import GameLogic

cont = GameLogic.getCurrentController()

me = cont.getOwner()

print dir(me)

sensor   = cont.getSensor("sensor")
actuator = cont.getActuator("act")
```

File Edit Format   AB   TX:GetDocs   X   Screen 15   Tab: 4   Text: Internal

The Text Window can be displayed with **SHIFT**-**F11** or by adjusting the Window Type menu in the Window Header.

In the Text Window Header there is the file menu for opening, saving and executing Python scripts. In the Edit menu you can find the common functions to copy&paste, search&replace etc. The Format menu will assist you in formating the code which is especially important because Python uses the indentation to mark code blocks.

The first Icon in the Text Window Header will make the Text Window fullscreen, this can also be done with the keyboard **CTRL**-**UP** and **CTRL**-**DOWN**.

The next icon switches on the line numbers, which is very helpful for programming and debugging.

The icon to the right of the line number will enable a word wrap, good for typing longer texts in the Text Window.

The "AB" buttons enables syntax highlighting for python keywords.

The icon with the (Python-)snake on it enables the use of Python text plug ins.

The next buttons can be used to browse between text files, open new ones or add new text buffers. The "X"-shaped Button deletes a text buffer.

With the Button (labeled "Screen 15" in the figure above) on the right side you can change the font used to display the text.

You can scroll the text using the scrollbar on the left, using **SHIFT**-**MMB** and mouse movements or using the mouse wheel.

By holding **LMB** and then dragging the mouse you can mark ranges of text for the usual cut, copy & paste functions. The key commands are:

ALT-**C** Copies the marked text into a buffer

ALT-**X** Cuts out the marked text into a buffer

ALT-**V** Pastes the text from buffer to the cursor in the Text Window

ALT-**O** Loads a text, a FileWindow appears

CTRL-**R** Reloads the current text, very useful for editing with an external editor

SHIFT-**ALT**-**F** Pops up the Filemenu for the Text Window

ALT-**F** Find function

ALT-**J** Pops up a Number Button where you can specify a line number that the cursor will jump to

ALT-**U** Unlimited Undo for the Text Window

ALT-**R** Redo function, recovers the last Undo

ALT-**A** Marks the whole text

BGE Python

With Python integrated into the game engine you can influence Logic Bricks, change their parameters and react to events triggered by the Logic Bricks.

Besides that you can influence the GameObject that carries the Python Controller directly. This means moving it, applying forces or getting information from this object.

In addition to the Python in the game engine, Blender includes Python for modeling and animation tasks, which is not covered here.

Basic Blender Game Engine Python

The first step for using Blender game engine (BGE) Python is to add at least a Sensor and a Python Controller to an object. Then add a new text file in the Text Window. Fill in the name of that text file into the "Script:" field of the Python Controller. You should now have a game logic setup like in this Figure.

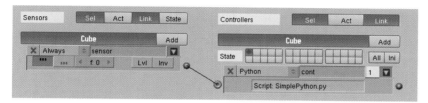

Logic Bricks for a first game Python script.

Now enter the following script into the Text Window (you don't need to type the lines starting with "#", these are comments).

```
1.    # first BGE Python script
2.    # gets the position of the object
3.    # and prints it to the console
4.
5.    import GameLogic
6.
7.    cont = GameLogic.getCurrentController()
8.    me   = cont.getOwner()
9.
10.   print me.getPosition()
```

First Simple Script

The result of the "print" command and errors from the Python interpreter will appear on the console from which you started Blender from, or in the DOS window, when running Blender from Windows. So it is helpful to size the Blender window in such a way that you can see the console window while programming Python.

This basic script only prints the position of the object that owns the Python Controller. Move your object and then restart the game engine with the **P** to see the results changing, or attach a Motion Actuator to the object to move it.

Now for an explanation of the script line by line. Line five is an important line. We import the "GameLogic" module which is the basis for all game Python in Blender.

In fact every script executed from the game engine will import this script without the need of this line. However it is good style to import it, so one can immediately see that this is a BGE Python. Also using "import GameLogic as GL" and writing "GL.xxx" later is a nice time saver.

In line seven we ask with "getCurrentController()" for a pointer to the Controller which executes the script and assign it to the variable "cont". You can see "getCurrentController()" is a function provided by the module "GameLogic".

In line eight we use the controller we got in line seven to get the owner, meaning the GameObject carrying the Logic Brick. You can see we use the method "getOwner()" provided by the controller to get the owner of our controller.

We now have a pointer to the owner of the Controller and we can use its methods to do things with it. Here in line 10 we use the "getPosition()" method to print the position of the GameObject as a matrix of the X, Y and Z values.

You may now wonder what other methods the PythonObjects have. Of course this is part of this documentation, but Python is "self" documenting, so we have other ways to get that information.

Add the following line to the end of the script from Figure 28-3:
```
print dir(owner)
```

Start the game engine again, stop it and look at the console window. You will see the following output:

```
[0.0, 0.0, 0.0]
  ['alignAxisToVect', 'applyImpulse', 'disableRigidBody',
'enableRigidBody', 'endObject', 'getAngularVelocity',
'getAxisVect', 'getChildren', 'getChildrenRecursive',
'getDistanceTo', 'getLinearVelocity', 'getMass', 'getMesh',
'getName', 'getOrientation', 'getParent', 'getPhysicsId',
'getPosition', 'getPropertyNames', 'getReactionForce',
'getState', 'getVectTo', 'getVelocity', 'getVisible', 'isA',
```

```
'rayCast', 'rayCastTo', 'removeParent', 'restoreDynamics',
'setAngularVelocity', 'setCollisionMargin', 'setLinearVelocity',
'setOrientation', 'setParent', 'setPosition', 'setState',
'setVisible', 'suspendDynamics']
```

The first line shows the position of the object, the next lines show the methods, that the "owner" provides. For example you see a ‚getMass' method, which will return the mass of a dynamic object. With the knowledge of the "dir()" function you can ask Python objects for information, without consulting external documentation.

Examples:

- **FirstBGEPython.blend**
- **FirstBGEPython1.blend**

Actuator Access

The next step for our quick introduction to BGE Python is the access for Actuators. Generally it is possible to change values in the Actuators and to activate or deactivate the Actuator from within Python.

Build a logic as shown in the figure on the previous page. Make sure that you enter a value for "Rot", or nothing will move in our example. Then change the python script or enter a new one as shown in the listing below.

It is a good style to name the Logic Bricks to make the logic clear and to avoid errors in scripts

```
1.    # BGE Python script
2.    #
3.    # Access to the  Actuator
4.
5.    import GameLogic
6.
7.    cont = GameLogic.getCurrentController()
8.    me   = cont.getOwner()
9.
10.   moveit = cont.getActuator("Moveit")
11.   GameLogic.addActiveActuator(moveit,1)
```

Actuator Access

In line 10 you can see how an Actuator is accessed. The Controller variable "cont" provides a "getActuator()" function. We pass it the name of the Actuator as a string. It is possible to have numerous Actuators connected to a Controller, so a good talking name will help here to avoid confusion. The next line now uses a function from the

GameLogic module "addActiveActuator()" to enable the Actuator. The parameters are first the variable holding the Actuator and a "1" to enable the Actuator. In the rare case where you need to stop an Actuator you would pass a "0".

When everything is entered correctly and the Logic Bricks are connected the right way (and named according to the script), you can press **P** to start the game engine. The cube should now rotate. Of course this is much easier with a simple AND-Controller, but in the next step we will do something which is not possible with only Logic Bricks.

Properties and Actuators

Imagine you want to speed up an object slowly. With Logic Bricks there is no simple way to achieve this, but with some Python it is easy to do.

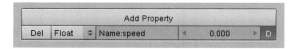

First we add a Property (see Properties) by clicking on the "Add Property" button left of the Logic Bricks of our small testscene. Leave the type to "Float" and name the property "speed", this Property will hold the current speed (I will use rotation speed) of our object. You should also activate the "D" button, this will show the property in the 3D View while the game is running. This is usually only done when the 3DView is not in textured mode, so check that you are in wireframe or solid mode. If you want to see the Debug output also in textured mode use the Game-menu to activate "Show Debug Properties".

Now change the existing script:

Properties and
changing Actuators

```
1.    # BGE Python script
2.    #
3.    # Access to the  Actuator
4.
5.    import GameLogic
6.
7.    cont = GameLogic.getCurrentController()
8.    me   = cont.getOwner()
9.
10.   moveit = cont.getActuator("Moveit")
11.
12.   me.speed = me.speed + 0.0005
13.
```

```
14.    moveit.setDRot(0,0,me.speed,1)
15.    GameLogic.addActiveActuator(moveit,1)
```

You may have wondered what line 8 was used for in the previous script, it was just left in for convenience, but now we use the variable "me" which is holding a pointer to our object to access the Property we created in the Logic Buttons. In line 12 we add "0.0005" every time the script is called to the property "speed". This will make "speed" count up in very small steps, however, since the script gets called every 1/60th of a second it will count up quite fast.

In line 14 we now set the Rot value for the Z-axis with the "speed" value. The first three argument values to "setDRot()" are the rotation around X, Y and Z. The fourth argument denotes if the rotation should be around the local axis ("1") or global axis ("0"). This is the Python counterpart to the "L" button in the Motion Actuator.

Sensor Access

For completeness I will now demonstrate how to access a sensor from Pyton:

```
1.    # BGE Python script                              Sensor Access
2.    #
3.    # Access to the  Actuator
4.
5.    import GameLogic
6.
7.    cont = GameLogic.getCurrentController()
8.    me   = cont.getOwner()
9.
10.   moveit = cont.getActuator("Moveit")
11.   always = cont.getSensor("Always")
12.
13.   if always.isPositive():
14.     me.speed = me.speed + 0.0005
15.
16.    moveit.setDRot(0,0,me.speed,1)
17.    GameLogic.addActiveActuator(moveit,1)
```

This looks very similar like the Actuator Access. In line 11 we get a pointer to the Sensor named "Always" into a variable and can now use its functions. Here we just use "isPositive()" which will only return "true" if the Sensor fires a positive event. In this case it is again just for demonstrating and will not provide extra functionality. But in the case of other sensor types or the case that there are more sensors connected to the Python-Controller this function will help us very much.

See the file **FirstBGEPython6.blend** for an example with two KeyboardSensors controlling the rotational speed of the object.

GameLogic Module

The GameLogic module is the base of all game logic by Python.

RETURNS	FUNCTION	EXPLANATION
	addActiveActuator (actuator,bool)	Adds an active actuator
string	expandPath(path)	Converts a blender internal path into a proper file system path. path - the string path to convert. Use / as directory separator in path You can use ,//' at the start of the string to define a relative path; Blender replaces that string by the directory of the startup .blend or runtime file to make a full path name (doesn't change during the game, even if you load other .blend). The function also converts the directory separator to the local file system format.
int	getAverageFrameRate()	Gets the estimated average frame rate.
list	getBlendFileList(path)	Gets a list of blend files in the same directory as the current blend file or the list from "path"
controller	getCurrentController()	Gets the current controller (the one "owning" the script).
scene	getCurrentScene()	Gets a reference to the current scene.
integer	getLogicTicRate()	Gets the logic tic rate.
integer	getPhysicsTicRate()	Gets the physics tic rate.
float	getRandomFloat()	Returns a random floating point value in the range [0..1]

RETURNS	FUNCTION	EXPLANATION
dict	globalDict()	dict() → new empty dictionary. dict(mapping) → new dictionary initialized from a mapping object's (key, value) pairs. dict(seq) → new dictionary initialized as if via: d = {} for k, v in seq: d[k] = v dict(**kwargs) → new dictionary initialized with the name=value pairs in the keyword argument list. For example: dict(one=1, two=2).
	setGravity(x,y,z)	Set Gravitation.
	setLogicTicRate()	Sets the logic tic rate.
	setPhysicsTicRate()	Sets the physics tic rate

Rasterizer Module

RETURNS	FUNCTION	EXPLANATION
	disableMotionBlur()	Disable motion blur.
	enableMotionBlur()	Enable motion blur.
	enableVisibility()	Enable visibility.
float	getEyeSeparation()	Get the eye separation for stereo mode.
float	getFocalLength()	Get the focal length for stereo mode.
string	getGLSLMaterialSetting (string)	Get the state of a GLSL material setting.
	getMaterialMode()	Get the material mode being used for OpenGL rendering.
integer	getWindowHeight()	Get window height (see Trackball.blend).
integer	getWindowWidth()	Get window width.
	makeScreenshot (path)	Make screenshot, saved in format as denoted in the Display Buttons.
	setAmbientColor ("[r,g,b,a]")	Set Ambient Color.
	setBackgroundColor ("[r,g,b,a]")	Set Background Color.
	setEyeSeparation (float)	Set the eye separation for stereo mode.

RETURNS	FUNCTION	EXPLANATION
	setFocalLength(float)	Set the focal length for stereo mode.
	setGLSLMaterialSetting()	Set the state of a GLSL material setting.
	setMaterialMode()	Set the material mode to use for OpenGL rendering.
	setMistColor()	Set Mist Color (rgb).
	setMistEnd()	Set Mist End(rgb).
	setMistStart()	Set Mist Start(rgb).
	setMousePosition(x,y)	Set mouse position.
	showMouse(bool)	Show mouse in game engine mode.

GameLogic.globalDict

This is a place where data can be stored even when new blend files are loaded. This was developed for Apricot, so Frankie can go into levels in new blendfiles keeping his inventory.

The GameLogic.globalDict is a Python directory, dictionaries are sometimes found in other languages as "associative memories" or "associative arrays". Unlike sequences, which are indexed by a range of numbers, dictionaries are indexed by keys, which can be any immutable type

Here is a small example using a dictionary (from the official Python documentation at **http://www.python.org/doc/2.5.2/tut/node7.html** , section 5.5):

```
>>> tel = {'jack': 4098, 'sape': 4139}
>>> tel['guido'] = 4127
>>> tel
{'sape': 4139, 'guido': 4127, 'jack': 4098}
>>> tel['jack']
4098
>>> del tel['sape']
>>> tel['irv'] = 4127
>>> tel
{'guido': 4127, 'irv': 4127, 'jack': 4098}
>>> tel.keys()
['guido', 'irv', 'jack']
>>> tel.has_key('guido')
True
```

```
>>> 'guido' in tel
True
```

Loading and saving the GameLogic.globalDict can be done with the Game Actuator. You can access the global data with Python like this:

```
# Save data before changing levels
# gets data from a Property to globalDict
GameLogic.globalDict['SavedScore'] = me.actualscore
```

Don't forget a "Save GameLogic.globalDict" with the Game Actuator before changing levels. In the new level we now have to do "Load GameLogic.globalDict" with the Game Actuator and can then access the saved data:

```
# load data after loading a level
# gets data from globalDict to a Property
me.actualscore = GameLogic.globalDict['SavedScore']
```

Examples:

- **GlobalDict_L1.blend** (press A to "score", loads the next level at score=5 and the score is keept in Level 2)
- **GlobalDict_L2.blend** (Level 2)

GameKeys Module

This module holds key constants for the Keyboard Sensor.

PhysicsConstraints Module

This python module, PhysicsConstraints, gives access to internal physics settings that influence quality of the rigid body dynamics

createConstraint (Edge Constraint)

createConstraint(obj1_PhysicsID, obj2_PhysicsID, constraintType, edgePos_x, edgePos_y, edgePos_z, edgeAngle_x, edgeAngle_y, edgeAngle_z)

obj1_PhysicsID: integer (The physics ID of object 1)

obj2_PhysicsID: integer (The physics ID of object 2)

constraintType: integer 0 = No constraint. 1 = Point constraint. 2 = Edge constraint. 11 = Vehicle constraint

edgePos_x: float (Blender unit) edgePos_y: float (Blender unit) edgePos_z: float (Blender unit)

edgeAngle_x: float (Range: -1.0 to 1.0) edgeAngle_y: float (Range: -1.0 to 1.0) edgeAngle_z: float (Range: -1.0 to 1.0)

Position (edgePos_x, edgePos_y, edgePos_z) Where do you want the center of the edge to be located? (Distance from obj1's object center)

Angle (edgeAngle_x, edgeAngle_y, edgeAngle_z) In what direction do you want the edge to point? (Uses obj1's axis)

Sample Code:

```
1.    # import PhysicConstraints Module
2.    import PhysicsConstraints
3.
4.    # get object list
5.    objList = GameLogic.getCurrentScene().getObjectList()
6.
7.    # get object named Obj_1
8.    obj1 = objList["OBObj_1"]
9.
10.   # get object named Obj_2
11.   obj2 = objList["OBObj_2"]
12.
13.   # want to use Edge constraint type
14.   constraintType = 2
15.
16.   # get Obj_1 physics ID
17.   obj1_ID = obj1.getPhysicsId()
18.
19.   # get Obj_2 physics ID
20.   obj2_ID = obj2.getPhysicsId()
21.
22.   # Use bottom right edge of 0bj_1 for hinge position
23.   edgePos_x = 1.0
24.   edgePos_y = 0.0
25.   edgePos_z = -1.0
26.
27.   # use Obj_1 y axis for angle to point hinge
```

```
28.    edgeAngle_x = 0.0
29.    edgeAngle_y = 1.0
30.    edgeAngle_z = 0.0
31.
32.    # create an edge constraint
33.    PhysicsConstraints.createConstraint( obj1_ID, obj2_ID,
34.        constraintType,
35.        edgePos_x, edgePos_y, edgePos_z,
36.        edgeAngle_x, edgeAngle_y, edgeAngle_z )
```

Example:

- **EdgeConstraint.blend**

createConstraint (Point Constraint)

createConstraint(obj1_PhysicsID, obj2_PhysicsID, constraintType, pointPos_x, pointPos_y, pointPos_z)

obj1_PhysicsID: integer (The physics ID of object 1)

obj2_PhysicsID: integer (The physics ID of object 2)

constraintType: integer 0 = No constraint. 1 = Point constraint. 2 = Edge constraint. 11 = Vehicle constraint

pointPos_x: float (Blender unit) pointPos_y: float (Blender unit) pointPos_z: float (Blender unit)

Point Position (pointPos_x, pointPos_y, pointPos_z) Where do you want the pivot point to be located? (Distance from obj1's object center)

Sample Code:

```
1.    # import PhysicConstraints Module
2.    import PhysicsConstraints
3.
4.    # get object list
5.    objList = GameLogic.getCurrentScene().getObjectList()
6.
7.    # get object named Obj_1
8.    obj1 = objList["OBObj_1"]
9.
```

```
10.    # get object named Obj_2
11.    obj2 = objList["OBObj_2"]
12.
13.    # want to use point constraint type
14.    constraintType = 1
15.
16.    # get Obj_1 physics ID
17.    obj1_ID = obj1.getPhysicsId()
18.
19.    # get Obj_2 physics ID
20.    obj2_ID = obj2.getPhysicsId()
21.
22.    # Use bottom right front corner of obj1 for point position
23.    pointPos_x = 1.0
24.    pointPos_y = -1.0
25.    pointPos_z = -1.0
26.
27.    # create a point constraint
28.    PhysicsConstraints.createConstraint( obj1_ID, obj2_ID,
29.        constraintType,
30.        pointPos_x, pointPos_y, pointPos_z)
```

Example blend:

- **PointConstraint.blend**

createConstraint (Vehicle Constraint)

createConstraint(obj1_PhysicsID, obj2_PhysicsID, constraintType)

obj1_PhysicsID: integer (The physics ID of the vehicle)

obj2_PhysicsID: integer (Set this to zero)

constraintType: integer 0 = No constraint. 1 = Point constraint. 2 = Edge constraint. 11 = Vehicle constraint.

Sample Code:

```
1.    # import PhysicConstraints Module
2.    import PhysicsConstraints
3.
```

```
4.    # get object list
5.    objList = GameLogic.getCurrentScene().getObjectList()
6.
7.    # get object named Car
8.    objCar = objList["OBCar"]
9.
10.   # want to use vehicle constraint type
11.   constraintType = 11
12.
13.   # get car physics ID
14.   carID = objCar.getPhysicsId()
15.
16.   # create a vehicle constraint
17.   PhysicsConstraints.createConstraint( carID, 0, constraintType)
```

Example blend:

- **VehicleConstraint.blend**

getAppliedImpulse

getAppliedImpulse(constraintId)

Returns the applied impulse.

Return type: float constraintId: integer

Save the constraintID when the constraint is created.

Sample Code:

1st script

```
1.    # import PhysicConstraints Module
2.    import PhysicsConstraints
3.
4.    # get object list
5.    objList = GameLogic.getCurrentScene().getObjectList()
6.
7.    # get object named Car
8.    objCar = objList["OBCar"]
9.
```

```
10.    # want to use vehicle constraint type
11.    constraintType = 11
12.
13.    # get car physics ID
14.    car_ID = objCar.getPhysicsId()
15.
16.    # create a vehicle constraint
17.    carConst = PhysicsConstraints.createConstraint( car_ID, 0, constraintType)
18.
19.    # get the constraint ID
20.    carConst_ID = carConst.getConstraintId()
21.
22.    # save the constraint ID as a objCar variable
23.    objCar.constraint_ID = carConst_ID
24.
25.    #### rest of script
```

2nd script

```
1.    # import PhysicConstraints Module
2.    import PhysicsConstraints
3.
4.    # get object list
5.    objList = GameLogic.getCurrentScene().getObjectList()
6.
7.    # get object named Car
8.    objCar = objList["OBCar"]
9.
10.    # get car constraint ID that was saved
11.    carConst_ID = objCar.constraint_ID
12.
13.    # get the applied impulse
14.    appliedImpulse = PhysicsConstraints.getAppliedImpulse(carConst_ID)
```

getVehicleConstraint

getVehicleConstraint(constraint_ID)

Returns the vehicle constraint ID.

constraint_ID: integer

Sample Code:

```
1.    # import PhysicConstraints Module
2.    import PhysicsConstraints
3.
4.    # get object list
5.    objList = GameLogic.getCurrentScene().getObjectList()
6.
7.    # get object named Car
8.    objCar = objList["OBCar"]
9.
10.   # want to use vehicle constraint type
11.   constraintType = 11
12.
13.   # get car physics ID
14.   car_ID = objCar.getPhysicsId()
15.
16.   # create a vehicle constraint
17.   carConst = PhysicsConstraints.createConstraint( car_ID, 0, constraintType)
18.
19.   # get the constraint ID
20.   carConst_ID = carConst.getConstraintId()
21.
22.   # get vehicle constraint
23.   car = PhysicsConstraints.getVehicleConstraint(carConst_ID)
```

removeConstraint

```
removeConstraint(constraint_ID)
```

Removes the constraint.

```
constraint_ID: integer
```

Save the constraintID when the constraint is created.

This removes the constraint between 2 game objects (point and edge constraints). It does not remove vehicle constraints.

Sample Code:

Part 1: Create a Point Constraint

```
1.    #########  PointConstraint.py
```

```
2.
3.    # import PhysicConstraints Module
4.    import PhysicsConstraints
5.
6.    # get object list
7.    objList = GameLogic.getCurrentScene().getObjectList()
8.
9.    # get object named Obj_1
10.   obj1 = objList["OBObj_1"]
11.
12.   # get object named Obj_2
13.   obj2 = objList["OBObj_2"]
14.
15.   # want to use point constraint type
16.   constraintType = 1
17.
18.   # get Obj_1 physics ID
19.   obj1_ID = obj1.getPhysicsId()
20.
21.   # get Obj_2 physics ID
22.   obj2_ID = obj2.getPhysicsId()
23.
24.   # Use bottom right front corner of obj1 for point position
25.   pointPos_x = 1.0
26.   pointPos_y = -1.0
27.   pointPos_z = -1.0
28.
29.   # create a point constraint
30.   constraint = PhysicsConstraints.createConstraint( obj1_ID, obj2_ID,
31.       constraintType,
32.       pointPos_x, pointPos_y, pointPos_z)
33.
34.   # get the constraint ID
35.   constraint_ID = constraint.getConstraintId()
36.
37.   # save the constraint ID as an Obj_1 variable
38.   obj1.constraint_ID = constraint_ID
```

Part 2: Remove constraint script

```
1.    ###########  RemoveConstraint.py
2.
3.    # import PhysicConstraints Module
```

```
4.     import PhysicsConstraints
5.
6.     # get object list
7.     objList = GameLogic.getCurrentScene().getObjectList()
8.
9.     # get object 1
10.    obj1 = objList["OBObj_1"]
11.
12.    # get constraint ID that was saved as an Obj_1 variable
13.    # when the constraint was created
14.    constraint_ID = obj1.constraint_ID
15.
16.    # remove constraint
17.    PhysicsConstraints.removeConstraint(constraint_ID)
```

Example blend:

- **RemoveConstraint.blend**

setDeactivationTime

setDeactivationTime(time)

Time (in seconds) after objects with velocity less then thresholds (see below) are deactivated

time:float

This affects every object in the scene, except for game objects that have ,No sleeping' turned on.

Sample Code:

```
1.    # import PhysicConstraints Module
2.    import PhysicsConstraints
3.
4.    # set the deactivation time
5.    PhysicsConstraints.setDeactivationTime(1.0)
```

setDeactivationLinearTreshold

setDeactivationLinearTreshold(linearTreshold)

Sets the linear velocity that an object must be below before the deactivation timer can start.

`linearTreshold:float`

This affects every object in the scene, except for game objects that have ‚No sleeping' turned on.

Sample Code:

```
1.    # import PhysicConstraints Module
2.    import PhysicsConstraints
3.
4.    # set the deactivation linear velocity threshold
5.    PhysicsConstraints.setDeactivationLinearTreshold(1.0)
```

setDeactivationAngularTreshold

`setDeactivationAngularTreshold(angularTreshold)`

Sets the angular velocity that an object must be below before the deactivation timer can start.

`angularTreshold:float`

This affects every object in the scene, except for game objects that have ‚No sleeping' turned on.

Sample Code:

```
1.    # import PhysicConstraints Module
2.    import PhysicsConstraints
3.
4.    # set the deactivation angular velocity threshold
5.    PhysicsConstraints.setDeactivationAngularTreshold(1.0)
```

setGravity

`setGravity(gx, gy, gz)`

Sets the gravity for the scene.

gx: float (force of gravity on world x axis) gy: float (force of gravity on world y axis)
gz: float (force of gravity on world z axis)

This affects every object in the scene that has physics enabled.

Sample Code:

```
1.    # import PhysicConstraints Module
2.    import PhysicsConstraints
3.
4.    # Beam me up!!
5.    # set gravity to a +10.0 on z axis
6.    PhysicsConstraints.setGravity( 0.0, 0.0, 10.0)
```

Example blend:

- **SetGravity.blend**

setLinearAirDamping

setLinearAirDamping(damping)

Sets the linear air resistance for all objects in the scene.

damping: float

Sample Code:

```
1.    # import PhysicConstraints Module
2.    import PhysicsConstraints
3.
4.    # set linear air resistance to 30.0
5.    PhysicsConstraints.setLinearAirDamping(30.0)
```

Simple script to get the message body

setNumIterations

setNumIterations(numIter)

Sets the number of times an iterative constraint solver is repeated. Increasing the number of iterations improves the constraint solver. It will decrease performance.

numIter: integer

Sample Code:

```
1.    # import PhysicConstraints Module
2.    import PhysicsConstraints
3.
4.    # repeat iterative solvers 10 times
5.    PhysicsConstraints.setNumIterations(10)
```

setNumTimeSubSteps

```
setNumTimeSubSteps(numSubStep)
```

Increasing the number of time substeps improves the quality of the entire physics simulation, including collision detection and constraint solving. It will decrease performance. Set the number of timesubsteps to 0 to suspend simulation

```
numSubStep:integer
```

Sample Code:

```
1.    # import PhysicConstraints Module
2.    import PhysicsConstraints
3.
4.    # set time sub steps to 2
5.    PhysicsConstraints.setNumTimeSubSteps(2)
```

Message Body

One of the most asked things with the messaging system in Blender is how to get the message body. In the Message Actuator we can send a text or the content of a Property but there is no function to retrieve this with Logic Bricks.

So here we need a small script.

```
1.    # The message sensor has to be named "message"
2.    # body will go in existing Property "mbody"
3.    # The message body will be converted to the type of the Property
4.
5.    # Only the last (if there are more than one messages sent)
6.    # body will be stored!
7.
8.    from types import *
```

```
9.
10.    cont = GameLogic.getCurrentController()
11.    mess = cont.getSensor("message")
12.    me   = cont.getOwner()
13.
14.    if mess.isPositive():
15.      bodies = mess.getBodies()
16.      if bodies!=None:
17.          for body in bodies:
18.              if type(me.mbody) is StringType:
19.                  me.mbody = body
20.              else:
21.                  me.mbody = float(body)
```

This needs to be connected to a Message Sensor called "message". Fill in the Subject field as needed. However, this simple script will not work properly if more than one message arrives in one frame. All but the last message will be discarded. See the score counting mechanism in the pinball tutorial files for how to avoid this.

Example:

- **MessageBody.blend**
- See also in the Pinball Tutorial files

APPENDIX

CHAPTER 14

Getting Blender

The central place to get Blender is at **http://www.blender.org/download/get-blender/** . For this book it is recommended to use Blender 2.48a for which the book was written. Future Blender versions may contain enhancements or changes which can be confusing for beginners.

Installation of Blender

To install Blender, download the appropriate package for your platform to your computer. The Windows version comes with an optional self-extracting installer, for other operating systems you can unpack the compressed file to the location of your choice.

Provided the Blender binary is in the original extracted directory, Blender will run straight out of the box. No system libraries or system preferences are altered.

If you are unsure which version to choose use the 32-bit Installer for Windows or use the Blender package provided by your Linux distribution.

Getting Support

The download packages contain a blender.html file with installation instructions and a quick survival guide for new users.

All support links are collected at **http://www.blender.org/education-help/**

The support is done mostly on user forums and irc chat, so don't hesitate to ask there! Links to the major sites are in the link section.

Of course there is a huge list of Blender books and tutorial CDROMs which can be bought in the Blender e-shop or at your local book store.

Blender Foundation and Institute

Goals

The Blender Foundation is an independent organisation (a Dutch "stichting"), acting as a non-profit public benefit corporation, with the following goals:

- To establish services for active users and developers of Blender
- To maintain and improve the current Blender product via a public accessible source code system under the GNU GPL license
- To establish funding or revenue mechanisms that serve the foundation's goals and cover the foundation's expenses
- To give the worldwide Internet community access to 3D technology in general, with Blender as a core

Organization

The Blender Foundation has offices in the Amsterdam Blender Institute. Revenues from e-shop and publishing enable Ton Roosendaal and a small staff to work full-time on Blender, organize activities like for Siggraph or the Blender Conference, support development/documention projects, and pay for bookkeeping and administration expenses. The main activities for Blender are organized in boards and projects.

Blender Community, Books, Websites

- The official Blender Website: **http://blender.org**
- Blender Multiplayer Game and Tutorial: **http://www.wsag.ch.vu/**
- Download some example files for soft bodies: **http://download.blender.org/ demo/test/gamesoftbody-samples.zip**
- Blender Artists Forum: **http://blenderartists.org/forum/**
- Bullet Physics Library: **http://bulletphysics.com**
- CGTextures: **http://cgtextures.com/**
- Blender Nation: **http://www.blendernation.com/**
- Blender Artists: **http://blenderartists.org/**
- Blendpolis, big german community: **http://blendpolis.de/f/blender.php**

Books and CDROMs

You can get most of the Blender Foundation-Released Books, DVDs and CD-ROMs in the Blender e-shop: **http://www.blender3d.org/e-shop/**

Glossary

Active

Blender makes a distinction between selected and active. Only one Object or item can be active at any given time, for example to allow visualization of data in buttons.

See Also: Selected.

Actuator

A LogicBrick that acts like a muscle of a lifeform. It can move the object, or also make a sound.

See Also: LogicBrick, Sensor, Controller.

APPENDIX

Alpha

The alpha value in an image denotes opacity, used for blending and antialiasing.

Anti-aliasing

An algorithm designed to reduce the stair-stepping artifacts that result from drawing graphic primitives on a raster grid.

Back-buffer

Blender uses two buffers in which it draws the interface. This double-buffering system allows one buffer to be displayed, while drawing occurs on the back-buffer. For some applications in Blender the back-buffer is used to store color-coded selection information.

Bevel

Beveling removes sharp edges from an extruded object by adding additional material around the surrounding faces. Bevels are particularly useful for flying logos, and animation in general, since they reflect additional light from the corners of an object as well as from the front and sides.

Bounding box

A six-sided box drawn on the screen that represents the maximum extent of an object.

Channel

Some DataBlocks can be linked to a series of other DataBlocks. For example, a Material has eight channels to link Textures to. Each IpoBlock has a fixed number of available channels. These have a name (LocX, SizeZ, enz.) which indicates how they can be applied. When you add an IpoCurve to a channel, animation starts up immediately.

Child

Objects can be linked to each other in hierarchical groups. The Parent Object in such groups passes its transformations through to the Child Objects.

Clipping

The removal, before drawing occurs, of vertices and faces which are outside the field of view.

Controller

A LogicBrick that acts like the brain of a lifeform. It makes decisions to activate muscles (Actuators), either using simple logic or complex Python scripts. See Also: LogicBrick, Sensor, Python, Actuator.

DataBlock (or „block")

The general name for an element in Blender's Object Oriented System.

Doppler effect

The Doppler effect is the change in pitch that occurs when a sound has a velocity relative to the listener. When a sound moves towards the listener the pitch will rise. when going away from the listener the pitch will drop. A well known example is the sound of an ambulance passing by.

Double-buffer

Blender uses two buffers (images) to draw the interface in. The content of one buffer is displayed, while drawing occurs on the other buffer. When drawing is complete, the buffers are switched.

Edit Mode

Mode to select and transform vertices of an object. This way you change the shape of the object itself. Hotkey: **TAB**.

See Also: Vertex (pl. vertices).

Extend select

Adds new selected items to the current selection (**SHIFT**-**RMB**)

Extrusion

The creation of a three-dimensional object by pushing out a two-dimensional out-line and giving it height, like a cookie-cutter. It is often used to create 3-D text.

Face

The triangle and square polygons that form the basis for Meshes or for rendering.

Flag

A programming term for a variable that indicates a certain status.

Flat shading

A fast rendering algorithm that simply gives each facet of an object a single col-or. It yields a solid representation of objects without taking a long time to render. Pressing **Z** switches to flat shading in Blender.

FPS

Frames per second. All animations, video, and movies are played at a certain rate. Above ca. 15fps the human eye cannot see the single frames and is tricked into see-ing a fluid motion. In games this is used as an indicator of how fast a game runs.

Frame

A single picture taken from an animation or video.

Gouraud shading

A rendering algorithm that provides more detail. It averages color information from adjacent faces to create colors. It is more realistic than flat shading, but less realistic than Phong shading or ray-tracing. The hotkey in Blender is **CTRL-Z**.

Graphical User Interface (GUI)

The whole part of an interactive application which requests input from the user (keyboard, mouse etc.) and displays this information to the user. Blenders GUI is designed for a efficient modeling process in an animation company where time equals money. Blenders whole GUI is done in OpenGL.

See Also: OpenGL.

Hierarchy

Objects can be linked to each other in hierarchical groups. The Parent Object in such groups passes its transformations through to the Child Objects.

Ipo

The main animation curve system. Ipo blocks can be used by Objects for movement, and also by Materials for animated colors.

Ipo Curve

The Ipo animation curve.

Item

The general name for a selectable element, e.g. Objects, vertices or curves.

APPENDIX

Keyframe

A frame in a sequence that specifies all of the attributes of an object. The object can then be changed in any way and a second keyframe defined. Blender automatically creates a series of transition frames between the two keyframes, a process called „tweening."

Layer

A visibility flag for Objects, Scenes and 3DWindows. This is a very efficient method for testing Object visibility.

Link

The reference from one DataBlock to another. It is a „pointer" in programming terminology.

Local

Each Object in Blender defines a local 3D space, bound by its location, rotation and size. Objects themselves reside in the global 3-D space.

A DataBlock is local, when it is read from the current Blender file. Non-local blocks (library blocks) are linked parts from other Blender files.

Logic Brick

A graphical representation of a functional unit in Blender's game logic. LogicBricks can be Sensors, Controllers or Actuators.

See Also: Sensor, Controller, Actuator.

Mapping

The relationship between a Material and a Texture is called the ‚mapping'. This relationship is two-sided. First, the information that is passed on to the Texture must be specified. Then the effect of the Texture on the Material is specified.

Mipmap

Process to filter and speed up the display of textures.

ObData block

The first and most important DataBlock linked by an Object. This block defines the Object type, e.g. Mesh or Curve or Lamp.

Object

The basic 3-D information block. It contains a position, rotation, size and transformation matrices. It can be linked to other Objects for hierarchies or deformation. Objects can be „empty" (just an axis) or have a link to ObData, the actual 3-D information: Mesh, Curve, Lattice, Lamp, etc.

OpenGL (OGL)

OpenGL is a programming interface mainly for 3D applications. It renders 3-D objects to the screen, providing the same set of instructions on different computers and graphics adapters. Blenders whole interface and 3-D output in the real-time and interactive 3-D graphic is done by OpenGL.

Parent

An object that is linked to another object, the parent is linked to a child in a parent-child relationship. A parent object's coordinates become the center of the world for any of its child objects.

Perspective view

In a perspective view, the further an object is from the viewer, the smaller it appears.

Pivot

A point that normally lies at an object's geometric center. An object's position and rotation are calculated in relation to its pivot-point. However, an object can be moved off its center point, allowing it to rotate around a point that lies outside the object.

Pixel

A single dot of light on the computer screen; the smallest unit of a computer graphic. Short for „picture element."

Plug-In

A piece of (C-)code loadable during runtime. This way it is possible to extend the functionality of Blender without a need for recompiling. The Blender plugin for showing 3D content in other applications is such a piece of code.

Python

The scripting language integrated into Blender. Python is an interpreted, interactive, object-oriented programming language.

Render

To create a two-dimensional representation of an object based on its shape and surface properties (i.e. a picture for print or to display on the monitor).

Rigid Body

Option for dynamic objects in Blender which causes the game engine to take the shape of the body into account. This can be used to create rolling spheres for example.

Selected

Blender makes a distinction between selected and active objects. Any number of objects can be selected at once. Almost all key commands have an effect on selected objects. Selecting is done with the right mouse button.

See Also: Active, Selected, Extend select.

Sensor

A LogicBrick that acts like a sense of a lifeform. It reacts to touch, vision, collision etc.

See Also: LogicBrick, Controller, Actuator.

Single User

DataBlocks with only one user.

Smoothing

A rendering procedure that performs vertex-normal interpolation across a face before lighting calculations begin. The individual facets are then no longer visible.

Transform

Change a location, rotation, or size. Usually applied to Objects or vertices.

Transparency

A surface property that determines how much light passes through an object without being altered.

See Also: Alpha.

User

When one DataBlock references another DataBlock, it has a user.

Vertex (pl. vertices)

The general name for a 3-D or 2-D point. Besides an X,Y,Z coordinate, a vertex can have color, a normal vector and a selection flag. Also used as controlling points or handles on curves.

Wireframe

A representation of a three-dimensional object that only shows the lines of its contours, hence the name „wireframe."

X, Y, Z axes

The three axes of the world's three-dimensional coordinate system. In the FrontView, the X axis is an imaginary horizontal line running from left to right; the Z axis is a vertical line; and Y axis is a line that comes out of the screen toward you. In general, any movement parallel to one of these axes is said to be movement along that axis.

X, Y, and Z coordinates

The X coordinate of an object is measured by drawing a line that is perpendicular to the X axis, through its centerpoint. The distance from where that line intersects the X axis to the zero point of the X axis is the object's X coordinate. The Y and Z coordinates are measured in a similar manner.

Z-buffer

For a Z-buffer image, each pixel is associated with a Z-value, derived from the distance in ,eye space' from the Camera. Before each pixel of a polygon is drawn, the existing Z-buffer value is compared to the Z-value of the polygon at that point. It is a common and fast visible-surface algorithm.

APPENDIX

Index

THE ESSENTIAL BLENDER
Guide to 3D Creation with the Open Source Suite Blender

edited by ROLAND HESS

Blender is the only free, fully integrated 3D graphics creation suite to allow modeling, animation, rendering, post-production, and real time interactive 3D with cross-platform compatibility. *The Essential Blender* covers modeling, materials and textures, lighting, particle systems, several kinds of animation, and rendering. It also contains chapters on the compositor and new mesh sculpting tools. For users familiar with other 3D packages, separate indices reference topics using the terminology in those applications. The book includes a CD with Blender for all platforms, as well as the files and demos from the book.

SEPTEMBER 2007, 376 PP. W/CD, $44.95   ISBN 978-1-59327-166-4

THE ARTIST'S GUIDE TO GIMP EFFECTS
Creative Techniques for Photographers, Artists, and Designers

by MICHAEL J. HAMMEL

The GIMP, an image editor whose power and ease-of-use rivals that of Adobe Photoshop, is one of the world's most popular free software projects. *The Artist's Guide to GIMP Effects* shows you how to harness the GIMP's powerful features to produce professional-looking advertisements, impressive photographic effects, as well as logos and text effects. The book's extensively illustrated step-by-step tutorials are perfect for hands-on learning and experimentation.

AUGUST 2007, 360 PP., $44.95   ISBN 978-1-59327-121-3

UBUNTU FOR NON-GEEKS, 3RD EDITION
A Pain-Free, Project-Based, Get-Things-Done Guidebook

by RICKFORD GRANT

The new edition of this best-selling guide to Ubuntu Linux for beginners covers Ubuntu 8.04, Hardy Heron. Step-by-step projects have readers interact with their system, rather than just read about it, as they build upon previously learned concepts. *Ubuntu for Non-Geeks* covers topics likely to be of interest to the average desktop user, such as installing new software via Synaptic; Internet connectivity; working with removable storage devices, printers, and scanners; burning DVDs, playing audio files, and even working with iPods. This edition features increased coverage of Bluetooth, wireless networking, modems, and, of course, coverage of the significant new features in the 8.04 release.

JUNE 2008, 360 PP., W/CD $34.95   ISBN 978-1-59327-180-0

THE MANGA GUIDE TO DATABASES

by MANA TAKAHASHI, SHOKO AZUMA, AND TREND-PRO CO., LTD.

With its unique combination of Japanese-style manga and serious educational content, *The Manga Guide to Databases* is an entertaining and effective guidebook to learning how to design, build, and manage databases. The book begins with stressed out Princess Ruruna's predicament: with the king and queen away, she has to manage the Kingdom of Kod's humongous fruit-selling empire all by herself, and all of the data is a confusing mess. But a mysterious book and a helpful fairy promise to solve her organizational problems. Readers follow along as Tico teaches Ruruna how to design a relational database, perform basic operations, secure a database, and eventually perform more advanced tasks.

JANUARY 2009, 224 PP., $19.95   ISBN 978-1-59327-190-9

THE MANGA GUIDE TO ELECTRICITY

by KAZUHIRO FUJITAKI, MATSUDA, AND TREND-PRO CO., LTD.

The Manga Guide to Electricity teaches readers the fundamentals of how electricity works through authentic Japanese manga. Readers follow Rereko, a denizen of Electopia, the Land of Electricity, as she is exiled to Tokyo to learn more about electricity. In no time, graduate student Hikaru is teaching her the essentials, such as static electricity and Coloumb's law; the relationship between voltage, resistance, and current; and the difference between series and parallel electrical circuits. Using real-world examples like flashlights and home appliances, *The Manga Guide to Electricity* combines a whimsical story with real educational content so that readers will quickly master the core concepts of electricity with a minimum of frustration.

MARCH 2009, 224 PP., $19.95   ISBN 978-1-59327-197-8

PHONE:
800.420.7240 OR
415.863.9900
MONDAY THROUGH FRIDAY,
9 AM TO 5 PM (PST)

FAX:
415.863.9950
24 HOURS A DAY,
7 DAYS A WEEK

EMAIL:
SALES@NOSTARCH.COM

WEB:
WWW.NOSTARCH.COM

MAIL:
NO STARCH PRESS
555 DE HARO ST, SUITE 250
SAN FRANCISCO, CA 94107
USA